W9-CEW-129

The Personalism of JOHN HENRY NEWMAN

The Personalism of JOHN HENRY NEWMAN

JOHN F. CROSBY

THE CATHOLIC UNIVERSITY OF AMERICA PRESS
Washington, D.C.

The paper used in this publication meets the minimum requirements of American National Standards for Information Science—Permanence of Paper for Printed Library Materials, ANSI Z39.48-1984.
∞

Library of Congress Cataloging-in-Publication Data
Crosby, John F., 1944–
The personalism of John Henry Newman / John F. Crosby.
pages cm
Includes bibliographical references and index.
ISBN 978-0-8132-2689-7 (cloth : alk. paper)
1. Newman, John Henry, 1801–1890. I. Title.
BX4705.N5C69 2014
230'.2092–dc23 2014018250

FOR MY CHILDREN, Michael, Jane, John Paul, Maria, Josef, and John Henry, my first-born, named for Blessed John Henry Newman

I AM FAR FROM denying the real force of the arguments in proof of a God … but these do not warm me or enlighten me; they do not take away the winter of my desolation, or make the buds unfold and the leaves grow within me, and my moral being rejoice.

John Henry Newman

Contents

Acknowledgments

I thank Franciscan University of Steubenville for granting me a sabbatical semester in the spring of 2011, during which this book was drafted.

I thank the Catholic University of America Press for permission to use, in chapter 4, a few pages from my *Personalist Papers* (2004).

Special thanks go to my wife, Pia, who carefully reviewed each chapter as it was drafted and gave me much encouragement along the way.

I also have an acknowledgment of an entirely different kind to make: I want to pay tribute to the memory of my revered grandfather, John F. Crosby (1889–1962), who first directed me to Newman when I was still a boy and who sowed a seed that has borne much fruit for me.

Abbreviations

The works published by Newman during his lifetime are quoted according to the uniform edition that was published by Longmans, Green of London between 1868 and 1881. This is the edition of his works that is used by *www.newmanreader.org*.

Newman's letters are quoted according to the thirty-two-volume edition published by Oxford University Press under the title *Letters and Diaries of John Henry Newman*.

I abbreviate titles as follows:

Apol.	*Apologia Pro Vita Sua*
Arians	*The Arians of the Fourth Century*
DA	*Discussions and Arguments on Various Subjects*
DD	*An Essay on the Development of Christian Doctrine*
DMC	*Discourses Addressed to Mixed Congregations*
ECH	*Essays Critical and Historical*, I and II
GA	*An Essay in Aid of a Grammar of Assent*
HS	*Historical Sketches*, I–III
Idea	*The Idea of a University*
LD	*Letters and Diaries of John Henry Newman*
LJ	*Lectures on the Doctrine of Justification*
OUS	*Fifteen Sermons Preached before the University of Oxford*

PPC	*Lectures on the Present Position of Catholics in England*
PPS	*Parochial and Plain Sermons,* I–VIII
SD	*Sermons Bearing on Subjects of the Day*
SVO	*Sermons Preached on Various Occasions*
VM	*Via Media of the Anglican Church,* I and II
VV	*Verses on Various Occasions*

Introduction

At the end of his study of John Henry Newman as philosopher, Edward Sillem gives an overall assessment of Newman among the philosophers, and he concludes by saying something very significant: "As far as philosophy is concerned he was no Augustine, Aquinas nor Scotus in stature. His real work lay in other fields. *But he stands at the threshold of the new age as a Christian Socrates, the pioneer of a new philosophy of the individual Person and Personal Life.*"[1] In this book I want to draw out this personalist originality of Newman. I want to present and interpret, perhaps develop a little, and above all show the fruitfulness of the pioneering personalism of which Sillem speaks.

My Personal Path to This Study

I came to this project through my own work in personalist philosophy. I kept finding in Newman a major source of personalist insight. I kept quoting him in my own writings. Newman seemed to me to be a forerunner of the great twentieth-century Christian personalists, thinkers such as Soren Kierkegaard, Max Scheler, Emmanuel Mounier, Gabriel Marcel, Jacques Maritain,

1. Edward Sillem, *The Philosophical Notebook* (Louvain: Nauwaelerts, 1961), I, 250. My italics.

Romano Guardini, Dietrich von Hildebrand, Edith Stein, and Karol Wojtyla. So I conceived the following plan: I would write a study in which I would not use Newman as a source for my own philosophical projects, but center the study around Newman and his personalism. What especially drew me to this project was my growing realization that his personalism is fundamental to his thought; I realized that a study of Newman's personalism would be a study leading into the heart of Newman, and would thus be a good way of introducing Newman to those who do not yet know him, and a new way of thinking about the unity of his thought for those who do already know him.

There is also another, quite different personal path by which I have been led to this study of Newman. This other path reveals a great deal more about the focus of my study, and even explains why my first chapter deals with something other than his personalism. When I first encountered Newman in my teens and early twenties, I was drawn to him mainly by the radical Christianity that he preached in Oxford during the years of the Oxford Movement. He challenged what he called "the religion of the day," a Christianity that, having been long established in England, was taken for granted by everyone but taken seriously by very few. Like Kierkegaard in Denmark, Newman in England exposed the hollowness of a Christianity that had become merely conventional and had lost its savor. The Christianity that he found all around him was harmless, mediocre. He was on fire with the radical Christianity he had found in the apostolic age and in the Greek fathers of the Church. He cast this fire onto Oxford and England and ignited the Oxford Movement. He preached about the fear of God, zeal for God's honor; he preached about sin and conversion; he preached about self-denial and self-discipline. He evoked with great power for his listeners the "invisible world" of God, the angels, the souls of the dead, the world to come. In an age when Christianity had become soft and self-indulgent, he revealed the demanding edge of it. He announced the Gospel unadulterated, in all its power to upend and to overthrow human-all-too-human patterns of thinking. He announced without compromise the antagonism between the Gospel and the world. He would often preach with the fierceness of an Old Testament prophet, as in the sermon "Jewish Zeal, a Pattern for Christians." Of course, he was not just another preacher threatening his congregation with hellfire; he was Newman, a man of the highest culture and the most exquisite sensibilities and the most penetrating insight into human and divine things. I responded to Newman's preaching just like many Oxford undergraduates in his day; I was deeply convicted by the authentic Christianity that he proclaimed. I rejoiced to encounter real Christianity proclaimed so convincingly. I could never be the same after hearing Newman preach.

But I had not yet really encountered that side of his mind that centers around subjectivity, experience, the heart, personal influence, imagination. The Newman I first knew presented a severe objectivity, a radical theocentrism; he affirmed "the dogmatical principle" and regarded theological liberalism as his archenemy. It was only later that I got to know him as "the pioneer of a new philosophy of the individual person and personal life," and to see him in relation to the great Christian personalists of the twentieth century, and to experience him as a rich source of my own work in personalist philosophy. And when I did get to know this side of Newman I realized that the drama of Newman's thought lies in the fruitful tension of these two sides of his mind and personality. Newman once wrote, "But one aspect of Revelation must not be allowed to exclude or to obscure another; and Christianity is dogmatical, devotional, practical all at once; it is esoteric and exoteric; it is indulgent and strict; it is light and dark; it is love, and it is fear."[2] We can appropriate this for our study of Newman, and we can say that one aspect of his mind must not be allowed to obscure another, and that Newman combines in himself subjectivity and objec-

2. John Henry Newman, *Essay on the Development of Christian Doctrine* (London: Longmans, Green, 1868–1881), 36 (hereafter, DD).

tivity, heart and intellect, experience and doctrine, modernity and antiquity. Theologians sometimes speak of the *coincidentia oppositorum* in God and in the saints. Well, there is a *coincidentia oppositorum* in Newman, and this is part of the reason for the inexhaustible plenitude of his thought. So I realized that a study of Newman's personalism is possible only if the personalism is seen in relation to his radical theocentrism, only if the fruitful tension of these apparent opposites is preserved. This is why the first chapter of this study is a chapter on his theocentrism; only then do I proceed to the chapters on his personalism, and in those later chapters I do not forget the first chapter.

There are interpreters of Newman who deny that his theocentrism and his personalism exist in a fruitful tension, that they form a real unity; they say that these two sides of Newman's thought contradict each other. They say this because personalism is, as I just remarked, explicated in terms of subjectivity, experience, the heart, personal influence, and imagination; and these things, when they become strong in a thinker, tend to undermine the doctrinal commitments of a theocentric thinker like Newman. Thus one interpreter of Newman, W. R. Inge, one of the first to speak of Newman's personalism, writes that Newman introduced "into the Roman Church a very dangerous and essentially alien habit of thought, which has since developed into Modernism," a habit of thought which "when logically drawn out, must lead away from Catholicism in the direction of an individualistic religion of experience, and a substitution of history for dogma."[3] This critic is aware of the theocentric Newman; what he wants to say is that Newman's thought, through its personalism, is divided against itself. And Inge is not the first to say this; at the time of the Modernist controversy within the Catholic Church at the beginning of the twentieth century—this is what Inge refers to—some Modernists invoked Newman as their chief source of inspiration. People were perplexed that a

3. William Ralph Inge, *Outspoken Essays* (London: Longmans, Green, 1923), 201–2.

man of Newman's uncompromising orthodoxy could give the impetus to something so foreign to orthodoxy as Modernism. Thus by seeking to understand the unity of Newman's theocentrism and his personalism, or rather the unity of his theocentrism and *the rest of* his personalism, we will not only enter into the drama of Newman's thought; we will also protect it against what I take to be a capital misunderstanding of it. Newman's personalist thought is indeed distinctly modern, but is not modernist in the theological sense. I return to this important issue at the end of this study.

Personalism

Personalism has emerged in response to the sense that persons and their dignity are endangered. Thus Karol Wojtyla, telling a friend about writing his personalist treatise, *The Acting Person,* said: "The evil of our times consists in the first place in a kind of degradation, indeed in a pulverization, of the fundamental uniqueness of each human person.... To this ... we must propose, rather than sterile polemics, a kind of 'recapitulation' of the inviolable mystery of the person."[4] Wojtyla felt driven to develop his personalism as a way of defending the violated dignity of persons. Personalism also emerges in response not only to the violation of persons but also in response to the theoretical underpinnings of such violation; thus it emerges in response to a reductionistic, naturalistic image of man. When natural science claims to give an exhaustive account of the human condition, people feel threatened; the personalist impulse is to vindicate the freedom of persons by showing that human beings cannot be reduced without remainder to natural causes. But it is not only scientism that provokes a personalist reaction; personalism emerges in Europe at the end of the eighteenth century in the reaction to Hegel and in particular to Hegel's

4. Quoted by Henri DeLubac, *At the Service of the Church* (San Francisco: Ignatius Books, 1993), 172.

pantheism.[5] It is abhorrent to personalists to think of persons as parts or moments of God; they know that persons are abolished as persons by becoming parts or moments. Persons do not come out of God like a drop of water comes out of the sea, nor does it make any sense to speak of their being able to be dissolved back into God. A person is a being of its own, and this in a sense in which a part is not a being of its own. Personalists not only insist on human beings being persons but also on God being personal. They think that God is more than a dimension of the world; as Person He transcends the world with a being of His own. And they lay great stress on the interpersonal relations that exist between God and human persons, and especially on the unpredictable initiatives and elections of God.

The personalism that I hold is best represented by Karol Wojtyla, who was inspired by Max Scheler.[6] Wojtyla holds that each of us exists as subject, not just as object, or in other words, as someone, not just as something, or in still other words, as self-determining, not just determined. That is, each person lives his or her being "from within"; this is the subjectivity of the person. If we are to understand persons we must not only take them "from without," as objects; we have also to take them through their subjectivity, or interiority.[7] Some philosophers say it like this: we must take persons in their first-person being (as they live out of their own center), and not only in their third-person being (as others perceive them). Thus personalists see in the "turn to the subject" of modern philosophy not just the danger of lapsing into a subjectivism that they reject but also a new resource for understanding persons more deeply.

Personalists also hold that a human person, as a creature of

5. See Jan Bengtsson, *The Worldview of Personalism* (Oxford: Oxford University Press, 2006), 8.

6. Bengtsson calls Wojtyla "perhaps the greatest twentieth century personalist" (281).

7. This thought is developed by Karol Wojtyla in his seminal paper "Subjectivity and the Irreducible in the Human Being," found in his collection *Person and Community* (New York: Peter Lang, 1993).

interiority, does not exist just to provide an instance of the human kind, but exists as *this* unrepeatable person and so stands in a sense above the human kind, being always more than an instance of it. They are keenly aware of the inviolability of persons, that is, they understand why it is that none of us is ever rightly used and destroyed for the good of others. They are more sensitive than their ancestors to all the forms of manipulation and coercion that threaten our personhood. They also say that persons do not just exist, like the other animals, in a finite environment the contours of which are based on their needs, but that they exist in openness to the whole of being (an important feature of personhood to be discussed in the first chapter). And they reject the ancient distinction between Greek and barbarian, knowing that the birthright of a person belongs not to a select few but to every human being.

Personalists think that persons are beings of immeasurable dignity, and that they rank above all non-personal being. Personalists are not cowed by the immensity of space-time; they refuse to think of persons as specks within a vastness that renders persons negligible. The natural center of the world is the place where persons encounter each other.

Personalists resist an overly intellectualized view of the human person; they give special attention to the "heart" and to the affective dimension of personal existence, of course without depreciating the power of reason. They also have a distinctive understanding of social life, which they think of in terms of intersubjectivity. They say that we can no longer live in the social solidarity that was natural in earlier times. Thus we can no longer share the faith of our group merely out of a tribal loyalty to the group; as person each of us acts in his or her own name in making the basic commitments of one's life. Persons are just as little mere parts of a social group as they are of God. It may seem to follow from this that personalism is just another species of individualism and is sure to bring severe social fragmentation in its wake. But most personalists have been very sensitive to the sterility of individualism.[8] They have followed Buber in taking very seriously the interpersonal relations in which human persons live and move and have their being. Personalists refuse to think about social life only in terms of rights and of protection against intruders; they think of it mainly in terms of solidarity and co-responsibility.

Personalists think that this sense of personal existence has been powerfully awakening in the last couple of centuries, and that this awakening is an epochal event in humanity, a sea change in the way we understand ourselves. What I want to show in this study is that Newman is a significant voice in this epochal event; we can find in him much of the truth in this rising personalism. I do not mean to say that Newman knew the early personalists and was directly influenced by them, or that he called himself a "personalist"; nor do I mean that he gives a full philosophical account of these ideas, or that each of them can be found in him. He was rather a pioneer, "the pioneer of a new philosophy of the individual Person and of Personal Life." I also want to show that his pioneering personalism coheres entirely with and in fact stands in the service of his radically theocentric religion.[9]

The Personalist Teaching of Newman in Relation to His Personalist Ethos

Now personalism exists in Newman not only as a teaching that can be enunciated in propositions, but also as a personalist way of acting and being, including a personalist way of writing, of exercising influence on others, of proposing truth to others. When Newman chose as his cardinal's motto *cor ad cor loquitur,*

8. This is especially true of the French personalist Emmanuel Mounier in his *Personalism* (Notre Dame, Ind.: University of Notre Dame Press, no date). By the way, in the course of mentioning thinkers important for personalism, he says, after naming Buber and Berdyaev, "and one ought not to forget Newman" (xxviii).

9. In these paragraphs on personalism I have taken over some sentences from the longer account of personalism that I wrote for The Personalist Project; see www.thepersonalistproject.org/about_us/426.

he was expressing something about his way of addressing others, and this way of address was eminently personalist. We do not want to neglect this lived dimension of his personalism and to limit ourselves to his "theoretical" personalism, that is, to his personalist teachings. This is not just because Newman "practiced what he preached," but rather because the same writings that express his personalist teachings also express his personalist ethos. We are simply insisting on studying in all of its dimensions the personalism that we discern in his works. Let me explain.

It is an extraordinary thing about Newman that a great deal of his personalist teaching has an unintended "autobiographical" dimension to it. Thus in the sermon "Personal Influence, the Means of Propagating the Truth," he not only talks about personal influence in principle but he unwittingly reveals the kind of influence he exercised; or in his sermon "Unreal Words," he not only says things about a certain kind of shallow religious speech that are valid for all his listeners, but he himself speaks a language that eminently displays the "realness" for which he is pleading; or in his sermon "Jewish Zeal, a Pattern to Christians," he cannot help expressing the zeal that burned in himself. If we know about the influence he exercised, and then open the sermon on personal influence, we notice that the sermon is based on a kind of "knowledge by connaturality" (more on this in ch. 3). If we experience the solemn dignity of his religious speech, we find the sermon on unreal words to be written out of a "knowledge by connaturality." That is, Newman seems to understand human things through understanding his own heart; he knows human things through the medium of what he himself is. Therefore we should not be content in this study with the propositions that make up his personalist teaching; we should also look for the living person whose inner abundance is reflected in these propositions. This dependency of what he taught on who he is makes for a personalism all its own, a personalism that far exceeds a body of personalist teaching.

Newman's accuser, Charles Kingsley, once famously asked

him in public, "What then does Dr. Newman mean?" Newman began his response by saying, "He asks what I *mean;* not about my words, not about my arguments, not about my actions, as his ultimate point, but that living intelligence, by which I write, and argue, and act."[10] There is the personalism articulated in Newman's words and arguments, and there is the personalism embodied by the "living intelligence" that was Newman. In this study I want to try to capture both levels of his personalism, since both are expressed in his writings. I want to take him not just as a teacher of personalism, but also as a witness to personalism.

Final Preliminaries

I am a philosopher by training, and almost all of my previous published work would qualify as properly philosophical. I have always respected the power of philosophical reason to appeal to believer and non-believer alike, and to unite those who diverge at the level of faith. So I am strongly inclined to look for a personalism in Newman that can be expressed without expressing Newman's religious faith. But I have to acknowledge that Newman's personalism is so embedded in his faith that such a strictly philosophical approach would engage only a portion of his personalism, namely the portion that is laid out in the *Grammar of Assent.* I do better to take Newman as the Christian thinker that he was. I do better not even to claim that I am always speaking strictly as a philosopher. Thus I do not apologize for all the use I will be making of Newman's sermons. At the same time it must be said with emphasis that Newman's personalism is not just for believers; as with Kierkegaard, much that we find in Newman is such as to fascinate and to challenge non-Christians, and I want to give particular attention to this broader appeal of Newman's pioneering personalism.

There is another temptation to which my training in phi-

10. John Henry Newman, *Apologia Pro Vita Sua* (London: Longmans, Green, 1908), xxiv. Hereafter, Apol.

losophy exposes me. By my professional habits I am inclined to turn the teaching and witness of Newman into an object of scholarly investigation, and to keep myself out of view. I am inclined to avoid the first person and to speak as impersonally as possible. But there is a way of responding to Newman, and explaining what he has meant to me, that does not amount to an intrusion of me into my discourse on Newman, but is rather a way of showing forth Newman and his personalism. As I studied Newman and his times, I was surprised to see how much I could learn about him from the response of his contemporaries to him. It is not just that they help us to articulate what we ourselves already discern in Newman; seeing Newman with their eyes enlarges our sense of who Newman was. If that is true of his contemporaries in the nineteenth century, why should it not be true of us in the twentieth and twenty-first centuries who encounter Newman deeply? So I have written on the assumption that I can reveal Newman and his personalism not only by focusing on Newman, but also by sometimes speaking out of my own encounter with him. This personal way of engagement is perhaps the only adequate way to engage a personalist thinker.

And one final word about the focus of this study. It is not primarily a historical study. I am not in the first place concerned with Newman's place in the movement of thought known as personalism, nor am I much concerned with tracing contemporary personalist themes back to Newman; what concerns me, and stands at the center of this study, is the richness, the fruitfulness of his personalism and of the unity that it forms with his theocentric religious existence.[11]

11. My study presupposes some basic knowledge of Newman's life and times; the reader who lacks this may want to look, for a start, at the entry on Newman by William Barry in the *Catholic Encyclopedia* (1911), available at www.newmanreader.org/biography/biography.html. If the reader is looking for a short book-length introduction to Newman, he or she can do no better than to study C. S. Dessain, *John Henry Newman* (London: Thomas Nelson and Sons, 1966). But my book is not written just for Newman specialists; it means to serve as an introduction to the intellectual and spiritual world of Newman. This is why I quote so extensively from Newman throughout my book.

The Personalism of JOHN HENRY NEWMAN

1

Theocentric Religion

For the reason given in the Introduction, I begin my study of Newman's personalism with a chapter on a side of his mind and personality that seems in a sense antithetical to personalism. I call this the theocentrism of Newman, and I proceed to explore the different aspects of it.

"The Dogmatical Principle"

As I said, when I first encountered Newman I was drawn to him mainly by his affirmation of what he called "the dogmatical principle," or what he called in the negative his anti-liberalism. Here is an inspired statement of the dogmatical principle:

> That there is a truth then; that there is one truth; that religious error is in itself of an immoral nature; that its maintainers, unless involuntarily such, are guilty in maintaining it; that it is to be dreaded; that the search for truth is not the gratification of curiosity; that its attainment has nothing of the excitement of a discovery; that the mind is below truth, not above it, and is bound, not to descant upon it, but

to venerate it; that truth and falsehood are set before us for the trial of our hearts; that our choice is an awful giving forth of lots on which salvation or rejection is inscribed ... —this is the dogmatical principle, which has strength.

In the same place Newman states by way of contrast the principle of liberalism, which he abhorred with his whole being:

That truth and falsehood in religion are but matter of opinion; that one doctrine is as good as another; that the Governor of the world does not intend that we should gain the truth; that there is no truth; that we are not more acceptable to God by believing this than by believing that; that no one is answerable for his opinions; that they are a matter of necessity or accident; that it is enough if we sincerely hold what we profess; that our merit lies in seeking, not in possessing ... that belief belongs to the mere intellect, not to the heart also; that we may safely trust to ourselves in matters of Faith, and need no other guide,—this is the principle of philosophies and heresies, which is very weakness.[1]

This zeal for truth, and this abhorrence of the relativistic dissolution of truth, are absolutely fundamental to Newman. They stood at the center of his teaching and preaching as leader of the Oxford Movement. He never departed from the dogmatical principle. This is why he was able, speaking at the end of his life, to summarize the whole of it in terms of the defense of the dogmatical principle. In 1879 he said in Rome, on the occasion of his being elevated to the cardinalate: "For thirty, forty, fifty years I have resisted to the best of my powers the spirit of Liberalism in religion."[2] Many people have been drawn to Newman by the energy and power with which he taught the dogmatical principle, for he did not teach it with the pathos of a professor who is making an important point, but with the ardor of a confessor who is bearing witness.

Let me dwell on this ardor. What drew me to Newman was not just the affirmation of Christian doctrine, nor was it just the

1. DD, 357–58.

2. John Henry Newman, "The Biglietto Speech," in William Neville, ed., *Addresses to Cardinal Newman with His Replies* (London: Longmans, Green, 1905), 64.

fundamental affirmation of the supreme importance of truth in religion. What drew me was the radical theocentric spirit that seemed to me to express itself in the dogmatical principle.[3] In some of his sermons preached for Trinity Sunday he takes delight in the fact that the doctrine of the Trinity concerns not only the economy of our salvation, but also, and first of all, God as He exists in Himself. In one of them he says: "The Annunciation, the birth of Christ, His death on the Cross, His Resurrection, the descent of the Holy Ghost, are all mysteries; but we celebrate them, not on this account, but for the blessings which we gain from them. But today we celebrate, not an act of God's mercy towards us, but, forgetting ourselves, and looking only upon Him, we reverently and awfully, yet joyfully, extol the wonders, not of His works, but of His own Nature. We lift up heart and eyes towards Him, and speak of what He is in Himself."[4] Many say that the doctrine of the Trinity is barren and abstract and that it can be brought to life only by making it say something about us human beings and our redemption. So they say, for instance, that we have to think of the Father as our Creator, the Son as our Redeemer, and the Spirit as our Sanctifier, and that only then is the doctrine lifted for us out of indifference and able to play a role in our religious existence. We have to make the doctrine say as much about man as about God: only then does it light up with religious interest for us. In this sermon Newman makes a point of declining this anthropocentric support; he goes on to say, "Doubtless, from that deep mystery proceeds all that is to benefit and bless us. Without an Almighty Son we are not redeemed.... Yet, on this day, we celebrate the mystery for its own sake, not for our sake."[5]

3. See my study "What Is Anthropocentric and What Is Theocentric in Christian Existence? The Challenge of John Henry Newman," *Communio* 16 (Summer 1989), 244–55; also in German translation in the German *Communio,* "Anthropozentrismus und Theozentrismus im christlichen Leben," 19. Jahrgang, September 1990, 444–53.

4. Newman, *Parochial and Plain Sermons* VI (London: Longmans, Green, 1907), 327–28. Hereafter, PPS.

5. PPS, VI, 328.

Or consider another one of his Trinity Sunday sermons. At first we hear him expressing, in tones profoundly characteristic of him, his yearning for the rest and peace that he hopes for in eternity: "After the fever of life; after wearinesses and sicknesses; fightings and despondings; languor and fretfulness; struggling and failing, struggling and succeeding; after all the changes and chances of this troubled unhealthy state, at length comes death, at length the White Throne of God, at length the Beatific Vision ... —the sight of the Blessed Three, the Holy One; the Three that bear witness in heaven; in light unapproachable." And now Newman, speaking with hushed holy awe of what he apprehends through faith, speaks not of the shelteredness in God that he will find in eternity; instead, he spontaneously begins to recite, or rather to chant in adoration, the articles of the Athanasian Creed: "The Father God, the Son God, and the Holy Ghost God; the Father Lord, the Son Lord, and the Holy Ghost Lord; the Father uncreate, the Son uncreate, and the Holy Ghost uncreate; the Father incomprehensible, the Son incomprehensible, and the Holy Ghost incomprehensible. For there is one Person of the Father, another of the Son, and another of the Holy Ghost; and such as the Father is, such is the Son, and such is the Holy Ghost; and yet there are not three Gods, nor three Lords, nor three incomprehensibles, nor three uncreated; but one God, one Lord, one uncreated, and one incomprehensible."[6] This is the secret of Newman's dogmatical principle: the spirit of adoration in which Newman is led to use the Athanasian Creed as a psalm or hymn of praise. This is what caught my attention in the early years of my discipleship with Newman: the loss of this theocentric spirit in the world of contemporary religion, and the powerful presence of it in Newman's teaching. Indeed, Newman is a prophet of this theocentric spirit, and his dogmatical principle is best understood as an expression of this spirit.

6. PPS, VI, 369–70.

Theocentrism and Conscience

Newman's theocentric spirit begins at a level of his religious existence that is prior to his Trinitarian faith; it begins in his experience of conscience, which according to Newman gives us our most primordial religious knowledge. In chapter 7 we will examine this religious knowledge; for now let us just point out the theocentric structure of it.

For Newman conscience centers around *being morally obliged,* which is why he calls conscience "a magisterial dictate" and speaks of conscience warning and accusing us.[7] Here we have the reason why Newman's religion, insofar as it is based on conscience, is strongly theocentric. "And hence it is that we are accustomed to speak of conscience as a voice ... and moreover a voice, or the echo of a voice, *imperative and constraining, like no other dictate in the whole of our experience.*"[8] God is experienced as commanding us, and so is experienced as an authoritative sovereign, as Lord; he is in Newman's words experienced as *"a Supreme Governor, a Judge holy, just, powerful, all-seeing, retributive,"* as *"One who, not simply for the good of the offender, but as an end good in itself ... ordains that the offender should suffer for his offence."*[9] This is *not* a God who is experienced *merely* as a source of salvation, nor is it a God who is experienced *merely* as exercising a benevolent providence over us human beings and designing the economy of our redemption. Newman often teaches that we cannot think of God's action toward us exclusively in terms of "benevolence"; that He acts according to a justice that cannot be reduced to benevolence, as when He punishes as a matter of "retributive justice" and not merely for the reformation and healing of the wrongdoer.[10] Newman derives this teaching primarily from his experience of conscience.

7. Newman, *An Essay in Aid of a Grammar of Assent* (London: Longmans, Green, 1903), 105. Hereafter, GA.

8. GA, 107; my italics.

9. GA, 391; my italics.

10. See sermon 6 in his *Fifteen Sermons Preached before the University of Oxford* (London: Longmans, Green, 1909), sermon 6. Hereafter, OUS.

The psychologist Erich Fromm discusses conscience in one of his works, saying that in its healthy functioning it involves a "loving concern for oneself."[11] This is an account of conscience almost the opposite of Newman's. Newman would say that Fromm gives an account of conscience as something extremely self-absorbed and abandons all the self-transcendence that is achieved in taking seriously the call of conscience. Fromm for his part would reproach Newman with advocating what Fromm calls "authoritarian conscience," which is for him conscience deformed by an excess of obedience. This is the way Newman's theocentric view of conscience is bound to look to someone who approaches conscience without any reference to God. Once, however, we have done justice to conscience as a dictate, "imperative and constraining," and as calling for obedience and submission, then we can proceed, as I have tried to show in my paper on Fromm and Newman, to make sense of a certain "loving concern for oneself" in the experience of conscience. This self-concern belongs indeed to conscience, according to Newman, but not as the first and fundamental structure of conscience, as Fromm supposes.

We see, then, that the dogmatical principle, or rather the theocentric spirit of it, "begins" already in Newman in the experience of conscience. Already in conscience Newman is "broken open" to God, overwhelmed by the divine majesty, prostrate before the Holy One, freed from all eudaemonistic preoccupations with his own happiness as the ultimate end of existence. When Newman receives a revelation about the Trinitarian nature of God, he does not stipulate, as the condition of his taking an interest in it, that this revelation must concern the economy of his redemption; given his theocentric experience of conscience he is well prepared to venerate God as three-in-one for His own sake, and so to chant in adoration the articles of the Athanasian Creed.

11. I have elsewhere discussed this thesis of Fromm and have done so on the basis of Newman; see my study "Conscience and Superego," in *Personalist Papers* (Washington D.C.: The Catholic University of America Press, 2004).

Theocentric Stances: Fear, Zeal, and Love

I propose now to bring to light the radically theocentric strain in several great themes of Newman's preaching at Oxford: the fear of God, zeal for God's honor, and love for God.

Here is a powerful early sermon called "The Religion of the Day." After acknowledging the excess of fear and dread in the religion of barbarous ages, he examines the opposite deficiency of the religion in our own age, namely the complete loss of the fear of God, and he says:

What is the world's religion now? It has taken the brighter side of the Gospel,—its tidings of comfort, its precepts of love; all darker, deeper views of man's condition and prospects being comparatively forgotten. This is the religion natural to a civilized age, and well has Satan dressed and completed it into an idol of the Truth. As the reason is cultivated, the taste formed, the affections and sentiments refined, a general decency and grace will of course spread over the face of society, quite independently of the influence of Revelation.... Our manners are courteous; we avoid giving pain or offence; our words become correct; our relative duties are carefully performed.... Vice now becomes unseemly and hideous to the imagination, or, as it is sometimes familiarly said, "out of taste." Thus elegance is gradually made the test and standard of virtue.[12]

The "religion of the day" is for Newman an aestheticized religion; it is religion rendered harmless and trivialized by a certain aestheticist spirit. The overly fastidious hearts of believers shrink from the encounter with the living God; radical theocentrism seems to be in bad taste. Newman proceeds to speak of the erosion of conscience in the "religion of the day." Since conscience is such a source of theocentric religion, it will necessarily be eroded in the "religion of the day."

Conscience is no longer recognized as an independent arbiter of actions, its authority is explained away; partly it is superseded in the

12. PPS, I, 311–12.

> minds of men by the so-called moral sense, which is regarded merely as the love of the beautiful; partly by the rule of expediency, which is forthwith substituted for it in the details of conduct. Now conscience is a stern, gloomy principle; it tells us of guilt and of prospective punishment. Accordingly, when its terrors disappear, then disappear also, in the creed of the day, those fearful images of Divine wrath with which the Scriptures abound. They are explained away. Every thing is bright and cheerful. Religion is pleasant and easy; benevolence is the chief virtue; intolerance, bigotry, excess of zeal, are the first of sins.[13]

This deformation of religion in the "religion of the day" comes from losing a sense of the fear of God. As a result Christianity becomes harmless and trivial; it loses what Newman calls the "lasting taste of divine truth."[14]

It becomes something human-all-too-human. Now one might ask whether the loss of the fear of God is really a loss of the theocentric spirit. For one may say that in fearing God we fear the punishment of God, and that our fear, therefore, is not centered on God as He is in Himself, but on God only insofar as He threatens something harmful for us. Thus to recover religious fear would not be to recover the theocentric spirit.

Newman answers that there is a kind of fear of God that is just as centered on God as adoration is, just as centered on God as Newman shows himself to be when he chants the articles of the creed as a song of praise. "Now it must be observed that the existence of fear in religion does not depend on the circumstance of our being sinners; it is short of that. Were we pure as the Angels, yet in His sight, one should think, we could not but fear, before whom the heavens are not clean, nor the Angels free from folly. The Seraphim themselves veiled their faces while they cried, Glory!"[15] So for Newman religious fear means first of all the awe-filled shuddering of the creature before the infinite living God; it does not mean—not first of all—the dread of the guilty creature before the punishing hand of

13. PPS, I, 312.
14. PPS, I, 305.
15. PPS, V, 15–16.

the divine judge. Had Newman lived to read the work of Rudolf Otto, and especially his study *The Idea of the Holy* (1917), he would have responded strongly and warmly to Otto's distinction between numinous fear and natural fear. The latter is simply fear of some anticipated harm, whereas the former is fear in the presence of God who is experienced as *mysterium tremendum.* Numinous fear is so fundamentally theocentric that it is easily recognized as a moment in all adoration, which for its part is incontestably theocentric. When Newman chants the articles of the creed in adoration, he expresses numinous fear.

Perhaps the best way to see that there is a religious fear that is not self-regarding but radically God-regarding is to consider Newman's descriptions of deficient fear in religious persons. These descriptions are taken from Newman's sermon "Unreal Words," in which he thinks very concretely about the "unreality" that corrupts the speech of Christians. This unreality comes from a lack of religious fear, and it is clear from these descriptions that this lack does not consist only in failing to fear divine punishment. "Another instance of want of fear, is the bold and unscrupulous way in which men speak of the Holy Trinity and the Mystery of the Divine Nature. They use sacred terms and phrases, should occasion occur, in a rude and abrupt way, and discuss points of doctrine concerning the All-holy and Eternal, even (if I may without irreverence state it) over their cups, perhaps arguing against them, as if He were such a one as themselves." Here the lack of religious fear, as expressed in our way of talking, is simply a lack of respect for God, and respect for God is a thoroughly theocentric stance.

Newman continues: "Another instance of this want of fear is found in the peremptory manner in which men lay down what Almighty God must do, what He cannot but do, as if they were masters of the whole scheme of salvation, and might anticipate His high providence and will. And another is the confidence with which they often speak of their having been converted, pardoned, and sanctified, as if they knew their own state as well as God knows it."[16] Here religious fear is connected by Newman with wonder and awe, and not with dread of divine punishment. Newman continues: "And another [instance of this want of fear] is the familiarity with which many persons address our Lord in prayer, applying epithets to Him and adopting a strain of language which does not beseem creatures, not to say sinners."[17] Here religious fear is connected with our being creatures, not sinners. Thus religious fear in Newman is a theocentric stance in which God is venerated as God. The prominence of fear in his preaching helps to impart to his religion its strong theocentric character.

From Newman's preaching on religious fear I distinguish his preaching on zeal. In a sermon with the shocking title "Jewish Zeal, a Pattern for Christians," he says:

> What the Old Testament especially teaches us is this:—that zeal ... consists in a strict attention to His commands—a scrupulousness, vigilance, heartiness, and punctuality, which bears with no reasoning or questioning about them—an intense thirst for the advancement of His glory—a shrinking from the pollution of sin and sinners—an indignation, nay impatience, at witnessing His honour insulted—a quickness of feeling when His name is mentioned, and a jealousy how it is mentioned— ... a carelessness of obloquy, or reproach, or persecution, a forgetfulness of friend and relative, nay, a hatred (so to say) of all that is naturally dear to us, when He says, "Follow me."[18]

Many people are startled at Newman's expression of zeal; it is foreign to them, it does not make sense to them, it seems religiously primitive to them. They think that the only way we could really give "offense" to God would be by harming ourselves or others. They think that we are zealous for God's honor only insofar as we are concerned for man's well-being. But Newman envisions here an offense against God that is not explainable exclusively in terms of human well-being. He envisions a way of offending God that does not "pass through" the harming

16. PPS, V, 19.
17. PPS, V, 20.
18. PPS, III, 175.

of man. His understanding of zeal is not through and through anthropocentric; it is also theocentric. For instance, whenever Newman contends zealously against trivialized religion, against the "unreal words" in which it expresses itself, he is not just trying to avert harm for believers, but he is also resisting a way of being religious that dishonors God. This dishonoring of God is something all its own and is not reducible to (though of course it is closely connected with) the impoverishment of believers. Newman has some wise things to say about this impoverishment; thus he says, among other things, that our love of neighbor is damaged and trivialized when separated from zeal; he says in fact that our love of neighbor tends to become "languid unmeaning benevolence" when practiced apart from zeal.[19] But what concerns us at present is that zeal is a radically theocentric religious attitude. It is deeply akin to his commitment to the dogmatical principle, and in fact in many of Newman's affirmations of the dogmatical principle we can detect the ardor of his zeal. When Newman chants the articles of the creed in adoration, he burns with zeal.

Let me add just one other specimen of his zeal that is relevant to understanding his theocentrism. In his sermon "Faith and the World" he considers an objection some have made to Christianity, namely, that it imposes on men and women an unnatural life. He says that "there are a number of faculties and talents which seem only to exist in this world, and to be impossible in another. Consider the varieties of mental gifts ... such as talent for business, or talent for the useful arts, mechanical talent. Or, again, consider the talents which go to make up a great warrior. They seem as if evidently made for this world, and this world only."[20] The orientation of Christianity to the next world seems to do violence to all those abilities that connect us with this world, and this awakens the suspicion that Christianity is an

19. PPS, II, 286.

20. Newman, *Sermons Bearing on Subjects of the Day* (London: Longmans, Green,, 1902), 82. Hereafter, SD.

unnatural religion. As he turns to respond to this objection, it is significant that Newman resists the inclination to say that there are other abilities and faculties in human beings that cannot be fulfilled in this world, and that with a view to these abilities and faculties Christianity is eminently "natural." He makes this argument elsewhere (as in *Parochial and Plain Sermons,* IV, 14), but here shows a certain zeal as Christian teacher by granting the unnaturalness on which the objection is based.

> I answer by admitting that religion is in this sense unnatural; but I maintain that Christ came to bring in a higher nature into this world of men, and that this could not be done except by interfering with the nature which originally belongs to it. Where the spiritual system runs counter to the natural, the natural must give way. God has graciously willed to bring us to heaven; to practice a heavenly life on earth, certainly, is a thing above earth. It is like trying to execute some high and refined harmony on an insignificant instrument. In attempting it, that instrument would be taxed beyond its powers, and would be sacrificed to great ideas beyond itself. And so, in a certain sense, this life, and our present nature, is sacrificed for heaven and the new creature.[21]

This is spoken in the spirit of theocentric religion. He is saying that Christianity does not have to be justified exclusively in terms of human fulfillment; he has no hesitation to admit the aspect of "dis-fulfillment" that it also brings to believers. He continues in this theocentric vein on the next page, where he says that the Son of God's incarnation as man was no natural fulfillment of His divine nature, and so our being taken into His divine nature should not be expected to be all fulfillment for us. I repeat that Newman elsewhere says profound things about the fulfillment of the deepest aspirations of the human heart in Christianity, as all Christian teachers have done; but he speaks with a theocentric zeal when he sometimes declines the support of this argument and says that it is worth believing as a Christian even at the cost of considerable "dis-fulfillment."

While it is true that fear and zeal express the theocentric

21. SD, 87.

spirit of Newman, they are not the only religious stances that express it. Love, too, can express it. In fact, love is just as God-centered as fear and zeal. In the following, Newman anticipates the moment after death in which he and Christ will see each other face to face for the first time; it is the love with which Newman longs for this encounter that shows forth his theocentric spirit.

> to see His face, though for a moment! to hear His voice, to hear Him speak, though it be to punish! O Saviour of men, it [the soul] says, I come to Thee, though it be in order to be at once remanded from Thee; I come to Thee who art my Life and my All; I come to Thee on the thought of whom I have lived all my life long.... Yea, though I be now descending thither, into "a land desert, pathless and without water," I will fear no ill, for Thou art with me. I have seen Thee this day face to face, and it sufficeth; I have seen Thee, and that glance of Thine is sufficient for a century of sorrow, in the nether prison. I will live on that look of Thine, though I see Thee not, till I see Thee again, never to part from Thee. That eye of Thine shall be sunshine and comfort to my weary, longing soul; that voice of Thine shall be everlasting music in my ears.[22]

Newman does not express relief that he is saved, nor is he distressed at the prospect of suffering in purgatory; he has here eyes and ears only for the beauty of the God-man. This is love with theocentric ardor. If we think that Newman exaggerates the purgatorial suffering that awaits him, that exaggeration just serves to throw his theocentric spirit into relief; for the suffering that he anticipates does not prevent him from longing to see the God-man.

One of the Enemies of Theocentric Religion

Newman often does battle with those who depreciate the dogmatical principle and blunt the theocentric spirit of it. Of course,

22. Newman, *Discourses Addressed to Mixed Congregations* (London: Longmans, Green, 1906), 81–82. Hereafter, DMC.

"the religion of the day" depreciates it. But I want to examine one particular adversary of Newman, namely the one who makes so much of religious feelings as to lose interest in religious truth. The theocentrism of the dogmatical principle is here turned into its very opposite, namely into the self-absorption of one who is concerned with having certain religious feelings. Newman often identifies Martin Luther as one main source of this fateful religious subjectivism, as when he says:

> The old Catholic notion, which still lingers in the Established Church, was, that Faith was an intellectual act, its object truth, and its result knowledge.... But in proportion as the Lutheran leaven spread, it became fashionable to say that Faith was, not an acceptance of revealed doctrine, not an act of the intellect, but a feeling, an emotion, an affection, an appetency; and, as this view of Faith obtained, so was the connexion of Faith with Truth and Knowledge more and more either forgotten or denied. [Religious people increasingly said] that Religion was based, not on argument, but on taste and sentiment, that nothing was objective, every thing subjective, in doctrine. [They came to] think that Religion, as such, consisted in something short of intellectual exercises, viz., in the affections, in the imagination, in inward persuasions and consolations, in pleasurable sensations, sudden changes, and sublime fancies. They learned to believe and to take it for granted, that Religion was nothing beyond a supply of the wants of human nature, not an external fact and a work of God.[23]

We will see in later chapters that Newman takes "experience" and the "heart" very seriously in his personalism; by no means does he mean to set them aside as irrelevant to Christian existence. But in the setting of his theocentrism he warns against the great danger of religious subjectivism, the danger that experience and the heart become so prominent in our religious existence as to divert us from God to self.

Newman sometimes combats religious subjectivism under the title of "rationalism," as in his important tract "On the In-

23. Newman, *The Idea of a University* (London: Longmans, Green, 1907), 27–28. Hereafter, Idea.

troduction of Rationalistic Principles into Revealed Religion." At first glance the talk of rationalism seems strange, since this subjectivism seems to involve a defect of reason rather than an excess of it; we just heard Newman say that the subjectivists abandon the old idea that faith has to do with knowledge and truth, and this seems to be the very opposite of an excessive use of reason in religion. But Newman has a good reason for connecting rationalism and subjectivism, as we can see in his tract on rationalism. Speaking of the doctrine of the Atonement he says that in the perspective of rationalism: "It is chiefly to be regarded, not as a wonder in heaven, and in its relation to the attributes of God and to the unseen world, but in its experienced effects on our minds, in the change it effects when it is believed.... Not that the reality of the Atonement, in itself, is formally denied, but it is cast in the background, except so far as it can be discovered to be influential, viz., to show God's hatred of sin, the love of Christ, and the like; and there is an evident tendency to consider it as a mere Manifestation of the love of Christ, *to the denial of all real virtue in it as an expiation for sin.*"[24] One sees why Newman speaks of rationalism; his antagonist eliminates mystery in religion, and in this way acquires the title of rationalist. The Christian mysteries found with respect to the Atonement can be expressed like this: how does the death of the God-man put an end to our estrangement from God, how does it "satisfy" divine justice, whence its power to "take away" our sins? Newman is very insistent on saying that we cannot explain these things, that we have to venerate them as divine realities hidden in mystery. The rationalist, by contrast, thinks he can completely explain them; for to say that the whole meaning of the Atonement lies in God encouraging and reassuring man is to put the Atonement entirely within the realm of our experiencing (to be encouraged and to be reassured is some-

24. Newman, "On the Introduction of Rationalistic Principles into Revealed Religion," *Essays Critical and Historical,* I (London: Longmans, Green, 1907), 47–48; my italics. Hereafter, ECH.

thing that exists only as experienced). Thus the rationalist takes all mystery out of the Atonement. He treats the transmission of original sin in the same way, saying that the sin of Adam is passed on simply by bad example being given from one generation to the next, or by bad social structures enduring across the generations, as if there were not some more fundamental estrangement from God that is only expressed in the giving of bad example and in the endurance of bad social structures, but is not reducible to these. Thinking along these same lines the rationalist depreciates the real efficacy of the sacraments and contents himself with a mere psychological impact of them on himself. One sees that a rationalism based on subjectivism and tending toward liberalism is not so strange after all; it is an entirely "natural" form of rationalism.

But notice the kind of rationalism Newman is opposing. It is not just the rationalism that tries to prove too much in matters of revelation, as when St. Anselm argues that the number of the elect exactly equals the number of fallen angels. Newman is rather opposed to a rationalism that compromises the theocentrism of Christian belief. He is concerned to show that in acknowledging the Atonement and other Christian mysteries we are drawn out of our own minds and are led to an encounter with God in His otherness. In his tract on rationalism, in the course of distinguishing between subjective truth and objective truth, he says: "By Objective Truth is meant the Religious System considered as existing in itself, external to this or that particular mind: by Subjective, is meant that which each mind receives in particular, and considers to be such. To believe in Objective Truth is to throw ourselves forward upon that which we have but partially mastered or made subjective; to embrace, maintain, and use general propositions which are larger than our own capacity, of which we cannot see the bottom, which we cannot follow out into their multiform details; to come before and bow before the import of such propositions, as if we were contemplating what is real and independent of human judgment."[25] In other words, one sure way of cultivating the theocentric spirit is by gratefully acknowledging mystery in religion as something that transcends our experiencing, just as one sure way of falling into the bad anthropocentric spirit is by making our religious experiencing the measure of revelation. "As great then as is the difference between hanging upon the thought of God and resting in ourselves, lifting up the heart to God and bringing all things in heaven and earth down to ourselves, exalting God and exalting reason, measuring things by God's power and measuring them by our own ignorance, so great is the difference between him who believes in the Christian mysteries and him who does not."[26]

The Appeal of Newman's Theocentrism

The critics of Newman's theocentrism say that man, seen in the setting of his thought, is estranged from God. They might express themselves in the words of William James who, speaking of the "essential dualism of the theistic view," says that "Man being an outsider and a mere subject to God, not his intimate partner, a character of externality invades the field. God is not heart of our heart and reason of our reason, but our magistrate."[27] James speaks of "the difference between living against a background of foreignness and one of intimacy," and he pleads for "the vision of God as the indwelling divine rather than the external creator."[28] One might say that James is warning against

25. ECH, I, 34. In the continuation of this passage Newman proceeds to connect mystery in religion with the dogmatical principle and with his anti-liberalism: "Such a belief, implicit, and symbolized as it is in the use of creeds, seems to the Rationalist superstitious and unmeaning, and he consequently confines Faith to the province of Subjective Truth, or to the reception of doctrine, as, and so far as, it is met and apprehended by the mind, which will be differently, as he considers, in different persons, in the shape of orthodoxy in one, heterodoxy in another" (34–35).

26. PPS, IV, 293.

27. William James, *A Pluralist Universe,* in *Writings 1902–1910* (New York: Library Classics of the United States, 1987), 642.

28. Ibid., 644.

a kind of religion that is inherently heteronomous. It is certain that he would have seen the specter of heteronomy in Newman's theocentrism.

What James describes is a form of religion that is experienced as oppressive. But Newman does not experience the God whom he venerates as oppressive; he rather exults in God's greatness and is never so alive as in magnifying God in all His mysteriousness. What oppresses Newman is the rationalism that makes our minds the measure of God; what makes his heart expand is the theocentrism that lets God be the measure of our minds. In this chapter we have seen much evidence of Newman thriving in his way of venerating God. Let us now add the testimony of those who heard his theocentric preaching and were not oppressed by it, but fascinated by it and transformed by it.

A young man who heard Newman preach in Oxford wrote years later, expressing what many people have experienced: "The effect of his teaching on us young men was to turn our souls, as it were, inside out.... God the Creator was the first theme he taught us, and it contained ... all that followed. We never could be again the same as before."[29] Newman's preaching possessed life-transforming power. It did not come over as announcing a heteronomous sense of us existing outside of God, but it came over with an unearthly power. Even today we can experience this mysterious power in Newman's sermons. Now I want to say that his power and authority as a preacher comes in part from his radical theocentrism. It certainly also comes from the aspects of his personalism that we will examine later in this book, but not only from these; his theocentrism has a power all its own.

We can understand this power in light of what Newman said above about religious fear and the theocentrism proper to it. If we relate to God without any sense of Him as *mysterium tremendum,* if we divest Him of all that awakens numinous fear in us,

29. Willliam Lockhart, *Cardinal Newman: A Retrospect of Fifty Years* (London: Burns & Oates, 1891), 5–6.

if we let benevolence take over "unmixed" in our sense of who God is, and take over to the point of suppressing the divine *tremendum,* then we weaken, we trivialize God, we expose Him to scorn, we replace the living God with an emasculated substitute. Only a God whose lovingkindness is permeated by the *mysterium tremendum* is really God. Only such a God can fascinate us and can answer to the deepest aspirations of the human heart. This is why Newman's theocentric preaching had such a power to pierce the religious existence of his listeners.

Another contemporary of Newman who heard him preach in Oxford wrote in later years about one of his sermons: "Newman described closely some of the incidents of our Lord's passion; he then paused. For a few moments there was a breathless silence. Then, in a low, clear voice, of which the faintest vibration was audible in the farthest corner of St. Mary's, he said, 'Now, I bid you recollect that He to whom these things were done was Almighty God.' It was as if an electric stroke had gone through the church, as if every person present understood for the first time the meaning of what he had all his life been saying. I suppose it was an epoch in the mental history of more than one of my Oxford contemporaries."[30] Here we see Newman living out the dogmatical principle; for he is not only concerned with what the sufferings of Christ mean for us, he is also concerned with who it is who suffers, with the appalling fact that it is God Himself who suffers.[31] What I want to point out here is the power that this theocentric approach to Christ's sufferings had; it left a lasting mark on this listener, and, as he supposes, on others who heard the sermon.

Let us hear from one more member of Newman's Oxford

30. J. A. Froude, *Short Studies on Great Subjects,* vol. 4 (London: Longmans, Green, 1899), 286.

31. We are reminded here of one of the greatest sermons from Newman's Catholic period, "The Mental Sufferings of Our Lord in His Passion" (DMC, sermon 16). His theocentric spirit shows itself in this, that in this sermon Newman probes with great originality not what Christ's sufferings mean for us, but what they meant for Him.

congregation. This person inserts Newman into his age in a revealing way: "To an age which was set, as this age is, on material prosperity, easy living and all that gratifies the flesh, he [Newman] felt called to speak a language long unheard; to insist on the reality of the things of faith, and the necessity of obedience; to urge on men the necessity to crush self, and obey; to press home a severer, more girt-up way of living; to throw himself into strenuous conflict with the darling prejudices of his countrymen. It was in his *Parochial Sermons,* beyond all his other works, that he spoke out the truths which were within him—spoke them out with all the fervour of a prophet and the severe beauty of a poet."[32] This person is referring to what Newman called "the religion of the day," which for Newman was, as we saw, a religion too much accommodated to human need, too unwilling to challenge human self-indulgence; it was harmless Christianity, salt that had lost its savor, as we remarked in the Introduction. Newman saw it as his mission to challenge this established Christianity in the name of authentic, apostolical Christianity. He sometimes challenged it with the ferocity of an Old Testament prophet, as when he famously said in his sermon "The Religion of the Day," a sermon that was surely well known to this author: "Here I will not shrink from uttering my firm conviction, that it would be a gain to this country, were it vastly more superstitious, more bigoted, more gloomy, more fierce in its religion, than at present it shows itself to be. Not, of course, that I think the tempers of mind herein implied desirable, which would be an evident absurdity; but I think them infinitely more desirable and more promising than a heathen obduracy, and a cold, self-sufficient, self-wise tranquillity."[33]

It was Newman's theocentrism, with all its zeal for and fear of God, that made his religion real, serious, demanding, capable of

32. John Campbell Shairp, *Aspects of Poetry* (Oxford: Clarendon Press, 1881), 443. Of all the remembrances we have of Newman preaching, that of Shairp seems to me the most profound.

33. PPS, I, 320–21.

turning people's souls inside out, and hence made it the perfect antidote to the "religion of the day." Just as anthropocentrism and subjectivism and liberalism and rationalism tend to make religion mediocre and harmless, so Newman's theocentrism and anti-liberalism and anti-rationalism tend to impart to religion vigor and existential passion. What I want to call attention to at present is the deep appeal that Newman's theocentric preaching had for many people who had grown up in the barrenness of the established religion. Many of them aspired to something more in religion, and so Newman's call to conversion resonated deeply within them; it did not oppress them in the way in which theistic religion was oppressive for William James. By his preaching Newman spoke to their need like no other religious teacher in England in the nineteenth century.

The Personalist Basis of Newman's Theocentrism

Personalist philosophy offers us an illuminating way of thinking about the foundations of Newman's theocentric religion. It is true that Newman's personalism as presented in the following chapters stands in a relation of polarity with his theocentrism. But there is also a personalism *in* his theocentrism. Personalist thinkers such as Scheler and Buber, who explore the self-transcendence of human persons, have drawn a significant distinction that throws new light on Newman's theocentrism.

They have distinguished two realms in which human persons dwell: the "environment" and the "world."[34] My environment is constituted when I approach my surroundings using my needs as a principle of selection; I notice just those things

34. See Max Scheler, *Man's Place in Nature* (New York: Farrar, Straus and Cudahy, 1962), 35–55; Martin Buber, "Distance and Relation," in *The Knowledge of Man* (New York: Harper, 1966). One of the best presentations of the environment-world distinction is the one given by Josef Pieper, *Leisure* (New York: New American Library, 1963), ch. 2, "The Philosophical Act." I discuss the distinction in my book *The Selfhood of the Human Person,* ch. 5.4 and 5.5.

in my surroundings that promise to fulfill some need or that threaten to block the fulfillment of some need; whatever in my surroundings has no bearing on my needs is ignored and does not enter into my environment. Thus anything that could serve as food or shelter is prominent in my environment, to start with the most elementary needs; predatory animals are also prominent. My needs, from the most elementary ones to the most refined ones, are the measure and the center of my environment, and are reflected in its makeup. What the things in my surroundings are *in their own right and apart from my needs* is of no interest to me and thus finds no place in my environment. As environment-bound beings we humans are like the conscious animals, who also occupy an environment.

But we do not live only in an environment, nor do we differ from the conscious animals only by living in a more complex environment than they live in. We also live in another realm altogether, a realm to which the conscious animals have no access: we are "world-open" beings. Personalist thinkers usually characterize our world-openness in two ways. First, they say that we open to the world when a sense of the whole of reality awakens in us. This opening does not mean that we thematize the whole of reality in the sense of talking explicitly about "God and the world"; our sense of the whole is usually present as a frame of reference. For example, when we form the concept of environment, as we just did, and think of it as one realm in which we live, and then ask whether there are also other realms, we are asking on the background of "all possible realms in which a being can exist," which expresses an unsurpassable whole. An environment-bound being does not wonder about its environment as a realm of its own and ask what might lie beyond it; by asking like this—and asking even before an answer is found—this being has already passed from its environment into the "world." The second characteristic of our world-openness is intrinsically bound up with this sense of the whole: we are able to take an interest in things in their own right. Our power of taking an interest is no longer dominated by our needs; it is now de-centered; it can be captivated by the otherness of things. Instead of measuring things by our needs, we let ourselves be measured by them. We release things from our pragmatic grip and let them appear before us as they are. What something *really and ultimately is* can be understood only by inserting the thing in its place in the whole, and so this "objectivity" that we aim at as world-open beings, awakens in us that sense of the whole that also characterizes us as world-open beings.[35] We human persons live in both realms—not only in our environment, but also in the world. The matter-spirit duality of our being is expressed in the fact that we are citizens of both of these realms.

There is perhaps no more radical divergence in the understanding of the human person than the divergence of those who think of human persons as entirely environment-bound from those who acknowledge the world-openness of human persons. We can express the antagonism between Protagoras and Plato in these terms. In teaching that man is the measure of all things, Protagoras in effect confines man to his environment, where he is indeed the measure of all that appears in it. In teaching that God is the measure of man Plato performs that radical decentering of man that opens him to the world. The modern and contemporary descendants of Protagoras, such as Nietzsche and Rorty, acknowledge in effect only the environment. Even though they do not think of human needs only in terms of food and shelter, even though they expand the list of human needs, even to the point of speaking of religious needs, they still insist that our needs, however analyzed and counted, are the measure of all things. The one thing they cannot endure, the one thing that would be the undoing of their philosophies, is the idea of *things appearing as they are in their own right.*

Now it is illuminating to think of Newman's theocentric re-

35. It is important to distinguish these two aspects of world-openness; at the end of ch. 5 we will see that to these two correspond two aspects of Newman's theocentric religion.

ligion like this: it is religion built on a strong assertion of the world-openness of human persons. To understand this better we have to consider that religion can be corrupted by the "self-centeredness" that constitutes the human environment. The religious pragmatism of William James is full of such self-centeredness. At the end of his work *The Varieties of Religious Experience* he quotes approvingly from an author who says, "*God is not known, he is not understood; he is used* … sometimes as moral support, sometimes as friend, sometimes as an object of love. If he proves himself useful, the religious consciousness asks for no more than that. Does God really exist? How does he exist? What is he? are so many irrelevant questions. Not God, but life, more life, a larger, richer, more satisfying life, is, in the last analysis, the end of religion."[36] Our religious needs—not our survival needs, as above, but our religious needs—are the principle of selection; God is of interest to the religious pragmatist only insofar as He answers to these needs; the divine otherness is of no interest to him. It is the same logic whereby an animal constitutes its environment; the logic is simply transposed into human religion, that is all. What results is religion that is precisely devoid of world-openness.

But the religion proclaimed by Newman is charged with world-openness, and this is one main source of its theocentrism, even though he does not work with the pair of concepts environment-world. When he asserts his theocentrism he is often in debate with writers who are akin to the religious pragmatists. Above we heard this from Newman: "They learned to

36. William James, *The Varieties of Religious Experience*, in *William James: Writings 1902–1910* (New York: The Library of America, 1987), 453. More of the same is found at the very end of the book, where James backs away from the divine omnipotence on the grounds that our religious needs do not call for it: "The practical needs and experiences of religion seem to me sufficiently met by the belief that beyond each man and in a fashion continuous with him there exists a larger power which is friendly to him and to his ideals. All that the facts require is that the power should be both other and larger than our conscious selves. Anything larger will do, if only it be large enough to trust for the next step. It need not be infinite" (468). On the other hand, when we come to Newman's personalism we will find some points of striking convergence between Newman and James.

believe and to take it for granted, that Religion was nothing beyond a supply of the wants of human nature, not an external fact and a work of God."[37] This expresses exactly the dominance of our interests and needs and the resulting loss of a sense of divine realities as having a being of their own. We also heard this from his tract on rationalism: the doctrine of the Atonement "is chiefly to be regarded [by rationalist theologians], not as a wonder in heaven, and in its relation to the attributes of God and to the unseen world, but in its experienced effects on our minds ... as if His death took place merely ... to calm and assure us, *without any real connexion existing between it and God's forgiveness of our sins*."[38] This is what it means for the divine actions to be experienced in the medium of the environment, or in other words, according to the logic of the environment. In protesting against this religious self-centeredness Newman is in effect affirming what I have called the world-openness of authentic religious belief. Thus he expresses exactly what I mean by world-open religion when he admonishes us "to throw ourselves forward upon that which we have but partially mastered ... to embrace, maintain, and use general propositions which are larger than our own capacity, of which we cannot see the bottom ... as if we were contemplating what is real and independent of human judgment."[39]

And there are other achievements of personalist thought besides the environment-world distinction that help us to interpret Newman's theocentism. It would be fruitful to explore the ideas of value and value-response that were elaborated by Max Scheler and especially by Dietrich von Hildebrand. Here too it is the self-transcendence of the human person that these personalists want

37. Idea, 28.

38. ECH, I, 47–48.

39. ECH, I, 34. In the same world-open vein is this: Revelation is to be "entered into more or less by this or that mind, as it may be; and admitting of being apprehended more and more perfectly according to the diligence of this mind and that. It is one and the same, independent and real, of depth unfathomable, and illimitable in its extent." ECH, I, 41.

to stress. By a value-response von Hildebrand means a response given to a being in the consciousness that the being has some intrinsic excellence and is worthy of my response, calls for it, merits it.[40] Thus if I admire another as worthy of my admiration, or respect another as worthy of respect, then I give a value-response in the sense of von Hildebrand. Of course, the Christian tradition has long given attention to the flourishing that we achieve in acting toward others, as well as to the flourishing that others achieve through our acting toward them. These eudaemonist motives find their place in von Hildebrand, but he insists that it is all-important to be able to step beyond them and to achieve the self-transcendence of taking a value-responding stance to beings that are worthy of our response. When von Hildebrand develops the idea of value-response within our religious existence, he says that it is not enough to turn to God only as our protector, our refuge, our redeemer; we also have to turn to Him in adoration *as the One who is worthy.*

Now this spirit of value-response is most abundantly present in Newman. The three theocentric stances mentioned above are eminent value-responses. Newman's fear of God, that numinous fear that is prior to the fear of being punished, is simply a way of venerating God as He is in His own divine right, and is closely akin to adoration. As for Newman's zeal, we already stressed its character of value-response when we said that the person zealous for God's honor is not in the first place concerned with averting harm for human beings. And as for Newman's love we stressed that it is not awakened in the first place by the sight of the God-man as redeemer, but by the God-man in all His beauty. Recall too Newman's way of celebrating the mystery of the Trinity apart from any concern with the economy of our salvation: this is vintage value-response.

Perhaps we have here in these personalist ideas the reason for the profound resonance which Newman's theocentric

40. See Dietrich von Hildebrand, *Ethics* (Chicago: Franciscan Herald Press, 1973), ch. 1–3 and 17.

preaching and teaching found in the years of the Oxford Movement. If human persons really are constituted as persons by their capacity for world-openness and by their capacity for value-response, then they will not be able to be satisfied with religious pragmatism and religious subjectivism, and are sure to feel reinvigorated by a religious teacher who recovers the transcendence of world-open religion and of value-responding religion.

One might ask what exactly it is about the human person that makes him world-open. When in chapter 6 we examine Newman's thought on the interiority and subjectivity of persons, we will venture an answer to this question.

It follows from this analysis of the personalist foundations of Newman's theocentrism that we have to restate with greater precision the project of this book. The polarity in Newman that we are exploring is not exactly one obtaining *between* his theocentric religion and his personalism but is rather a polarity obtaining *within* his personalism, that is, a polarity obtaining between his personalist theocentrism and other, apparently antithetical aspects of his personalism. This study is in fact more comprehensive than I originally presented it; it deals not with an important part of Newman but with the whole Newman.

An Excess of Theocentrism?

Let me address this question by referring to Newman's thinking about the number of those who will be saved and the number who will likely be lost. He thought that very many will be lost, perhaps even most.[41] In fact in one place he surmises that at

41. "O misery of miseries! Thousands are dying daily; they are waking up into God's everlasting wrath ... and their companions and friends are going on as they did, and are soon to join them. As the last generation presumed, so does the present.... And thus it is that this vast flood of life is carried on from age to age; myriads trifling with God's love, tempting His justice, and like the herd of swine, falling headlong down the steep!" (DMC, 41) "The world goes on from age to age, but the holy Angels and blessed Saints are always crying alas, alas! and woe, woe! over the loss of vocations, and the disappointment of hopes, and the scorn of God's love, and the ruin of souls. One generation succeeds another, and whenever they look down

any time in history the elect are just seven thousand "and never more."[42] He never put this number into print; he mentions it only in a personal letter, in which he surely thought that he was expressing to a friend a "pious surmise." But it was for him no pious surmise that those lost were far more than those saved. This is certainly what St. Augustine and St. Thomas taught; Newman was following a long tradition of Christian thinkers who believed that they had strong scriptural support for a pessimistic theology of the number of the saved.[43]

It was a theocentric tradition in the sense that, given the everlasting loss of most human beings, one could hardly say that the happiness of human beings is the main point of creation. God would not allow such huge losses, according to the traditional theodicy, unless He could bring some greater good out of the losses, and this greater good must be some good other than the happiness of all human beings, since it is precisely a good that God brings out of the loss of this good. We recognize here the idea that we encountered above: God does not deal with us according what Newman calls "unmixed benevolence"; His benevolence is rather "mixed" with other principles like justice. What we add now is that He must have goals that are far "more important" to Him than human happiness, since He achieves them through the evil of most human beings becoming miserable. This train of thought deals a fatal blow to any anthropocentric conception of the economy of creation and redemption, and to that extent it reinforces a severe theocentric religion.

upon earth from their golden thrones, they see scarcely anything but a multitude of guardian spirits, downcast and sad, each following his own charge, in anxiety, or in terror, or in despair, vainly endeavouring to shield him from the enemy, and failing because he will not be shielded." (DMC, 122) It is clear that Newman means that most of those souls bewailed by the angels "fall headlong down the steep" into hell.

42. Charles Stephen Dessain et al., eds., *The Letters and Diaries of John Henry Newman* (Oxford: Clarendon Press, 1973), XXV, 453–54. Hereafter, LD.

43. But there is this difference between St. Augustine and Newman: the loss of a soul does not for Newman necessarily follow on the absence of baptism, for he envisioned the possibility of unbaptized pagans being counted among the elect. See his discussion of "the dispensation of paganism" in his *The Arians of the Fourth Century* (London: Longmans, Green, 1908), 79–89. Hereafter, Arians.

Newman did not just affirm in an abstract way the small number of saved souls; this small number entered into his way of perceiving people. Consider this mournful passage:

> What a scene is this life, a scene of almost universal disappointment! of springs blighted,—of harvests beaten down by the storm, when they should have been gathered into the storehouses! of tardy and imperfect repentances, when there is nothing else left to be done, of unsatisfactory resolves and poor efforts, when the end of life is come! O my dear children, how subdued our rejoicing in you is, even when you are walking well and hopefully! how anxious are we for you, even when you are cheerful from the lightness of your conscience and the sincerity of your hearts! how we sigh when we give thanks for you, and tremble even while we rejoice in hearing your confessions and absolving you! And why? because we know how great and high is the gift of perseverance.

Newman then tells of Hazael coming to the prophet Eliseus, who looked at him and broke out into tears at the premonition he had of the crimes that Hazael would commit in the future as king of Syria:

> the tears which the man of God shed, what if some Angel should be shedding the like over any of you, what time you are receiving pardon and grace from the voice and hand of the Priests of Christ! O, how many are there who pass well and hopefully through what seem to be their most critical years, and fall just when one might consider them beyond danger! How many are good youths, yet careless men.... How many, when led forward by God's unmerited grace, are influenced by the persuasions of relatives or the inducements of station or of wealth, and become in the event sceptics or infidels when they might have almost died in the odour of sanctity! How many, whose contrition once gained for them even the grace of justification, yet afterwards, by refusing to go forward, have gone backwards, though they maintain a semblance of what they once were, by means of the mere natural habits which supernatural grace has formed within them. What a miserable wreck is the world, hopes without substance, promises without fulfilment, repentance without amendment, blossom without fruit, continuance and progress without perseverance![44]

44. DMC, 140–43.

It is remarkable what Newman does and does *not* say on the following page, as he tries to keep his listeners from being overwhelmed with despair. He does not say that God is greater than our heart, he does not invite his readers to throw themselves on to the divine mercy. He says only this, that fearing for our final perseverance is salutary insofar as it can help us to avoid what we fear. The redemptive will of God seems here almost powerless; the dangers of damnation are portrayed as so many and so great that many a Christian reader closes this sermon (and others like it) with terror in his heart.

Why do I suggest that this side of Newman's theocentrism is excessive, when Newman is after all just speaking in line with an ancient Christian tradition? I suggest this because there is reason to think that this tradition is questionable. Pope Benedict himself puts this tradition into question when he teaches in his encyclical *Spe salvi:* "For the great majority of people—we may suppose—there remains in the depths of their being an ultimate interior openness to truth, to love, to God."[45] This "great majority" is destined for purgatory, he says, and not for hell. He envisions indeed the possibility of hell, but for relatively few: "There can be people who have totally destroyed their desire for truth and readiness to love, people for whom everything has become a lie, people who have lived for hatred and have suppressed all love within themselves.... In such people all would be beyond remedy and the destruction of good would be irrevocable: this is what we mean by the word *Hell.*"[46] I cannot enter here into all the issues raised by this papal teaching; but I see enough merit in it to be entitled to think that one does

45. Pope Benedict XVI, *Spe salvi,* paragraph 46.

46. *Spe salvi,* paragraph 45. No less a theologian than Hans Urs von Balthasar has put the "most are lost, few are saved" tradition into question. If he is right with his main claims in his book *Dare We Hope That All Men Be Saved?* (San Francisco: Ignatius Press, 1988), then the divine benevolence is not as "mixed" as it is in that tradition; Christianity is still theocentric, but not with the oppressive note that it takes on in that tradition. Pope Benedict does not go quite as far as von Balthasar, but he is much closer to him than to Newman on this issue. In his book von Balthasar engages Newman by name and makes what seem to me some telling criticisms of him (24–28).

not have to go all the way with Newman on the number of the damned in order to have a truly theocentric religion.

But Newman's theocentrism, even after we have acknowledged this limitation of it, remains a thing of great religious power. In this book I am interested in the fruitful tension arising within his personalism between the themes of the following chapters, and the core of religious truth that I acknowledge in his theocentrism.

My Encounter with Newman's Theocentrism

As I said in the Introduction, his theocentrism was the side of Newman that I first encountered. I experienced, and experienced strongly, what was experienced by the contemporaries of Newman quoted above. Given the moment in history in which I first read Newman, there was a rhyme and reason for me to seek out the theocentric Newman. For I first read Newman in the years immediately after the Second Vatican Council. It was a moment very different from 1833, when the Oxford Movement broke out. In the years of the Oxford Movement Newman spoke into a situation of religious torpor and mediocrity, whereas in the late 1960s Newman spoke, to those who read him, into a situation of religious *Aufbruch,* of religious turmoil. And yet in the late 1960s I needed nothing so much as Newman's sermons to find my bearings and keep my balance. Perhaps the reason for Newman's relevance for me was this: in the years immediately following the council there were many Christian voices calling for an accommodation with the world, for an adaptation to contemporary modes of thinking and living, and Newman's theocentrism is a powerful antidote to all the excesses committed in the name of such accommodation. His voice has prophetic force whether it is opposed to the worldliness that had crept up unawares on the Church of England, or opposed to the principled "turning to the world" that had many supporters in the wake of the council. However one explains it, it is undeniable that Newman's sermon

"The Religion of the Day," read in the setting of the post-conciliar ferment, seemed to challenge the Christian world in much the same way as that sermon challenged the Christian world in England when first preached in 1832.

I kept reading Newman, and I began to notice the personalist sides of his mind and personality. I began to absorb his profound thought on religious experience, on personal influence, on heart speaking to heart, on the imagination, on "the living intelligence" of each person. In fact, I eventually discovered a connection of his personalism with the council. In the interpretation of the council given by John Paul II, the council documents are full of personalism. When people speak of Newman as one who cleared the ground in the church for the council, as one who was present at the council as a "hidden" council father, they are referring among other things to his personalism. I came to see that Newman was just as important for discerning what has lasting validity in the council as he was for discerning the reckless interpretations of conciliar teaching.

I came to see something else; my path through Newman showed me the unity of his mind and personality. I saw that his theocentrism and his personalism (or rather the rest of his personalism), though antithetical on one level, form a unity at a deeper level, so that neither is rightly understood without the other. One could speak roughly of "objectivity" and "subjectivity" in Newman, and could say that they form a unity. I have long been struck by the *coincidentia oppositorum* in Newman's mind and personality; I have found this union of opposites at many levels in his thought, and I found it here.[47] This is why I have prefaced this study of his personalism with this chapter on his theocentrism, and why the results of this chapter will remain present to us through the subsequent chapters. We want to protect his personalism from the subjectivist dangers to which it would otherwise be vulnerable.

47. See my study "The *Coincidentia Oppositorum* in the Thought and in the Spirituality of John Henry Newman," *Anthropotes* (1990/2), 187–212.

2

Imagination and Intellect

Touching Truths into Life

Newman's religious situation was not unlike that of Kierkegaard in Denmark: he lived in a country in which Christianity, though established as the law of the land, was losing power over the lives of Christians. In one of his best-known Anglican sermons, "Unreal Words," Newman masterfully characterizes the religious barrenness of the established church; he does this by describing the kind of religious talk that is common among English Christians. Kierkegaard would have said that Newman was describing the way people talk in "Christendom." Newman speaks of

> the mode in which people speak of the shortness and vanity of life, the certainty of death, the joys of heaven. They have commonplaces in their mouths, which they bring forth upon occasions for the good of others, or to console them, or as a proper and becoming mark of attention towards them. Thus they speak to clergymen in a professedly serious way, making remarks true and sound, and in themselves deep, yet

> unmeaning in their mouths.... Or when they fall into sin, they speak of man being frail, of the deceitfulness of the human heart, of God's mercy, and so on:—all these great words, heaven, hell, judgment mercy, repentance, works, the world that now is, the world to come, being little more than 'lifeless sounds ...' in their mouths and ears ... as the proprieties of conversation, or the civilities of good breeding.[1]

Working in this pastoral situation Newman did not in the first place see himself called to give his countrymen greater theological precision, or to refute errors. He sought rather to make people *realize* the truths that they were so fruitlessly professing. He sought to make the sources of religious experience flow for them again. He sought to reawaken the religious imagination. He sought to appeal not only to the intellect but also to the heart, and in this way to stir up his listeners to action. He preached in a way that "pierced" the existence of his hearers, which means that he energized them existentially. That was the secret of his power.

His contemporaries attest to this power. We have already heard some of the accounts of his preaching, and here is another one of them:

> His power [as a preacher] showed itself chiefly in the new and unlooked-for way in which he touched into life old truths, moral or spiritual, which all Christians acknowledge, but most have ceased to feel.... As he spoke, how the old truth became new; how it came home with a meaning never felt before![2]

We often find evidence in the sermons that Newman is consciously aiming to "touch into life old truths." For example, in a very early sermon entitled "The Immortality of the Soul," Newman writes,

> In spite of our being able to speak [fluently] about it [the immortality of the soul] ... there seems scarcely room to doubt, that the greater number of those who are called Christians in no true sense *realize* it in

1. PPS V, 39–40.
2. J. C. Shairp, *John Keble* (1866; reprint by BiblioLife, 2008), 12–17.

their own minds at all. Indeed, it is a very difficult thing to bring home to us, and to *feel*, that we have souls; and there cannot be a more fatal mistake than to suppose we see what the doctrine means, as soon as we can use the words which signify it.[3]

Newman means to offer his listeners not just the truth about our immortality, but rather, and especially, the experiential and imaginative grasp of this truth:

I am not attempting by such reflections to prove that there is a future state; let us take that for granted. I mean, over and above our positive belief in this great truth, we are actually driven to a belief, *we attain a sort of sensible conviction of that life to come, a certainty striking home to our hearts and piercing them,* by this imperfection in what is present. The very greatness of our powers makes this life look pitiful; the very pitifulness of this life forces on our thoughts to another.[4]

Newman describes here from his point of view as preacher the very thing that his listeners and readers marveled at, his ability to touch old truths into new life.

But if we are really going to understand the experiential and the imaginative in Newman we will have to immerse ourselves in his sermons. A few well-chosen excerpts from Newman cannot really convey this feature of his thought.

Notional Apprehension and Real Apprehension

I want now to try to give an account, or rather to let Newman give an account, of just what he was doing in his sermons, and I want to do this by examining an important distinction that stands at the center of his most philosophical work, *An Essay in Aid of a Grammar of Assent.* In the first part of that work Newman distinguishes between *notional* and *real* apprehension of propositions, and also between *notional* and *real* assent to propositions. I will explain this distinction, and will try to develop it by bringing

3. PPS I, 17; my italics.
4. PPS V, 218; my italics.

it into contact with certain existentialist and phenomenological themes. I will then return to the sermons and show that the secret of his power is the ability to convert notional apprehension into real apprehension. I will also show that notional apprehension plays an important role of its own, and that real apprehension is inconceivable apart from it. Finally, I will explain why Newman is a personalist thinker as a result both of his teaching on notional and real apprehension, and of the way he lives out of real apprehension and can awaken it in us.

Here is an example of notional apprehension passing over into real apprehension. Take the true proposition that I will one day die. To apprehend it notionally is to apprehend it on the basis of the universal mortality of all living things. I think: all living things die, myself included. I subsume myself under universal mortality. But now suppose I have just gotten an ominous test result from my doctor: aggressive inoperable cancer. I know that I will soon die. My coming death is no longer abstract but pierces me with its concreteness. I experience myself not just as a logical part of "everyone" but almost as if I were the only human being; I experience my death as something supremely concerning me personally. I have a real apprehension of it, and I give a real assent to the proposition that I will soon die. I am filled with shuddering, whereas the notional assent leaves me unmoved, almost as if I were just a spectator of my own future death. Here we get a first impression of the abstractness of notional apprehension and the concreteness of real apprehension.

Here is one of Newman's own examples of making the transition from notional to real apprehension.

> Let us consider, too, how differently young and old are affected by the words of some classic author, such as Homer or Horace. Passages, which to a boy are but rhetorical commonplaces, neither better nor worse than a hundred others which any clever writer might supply, which he gets by heart and thinks very fine ... at length come home to him, when long years have passed, and he has had experience of life,

and pierce him, as if he had never before known them, with their sad earnestness and vivid exactness.[5]

The schoolboy apprehends the true sayings of the classical authors only notionally, but when he has grown up and has had some experience of life, he apprehends the same sayings not notionally but really. Now for the first time he understands what it means to say that these authors are classical authors, and why their utterances have been so cherished across the generations. Notice that Newman speaks of the power of real apprehension to "pierce" the boy who is now a man. Notional apprehension, by contrast, takes things abstractly and so keeps them at a greater distance from us; it has no such power to pierce us.

These two examples of the notional-real distinction are nonreligious examples; but of course the distinction is found within religion, and this is in fact the place where the distinction is of greatest interest to Newman. Just above we saw Newman contrasting a notional apprehension of our personal immortality with a real apprehension of it. In the *Grammar of Assent* Newman distinguishes between "the theological intellect" and "the religious imagination," which is simply the notional-real distinction as carried out in the setting of religious language, as we shall see in chapter 7.

Our task now is to try to give a philosophical account of this distinction. It is not enough to have a feel for it through revealing examples; we want, as Newman in the *Grammar of Assent* wanted, to understand it in a properly philosophical way. I will now develop five points of contrast—or one point of contrast considered under five different aspects—between notional and real apprehension/assent.[6] It will become apparent as I pro-

5. GA, 78–79.

6. I do not aim at a close study of the chapters in the *Grammar of Assent* in which Newman draws the distinction between real and notional, a study such as H. H. Price offers in his *Belief* (London: Allen & Unwin, 1969), 315–48. Rather, from the beginning I am interpreting the distinction with an eye to its personalist significance.

ceed how it is that Newman's concern with real apprehension and assent imparts a personalist spirit to his thought.

1. Let us begin with a point already mentioned, namely the *concreteness* that belongs to real apprehension and that forms a contrast with the *abstractness* or *generality* that belongs to notional apprehension. Newman explains the difference like this: notionally apprehended propositions "stand for certain [abstract] ideas existing in our own minds, and for nothing outside of them," and really apprehended propositions stand "for things simply external to us," "things that are unit and individual."[7] One sees what Newman wants to say, but one has to take exception to his way of saying it. His words seems to imply that when I apprehend my death notionally, I have as the object of my apprehension something abstract and general that serves as a replacement for my individual death. But this cannot be right, for the notional apprehension of my death is the apprehension of a concrete future event; thus the notional character found in this apprehension does not lie in the fact that an abstraction or a universal has replaced a concrete individual. In this notional apprehension there is indeed a characteristic abstractness, but the abstraction functions not as the object of the apprehension, but as a kind of conceptual lens through which my future death—itself a concrete individual fact—is apprehended.

One could express with well-known scholastic terms the problem in Newman that I am pointing to: *id quod* and *id quo*. A general concept, the scholastics said, is typically not *that which (id quod)* one speaks about in using the concept in a proposition, it is rather *that by or through which (id quo)* one speaks about something else. Newman tends to try to capture the notionality of a notional apprehension by picking out a general concept in the proposition that is notionally apprehended, and then taking this general concept as the object that is apprehended, whereas in fact that concept is the medium through which

7. GA, 9.

something else is apprehended.[8] Thus my notional apprehension of my mortality is not an apprehension directed to some universal mortality that replaces my individual mortality; it is directed to my individual mortality, but as "universalized," that is, taken not in its concrete plenitude but just under the aspect of mortality, or just as an instance of mortality.

And so we can summarize as follows what Newman really means: in the real apprehension of a proposition I apprehend something in all its concreteness, whereas in the notional apprehension of a proposition I typically apprehend something abstractly, universally. It may well be one and the same proposition that I apprehend now notionally, now really. Newman is aware of this possibility, but he cannot make sense of it as long as he thinks of the notional as an object of its own that replaces the concrete.

2. But this talk of taking things concretely is only the beginning of an account of real apprehension. We can get at the core of Newman's idea only if we consider that instead of real apprehension Newman often says "experiential" apprehension. Real is born of an experiential contact with concrete beings. It is not enough to *know about* concrete beings; we have to experience them in their concreteness, if we are ever to gain a real apprehension of the propositions expressing them. Notional apprehension, by contrast, always abridges experience, or bypasses it, keeping concrete things at a certain distance from us. If I virtually deduce my future death from the universal mortality of all men, then I can apprehend my death, concrete though it is, without having to encounter it in an experiential way—I can acknowledge it without being troubled by it.

Newman often reflects on different ways in which notional apprehension dries up experiential fullness. Thus he explains

8. A general concept ceases to function as a medium when we speak *about* it, as when we say, "'human mortality' is a general concept." But apart from such reflection on our meanings, they function as media rather than as objects of our intentions.

in one place how surgeons protect themselves against the reality of the dreadful diseases they have to deal with: they describe them with abstract Greek- and Latin-root names.[9] In this case there is a good reason for letting our notions block out experience. But in other cases, the deliberate use of notional apprehension can be distinctly dishonest, as George Orwell indicates in a famous essay. He says, "Defenceless villages are bombarded from the air, the inhabitants driven out into the countryside, the cattle machine-gunned, the huts set on fire with incendiary bullets: this is called *pacification*.... People are imprisoned for years without trial, or shot in the back of the neck or sent to die of scurvy in Arctic lumber camps: this is called *elimination of unreliable elements*."[10] Then Orwell says, "Such phraseology is needed if one wants to name things without calling up mental pictures of them," or as Newman would put it, if one wants to name things without eliciting any experiential sense of them, that is, any real apprehension of them. And one other sentence from this passage in Orwell, a sentence that might have been written by Newman: "A mass of Latin words falls upon the facts like soft snow, blurring the outlines and covering up all the details." This is a beneficent result for the physicians just mentioned, but a morally very suspect result when it is driven by insincerity. Real apprehension, by contrast, holds fast to the details; it lives from the concrete experience of them.

In notional apprehension we pick out some aspect of a thing or maybe several aspects of it, even though the full reality of the thing is always vastly more than these aspects, and indeed vastly more than the totality of all its aspects. Thus when I apprehend my future death in the notional way described above, I take it in one limited respect, namely, in respect of what it has in common with the mortality of all living beings. But there is very much about my death that exceeds this limited respect. I

9. GA, 22.

10. "Politics and the English Language," in *The Collected Essays, Journalism, and Letters of George Orwell*, vol. 4 (New York: Harcourt, Brace and World, 1968), 136.

am confronted with this excess when I begin to face my death as my personal death. Thus the notional apprehension keeps my death at a distance because it fixes on one limited aspect of it, leaving out of view the full human reality of it. This is why notional apprehension is perfectly adapted to the surgeons who want to keep a distance from the grim reality of disease, but also perfectly adapted to those insincere people who have an interest in hiding the sordid deeds in which they are complicit.

Perhaps we could bring in here the pair of terms made famous by a saying of Kant: *Begriff* (concept) and *Anschauung* (intuition). He said that concepts without intuition are empty and that intuition without concepts is blind. These terms correspond fairly closely to Newman's *notion* and *experience.* Newman might have said that in notional apprehension our relation to the world is entirely mediated by *Begriffe,* whereas in real apprehension it is relatively unmediated by them, it is born of *Anschauung.*[11] Newman was very concerned with avoiding that barrenness that comes from using concepts without sufficient support from intuition.

We are now in a position to explain why Newman has often been regarded as a kind of proto-phenomenologist. His defense of the rights of experience in connection with apprehension and assent makes for an obvious kinship with the phenomenologists. There is a well-known distinction made by the early Husserl that Newman would have found entirely congenial to his own mind; I refer to Husserl's distinction between "empty" and "fulfilled" intentions of the mind. For Husserl the mind can pick out facts, refer to them, make inferences from them, even assent to them, but without letting them unfold intuitively, or bringing them to evidence: these are the "empty" intentions of the mind. But if the mind lets things unfold intuitively before itself and lets them become present to itself, then the

11. Needless to say, we are not ascribing to Newman any part of Kant's elaboration of *Begriff* and *Anschauung* in the *Critique of Pure Reason,* such as Kant's restriction of *Anschauung* to the phenomenal world, or his subjectivization of *Begriff.*

intentions of the mind are "fulfilled."[12] The former intentions are akin to Newman's notional apprehension, and the latter to his real apprehension. When Husserl calls out to the philosophical world, "*zurück zu den Sachen selbst!*" (back to the things themselves), and pleads for a philosophy in which one restores to its proper place the intuitive presence of the objects of our intentions, and in which one recognizes in such presence the ultimate norm for all our philosophical assertions and assents, he speaks altogether in the spirit of Newman. Newman did not of course deal with the question of correct philosophical procedure, but if he had, his affinity with the experiential would have led him in the direction of phenomenology.

But one might ask here whether Newman's focus on the concrete individual does not make for a sharp contrast between Newman and the phenomenologists, who after all defended with their idea of "eidetic intuition" the intuitive presence not of individual but of universal states of affairs. It is true that Newman tends to limit experience to the concrete individual and to think of universals as products of the human activities of comparing and contrasting. He bears in himself some marks of the nominalist tradition of philosophy that he absorbed in England, and in this sense the phenomenologists with their idea of eidetic intuition would have presented a challenge to Newman. But it would have been a challenge made on grounds dear to him, namely grounds of experience.

But even if Newman had learned to recognize eidetic experience as a kind of experience all its own, irreducible to the experience of concrete individuals, he would have still continued to take an interest mainly in the latter, because this is the experience that can touch the heart and move us to action, as we will see directly below; the eidetic experience of the phenomenologists has no such power over us.

12. For a clear presentation of this phenomenological theme, see Robert Sokolowski, *Introduction to Phenomenology* (Cambridge: Cambridge University Press, 2000), 33–41.

In the next chapter we will see that the "experiential" takes on a deeper meaning in the case of what we will call "knowledge by connaturality," a kind of knowing that is highly developed in Newman.

3. Newman often calls real assent "imaginative" assent. In earlier drafts of the *Grammar* this was apparently his name for that which he later called real assent. He says that with real assent we have an "image in the imagination," whereas with notional assent we have a "notion in the intellect." Thus the real-notional contrast can be expressed as the contrast between an imaginative and a purely intellectual apprehension.

In the essay of Orwell just quoted we find a priceless example of this contrast. He picks out a well-known verse from Ecclesiastes, presenting it first in the venerable translation: "I returned and saw under the sun, that the race is not to the swift, nor the battle to the strong, neither yet bread to the wise, nor yet riches to men of understanding, nor yet favour to men of skill; but time and chance happeneth to them all." Then Orwell rewrites the verse in contemporary English: "Objective consideration of contemporary phenomena compels the conclusion that success or failure in competitive activities exhibits no tendency to be commensurate with innate capacity, but that a considerable element of the unpredictable must invariably be taken into account."[13] An imaginative element in the poetical original has clearly been sterilized in Orwell's rewrite; abstract thinking has extinguished imagination. We could as well say that an experiential element has been dried up by abstract thinking, or that a wholesome concreteness has been replaced by an unnatural abstractness.

One should note that "image" does not mean for Newman "visual image," it does not even mean "sensible image"; he recognizes all kinds of thoroughly non-sensible images. For instance, he speaks in one place about the image you can form

13. *The Collected Essays, Journalism, and Letters of George Orwell,* 133.

of the mind of St. Augustine from reading his works; Newman refers here to a concrete sense of Augustine's intellectual style, of the intellectual character that distinguishes Augustine from, say, Jerome. If imagination did not have some more-than-visual meaning for Newman, we would never be able to make sense of his talk of *the religious imagination* in contrast to *the theological intellect,* for what distinguishes the religious imagination is certainly not the presence of visual images, or of any kind of sense images.[14]

In speaking of real apprehension as imaginative Newman sometimes uses the expression "an image lighting up in the mind." With this he aims at an aspect of real apprehension that we have not yet had occasion to articulate. He seems to mean that by real apprehension I grasp the living unity of a thing, whereas a notional apprehension of the same thing gives me only fragments of the thing. He quotes a line from Virgil about a pontifex maximus in ancient Rome conducting a religious ceremony, and then remarks that a schoolboy reading Virgil may have "an abstract hold upon every word of the description, yet without the words therefore bringing before him at all the living image which they would light up in the mind of a contemporary of the poet, who had seen the fact described, or of a modern historian who had duly informed himself in the religious phenomena, and by meditation had realized the Roman ceremonial, of the age of Augustus."[15] The transition from notional to real apprehension is the transition from a group of fragments to the "living image" that knits them into one. He says that a person who never experienced falling in love will

14. It seems to me that H. H. Price's discussion of Newman's real apprehension (in his *Belief,* [London: Allen & Unwin, 1969], 315–48), competent and thoughtful as it is, suffers from thinking of the imaginative aspect of real apprehension too much in terms of sensible images. When he is forced to recognize that Newman's imagination surpasses all sensible images, he proposes an unsatisfactory distinction between imagining and imagining-that (or imagining-as). He seems never really to grasp the thoroughly non-sensible activities of the imagination in Newman's sense.

15. GA, 10.

be unable to understand from descriptions of it what it really is.[16] The descriptions will give her various aspects of falling in love, but they will light up no image in her mind until she has the experience. There is an act of imagination that she will be capable of only through having the experience.

If we consider what Newman says about the notional apprehension of God, we will find yet another example of this transition. In one place Newman discusses various "names" of God, such as "the Author, Sustainer, and Finisher of all things, the life of Law and Order, the Moral Governor; One who is Supreme and Sole; like Himself, unlike all things besides Himself which all are but His creatures; distinct from, independent of them all; One who is self-existing, absolutely infinite," etc.[17] Each one of them may be in some way understood, yet it may happen that no image lights up in the mind of the believer, whose apprehension of divine names remains notional. It is only a certain experience—we will examine it in chapter 7—that will light up an image of God in the believer, and only then has he moved from notional to real apprehension.

Newman thinks that the doctrine of the Trinity, by contrast, will always be for us only notional; there is nothing in our experience, he thinks,[18] that lets us imaginatively grasp the unity of the doctrinal affirmations about the individual divine persons.[19]

It is very interesting to consider the conspicuous absence of an image that makes various elements into one. The neurologist Oliver Sacks describes the neurological disruption of vision known as agnosia, and gives these examples of it. A patient of his, Dr. P., is presented with a rose, and the patient describes it

16. GA, 29.

17. GA, 101.

18. GA, 124–41.

19. One critic contrasts Newman with medieval Christians and explains the contrast in terms of the contrast between notional and imaginative apprehension. Harold Weatherby says that medieval Christians imaginatively apprehended the presence of God in creation, whereas Newman, distressed as he was by the hiddenness of God in creation, could apprehend His presence only notionally. *Cardinal Newman in His Age* (Nashville, Tenn.: Vanderbilt University Press, 1973), 19–21.

as "a convoluted red form with a linear green attachment" but cannot recognize it as a rose. The patient is presented with a glove and describes it as "a continuous surface infolded on itself with five outpouchings"; despite many hints given by the doctor the patient cannot recognize it as a glove. Sacks comments: "He construed the world as a computer construes it, by means of key features and schematic relationships. The scheme might be identified ... without the reality being grasped at all."[20] Newman would say: without any image lighting up in his mind, without any real apprehension of the thing in its unity. Sacks says that it was his patient's "absurd abstractness of attitude—absurd because unleavened with anything else—which rendered him incapable of perceiving identity, or particulars, rendered him incapable of judgment."[21] Newman would say: which rendered him incapable of imaginative apprehension. Sacks realizes that agnosia, though in the first place a visual impairment, can exist in analogous forms beyond physical vision; thus he says, "Our cognitive sciences are themselves suffering from an agnosia essentially similar to Dr. P.'s. Dr. P. may therefore serve as a warning and parable—of what happens to a science which eschews the judgmental, the particular, the personal, and becomes entirely abstract and computational."[22] One can easily think of Newman deprecating a kind of science so imaginatively impoverished that it eschews real apprehension and wants to live exclusively by notional apprehension.[23]

20. Oliver Sacks, *The Man Who Mistook His Wife for a Hat* (New York: HarperCollins, 1990), 15.

21. Ibid., 19.

22. Ibid., 20.

23. In a letter of 1872 Newman finds this imaginative aspect of real apprehension to be conspicuously lacking in the historical writing of the German historian Döllinger: "He does not throw himself into the state of things which he reads about—he does not enter into the position of Honorius, or of the council 40 years afterwards. He ties you down like Shylock to the letter of the bond, instead of *realizing what took place as a scene*" (my italics). LD XXVI, 120. Newman speaks in a similar vein when he criticizes a way of writing the lives of the saints that yields only fragments that "do not necessarily coalesce into the image of a person." *Historical Sketches* II (London: Longmans, Green, 1906), 228 (hereafter, HS II). Newman says

4. Notional apprehension is experienced as localized in one particular place in human nature, whereas real apprehension is experienced as the work of the whole human being. Newman sees notional apprehension as situated just in the intellect but he sees real apprehension as involving heart and will no less than intellect. Notice how he complains of the knowledge of God that is born of the traditional proofs for the existence of God; he once said that these proofs "do not warm me and enlighten me; they do not take away the winter of my desolation, or make the buds unfold and the leaves grow within me, and my moral being rejoice."[24] He means that these proofs do not touch him affectively because they yield only notional knowledge; Newman will settle for nothing less than the real knowledge of God that engages his whole being. "'There is a God,' when really apprehended, is the object of a strong energetic adhesion, which works a revolution in the mind; but when held merely as a notion, it requires but a cold and ineffective acceptance.... Such in its character is the assent of thousands, whose imaginations are not at all kindled, nor their hearts inflamed, nor their conduct affected, by the most august of all conceivable truths."[25]

It is because of the affective impact of real apprehension that it is so much more powerful than notional apprehension in moving us to act. We can acknowledge a truth notionally and yet keep it from ever getting close to our behavior, even though it has in fact consequences for our behavior. But real apprehensions, since they touch us affectively, have an impact on our behavior. In an often-quoted passage of the *Grammar of Assent* Newman says: "The heart is commonly reached, not through

here that if the saints do not speak in their own voice, no image will light up in the imagination of the reader; if they appear in hagiography always in the third person, so to say, then the thing that imparts unity to their deeds, namely their first-person self-understanding, is missing, and the hagiographer cannot avoid giving us a fragmentary narrative.

24. Apol., 241.

25. GA, 126.

the reason, but through the imagination, by means of direct impressions, by the testimony of facts and events.... Persons influence us, voices melt us, looks subdue us, deeds inflame us."[26]

It is clear that this aspect of real apprehension was of particular interest to Newman the preacher. The concreteness of real apprehension, the experiential character of it, and the imaginative character of it, are of interest to him insofar as they are related to the power of real apprehension to touch the heart and thereby to move persons to commit themselves in action.

In the next chapter we will unfold more fully Newman's thought on the place of the heart and of affective life within human existence.

5. From the fourth feature of real apprehension we are led to a fifth, though this fifth is not fully articulated by Newman. It emerges if we interpret Newman by way of Kierkegaard. Here is a well-known journal entry written by the young Kierkegaard in which he deplores a certain kind of intellectual barrenness.

> What would be the use of discovering so-called objective truth, of working through all the systems of philosophy and of being able, if required, to review them all and show up the inconsistencies within each system;—what good would it do me to be able to develop a theory of the state and combine all the details into a single whole, and so construct a world in which I did not live, but only held up to the view of others; what good would it do me to be able to explain the meaning of Christianity if it had *no* deeper significance *for me and my life;*—what good would it do me if truth stood before me, cold and naked, not caring whether I recognised her or not.

Kierkegaard says in this journal entry that he is not looking for any such objective truth but rather for a truth *"for which I can live and die."* He calls it truth "which grows together with the deepest roots of my life, through which I am, so to speak, grafted upon

26. GA, 92–93. Newman is here in fact quoting in 1870 from a work he had published back in 1841, a splendid polemical piece, "The Tamworth Reading Room," found in his collection *Discussions and Arguments on Various Subjects* (London: Longmans, Green, 1907); hereafter, DA.

the divine." And he says, "It is the divine side of man, his inward action which means everything, not a mass of information."[27] Kierkegaard is called the father of existentialism in philosophy; we can say that he expresses here a deep aspiration not for objective truth but for existential truth, that is, not for truth to be observed in the manner of a spectator, but truth to be dwelt in, to be lived, truth that stimulates our innermost action, truth that grows together with the deepest roots of our being.

Kierkegaard's objective truth is not hard to find in Newman. Notional apprehension is apprehension of objective truth in the sense of Kierkegaard; both thinkers are referring to a truth that is outside of me, at a distance from me, truth that leaves me cold even when acknowledged. Real apprehension closes this distance, giving me an experiential immediacy to the truth apprehended and enabling the truth to engage me as a whole person. Thus Newman's real apprehension clearly tends to converge with Kierkegaard's existential truth.

Just consider how natural it is to use Kierkegaard's language in interpreting one of our examples of notional and real apprehension that we used above. I can know that I will one day die and know this on the grounds that every living being in nature dies. Instead of saying that I notionally apprehend my death, one can as well say with Kierkegaard that my death is an objective fact outside of me that fails to engage me in a deep existential way. Suppose I now come to realize my future death in a personal way, shuddering at what awaits me. Instead of saying that I really apprehend my death, one can just as well say with Kierkegaard that my death is experienced with existential urgency, that it is experienced as *my* death, that it creates an earthquake in my subjectivity. When in the final chapter we study Newman's way of gaining a real apprehension of God through the experience of conscience, we will see that the experience is eminently existential in the sense of Kierkegaard.

27. Diary entry of August 1, 1835, in *The Journals of Kierkegaard,* trans. A. Dru (New York: Harper and Row, 1959), 44–45.

The edge of Kierkegaard's existential urgency is a certain relation of me to myself. As he said, "What good would it do me to be able to explain the meaning of Christianity if it had *no* deeper significance *for me and my life,*" if it did not "grow together with the deepest roots of my life." Kierkegaard wants to get away from being a mere spectator of truth and become a full participant in it. Now it is very helpful to think of Newman's contrast between notional and real in terms of spectator and participant. With the help of Kierkegaard we can in this way develop Newman's distinction beyond the letter of his text.

By way of anticipating what we will discuss at the end of this chapter let me point out that Kierkegaardian existentialism clearly has a personalist thrust to it. Just consider this relation to myself that distinguishes existential truth from objective truth, and that is expressed, in the case of my death, by speaking emphatically of *my* death. When, then, we bring Newman into relation with Kierkegaard we not only deepen our grasp of Newman's distinction between notional and real, but we also articulate better the personalism that is at work in the distinction. In fact, we understand this personalism better; the existential *tua res agitur* that goes with real apprehension brings out for us a personalist dimension of it that remains only implicit in the text of Newman.

I might add that this kinship of Newman with Kierkegaard is equally a kinship with some of the intellectual descendants of Kierkegaard. I think here first of all of Gabriel Marcel, the Christian existentialist. At the center of Marcel's thought stands the distinction between *problem* and *mystery.* To take something as a problem is to keep it outside of me, to take it as a mystery is to be a full participant in that thing. This is nothing but a variation on Kierkegaard's distinction between objective truth and existential truth, and on Newman's distinction between notional and real.

One might object that this Kierkegaardian depth is foreign to Newman. One might say that some of his own examples of real apprehension are devoid of such depth, such as "the sun shines" or "the prospect is charming."[28] Or this: "I am able as it were to gaze on Tiberius, as Tacitus draws him, and to figure to myself our James the First, as he is painted in Scott's Romance.... all this becomes a fact to me and an object of real apprehension."[29] Where is the existential urgency of Kierkegaard to be found here? I would grant to this objector that some of our five marks of real apprehension, and especially the fifth, do not hold for all of Newman's examples of real apprehension. But I would also say that the examples of real apprehension that most interest Newman are taken from the religious existence of persons, and that these examples do indeed instantiate this fifth, Kierkegaardian note of real apprehension, as we can see from the frequency with which Newman speaks of the heart being "pierced" by real apprehension. I would in addition urge against the objection that real apprehension *in the most proper sense,* that is, in its most revealing and eminent instances, always has this fifth note.

We can say in summary, then, that real apprehension takes things concretely and does not lose the concrete in the universal; it has an experiential immediacy and does not keep reality at a distance; it is imaginative and does not work merely with aggregates; and it engages the whole person, touching the heart, and does not engage merely the intellect; it has an existential urgency and does not take reality with a detached objectivity. One sees how these five aspects of real apprehension are variations on one theme.

We started in this chapter from Newman's sermons and from his power of touching into life articles of faith that have been long professed. Now the reader will understand why I said that his power consisted in taking the merely notional apprehensions of his listeners and converting them into real apprehensions. Recall this line that we quoted from one of his ser-

28. GA, 23.
29. GA, 27.

mons on the immortality of the soul: "It is a very difficult thing to bring home to us, and to *feel,* that we have souls; and there cannot be a more fatal mistake than to suppose we see what the doctrine means, as soon as we can use the words which signify it." In the contrast between feeling a truth and just uttering the propositions that express it, we recognize the contrast between real and notional apprehension. Whoever reads Newman's sermons knows that he has an almost preternatural ability to make you feel religious truths, to give you a real apprehension of them. One sees, then, that we have in Newman both a *teaching* on the notional and the real, and a *practice* of converting the notional into the real. His personalism exists at both levels: at the level of the teaching found in the *Grammar of Assent,* and at the level of the practice found throughout the sermons.[30]

The Excellence Proper to Notional Apprehension

As we get acquainted with Newman's strong affinity for real apprehension, we may get the impression that for him notional apprehension is something negative, something that can only interfere with real apprehension. Newman seems to countenance this sense of antagonism between the two modes of apprehension when he writes: "No one seems to look for any great devotion or fervour in controversialists, writers on Christian Evidences, theologians, and the like, it being taken for granted, rightly or wrongly, that such men are too intellectual to be spiri-

30. It is incomprehensible to me that Frank Turner in his massive *John Henry Newman* (New Haven, Conn.: Yale University Press, 2002) makes so little use of Newman's sermons. He claims to offer a major revisionist account of the Anglican Newman, and yet he neglects what is arguably the most important source for understanding the Anglican Newman. Everyone who has left a personal remembrance of Newman's influence during the Oxford Movement concurs with the remembrance of J. C. Shairp: "The centre from which his power went forth was the pulpit of St. Mary's" (Shairp, *John Keble,* 12). Turner makes little effort to understand this power, and he overrates the *Tracts for the Times* as a source for understanding Newman. The continuity of the Anglican Newman with the Catholic Newman, which Turner contests, becomes quite intelligible as soon as one does justice to Newman's preaching in Oxford.

tual, and are more occupied with the truth of doctrine than with its reality."[31] Those who are "more occupied with the truth of doctrine than with its reality" live by an excess of notional apprehension and a defect of real apprehension. It comes as a surprise, then, to find Newman expressing appreciation of the notional: "Each use of propositions [the real and the notional] has its own excellence and serviceableness, and each has its own imperfection," even though he adds, "however, real apprehension has the precedence."[32] It is important that we not think of Newman as denying the excellence proper to notional apprehension—important not only for the sake of preserving the balance of his thought on apprehension, but also for the sake of protecting him from a very serious misunderstanding, namely, the misunderstanding that he exalts experience at the expense of truth. This is the misunderstanding that leads to the idea that Newman is the father of theological modernism. In what follows I will admittedly not do a work of straightforward exposition; I will do a work of interpretation that tries to develop Newman's account of notional apprehension beyond the letter of the *Grammar of Assent,* so that it harmonizes better with the rest of his thought.[33]

To begin with, Newman says that notional apprehension has a certain breadth that real apprehension lacks. "On only a few subjects have any of us the opportunity of realizing in our minds what we speak and hear about."[34] That is, on only a few subjects is a real apprehension possible for us; as we range over the length and breadth of the world, touching on many subjects, our apprehension is mostly only notional. If we had no notional apprehension but only real apprehension, our world would be greatly

31. GA, 216.

32. GA, 34.

33. A very good discussion of Newman's appreciation of notional apprehension and assent is given by Terrence Merrigan in his *Clear Heads and Holy Hearts: The Religious and Theological Ideal of John Henry Newman* (Louvain: Peeters Press, 1991), part 2.

34. GA, 33.

contracted. The phenomenologists have made a similar point; they say that the intuition that fulfills our meaning-intentions is possible only with relatively few intentions; in most of them we have to deal with the absence rather than with the intuitive presence of that which we aim at.[35] In *The Idea of a University* Newman speaks of the "imperial intellect" and its sense of the whole of knowledge, and of the place of the different regions of knowledge within the whole. The imperial intellect has so great a reach only because it can apprehend things notionally.[36]

We can also gather from Newman some other excellences of notional apprehension, even though he does not put these forth explicitly when he appreciates notional apprehension. Let us recall that the real-notional distinction is a distinction that for Newman refers to propositions; the apprehension, whether real or notional, is always the apprehension of a proposition. And propositions consist not only of proper names but also of notions and concepts, each of which has some general meaning. So it is in no way an ideal for Newman that we should live only by experience and imagination, or that we should relate only to concrete individuals with as little conceptual mediation as possible. Real apprehension involves a collaboration of the conceptual and the experiential, since real apprehension is apprehension of a proposition, which is a conceptual structure.[37]

Let us consider how notional apprehension is implied in the very idea of religious *faith.* What Christians believe about the three persons of God and about the economy of redemption far exceeds what they experience, even when their belief is full of real apprehension. In other words, Christians still have many partially empty meaning-intentions, even after they have fallen under the influence of a Newman and have undergone a great religious awakening. This simply goes with living by faith, which

35. See Sokolowski, *Introduction to Phenomenology,* 33–41.

36. GA, 30–31.

37. This point is ably made by H. H. Price in his treatment of the notional-real distinction in *Belief,* the section entitled "Can assent be wholly un-notional?" 330–32.

means that we precisely lack the intuitive fulfillment of our beliefs. If we had no notional apprehension of truth that is not "covered" by real apprehension, we would not be able to live by faith. Newman does not make exactly this point, but when we make it we just develop his thought on apprehension and faith.

Let us also consider how, in matters of religion, notional apprehension brings a precision that real apprehension lacks. It is a precision that is not just an intellectual luxury but is religiously very necessary. In the last chapter of this study we will see how Newman finds a real apprehension of God in the experience that we have of moral obligation in conscience. But we find that certain religiously important questions about God cannot be answered only on the basis of the experience of conscience. For instance, does the divine authority that makes itself felt in conscience indicate one God only, or is it consistent with several gods? And again: is the God who "speaks" in conscience identical with the God who creates and sustains the world? The answers that we Christian monotheists give to these questions cannot be derived from the experience of conscience alone; we have to import them from other sources, such as speculative reason and revelation. Newman is in fact interpreting the experience of conscience in the light of these other sources when he discerns in conscience the God of Christian monotheism; he is really working with a certain composite of real and notional apprehension. Or to put it in phenomenological language, the claim of Christian monotheism is not completely "fulfilled" in the experience of conscience, not even if Newman is right in claiming that this experience is "the creative principle of religion";[38] we can make this claim in a justified way only if we have other sources of knowledge besides the experience of conscience. And we access these other sources of knowledge only by way of notional apprehension.

Recall Newman's "dogmatical principle," and especially his affirmation of mystery in revelation. We saw in the previous

38. GA, 110.

chapter how Newman resists the rationalism of theological liberalism, and how he exults in mystery. But of course mystery presupposes, just as faith does, religious beliefs that are not capable of complete intuitive fulfillment—beliefs that remain in large part empty meaning-intentions (in the phenomenological sense of empty). Without notional apprehension one could not enter with Newman's theocentric spirit into these mysteries and could not exult in them. Indeed, the entire theocentric dimension of Newman's spirituality would hardly be possible apart from notional apprehension and notional assent.

This is not to deny that Newman's sense of divine mystery is shot through with real apprehension, and that his real apprehension is in fact sometimes in excess of all that he apprehends notionally. When in chapter 7 we examine the "numinous" mystery that haunts Newman's sermons, we will encounter an experiential abundance that exceeds all that Newman notionally affirms of God, and we will find this precisely at the center of his experience of the divine mystery. So in relation to Christian mystery we have not only notional apprehension without real, but also real apprehension in excess of notional. Perhaps the sense of Christian mystery is conveyed to us in both ways; but it is in any case conveyed in the first way, that is in the way of unfulfilled notional apprehension. We have already mentioned Newman's view that the unity of the doctrinal statements about the three divine persons of the Trinity remains inevitably notional; we lack the experience that would let us have a real apprehension of this unity.[39] It is on the basis of this deficit of real apprehension that Newman speaks of the mystery of the Trinity.

We proceed to a serious misunderstanding of the notional element: one sometimes says that it is just a device of the human mind for organizing religious experience. This is what is meant: religion lives entirely from religious experience, but we need more rational structure in our religious experience than we can find in it; our religious experience, taken by itself, is too vague

39. GA, 124–41.

and amorphous for our religious needs, so we create order by imposing a certain rational form on our experience. Thus to affirm the unicity of God is for us to impose a certain subjective order on the experience of conscience. That it is a merely subjective order is seen from the fact that someone else may find sufficient order in his experience of conscience by assuming a plurality of gods. On this view the notional element is only pragmatically connected with the experience, and is subject to constant change. With this the door is opened to the theological modernism of which Newman has been accused. But Newman avoids this consequence by avoiding the subjectivist view of our notions and concepts. He does not think that they are merely auxiliary to our religious experience; they rather give expression to sources of religious knowledge that are independent of the experience that supports real apprehension. By means of our notions and concepts we make truth claims that we could not make on a subjectivistic basis, claims such as "God is really one, not several." We make no such real truth claim if we are just pragmatically ordering our experience by means of the concept of the divine unicity. These other sources of religious knowledge, such as metaphysical reflection or divine revelation, are irreducible to the religious experience of an individual and are underivable from it; they are accessed by notional apprehension, which therefore plays within the setting of Newman's thought a far greater role than it plays for the doctrinal subjectivist.

We can say, then, that notional apprehension (and notional assent) is appreciated by Newman as something indispensable for religious belief. It is not just a lack of real apprehension, but it is a mode of apprehension all its own, accomplishing important things that real apprehension cannot accomplish by itself. We should think of Newman's real and notional in terms of complementarity and polarity, not in terms of antagonism.[40] We

40. Cf. the Introduction to the third edition (1878) of his *The Via Media of the Anglican Church,* I (London: Longmans, Green), hereafter, VM; in the course of

should think of them as analogous to Kant's *Anschauung* and *Begriff:* Newman would agree that real apprehension without notional apprehension is blind, and that notional apprehension without real is empty. If in the *Grammar of Assent* Newman is pleading for real apprehension and not giving equal attention to notional and not fully articulating the significance of notional apprehension, this is not because of any principled disparagement of notional, but rather because of his personal affinity with real apprehension, and also because of his sense that Christians suffer from a conspicuous lack of real apprehension. He thinks that the religious awakening that they need can only come from deepening their real apprehension of the things of faith.

Personalism as Shown in the Real-Notional Distinction

We have already seen what is distinctly personalistic in Newman's commitment to real apprehension and to real assent. It was particularly apparent in the fourth and fifth point of contrast with notional apprehension, that is, in the affective power of real apprehension, and in the existential depth of it. The connection with Kierkegaard, the talk of Kierkegaardian *tua res agitur,* also brings to light the personalism in Newman. I now conclude this chapter by offering some further reflections on the personalism that lies in Newman's thought on notional and real apprehension.

Newman says that real assents "are of a personal character, each individual having his own, and being known by them."[41] He also says, "Real assent, then, as [well as] the experience which it presupposes, is proper to the individual, and, as such,

discussing the relation of theology to devotion and to the institutional church he says: "Theology is the fundamental and regulating principle of the whole Church system" (xlvii). If we think of theology as a notional work, and of devotion as something experiential and lived, then Newman seems to be affirming here almost a priority of notional over real apprehension.

41. GA, 83.

thwarts rather than promotes the intercourse of man with man."[42] Newman draws out the contrast to notional apprehension, of which he says that it "is in itself an ordinary act of our common nature. All of us have the power of abstraction, and can be taught either to make or to enter into the same abstractions; and thus to cooperate in the establishment of a common measure between mind and mind."[43] Thus the universal mortality of men is readily available to everyone, but that encounter with my own coming death which pierces me in a personal way and shakes me to the roots of my being, is something that each has to grow into for himself. If someone lacks a real apprehension of his death, I cannot easily transmit it to him, at least not in the way I can transmit to him information at the level of notional understanding; he has to gain it for himself. Or again: a notional apprehension of the truths contained in the Greek and Latin classics is readily available to almost everyone who reads them,[44] but that real apprehension which comes with age and wisdom is gained only by some, and those who gain it gain it each in his or her own personal way and own personal time and to his or her own personal degree. And if we think of real apprehension in terms of Kierkegaardian subjectivity, a certain "solitude" of the person in real apprehension becomes abundantly clear.

But more important is a second thought about the personalist implications of real apprehension. Newman's real apprehension is exactly what is needed for understanding persons. For a person is an individual being, and in fact a radically individual being as a result of the fact that each is unrepeatable.[45] That is, a person never exists as a copy of another person, nor does he or she ever exist as a mere instance or specimen of some type or

42. GA, 83–84.

43. GA, 83.

44. GA, 78–79.

45. None of the personalists has explored this dimension of personal being as deeply as Max Scheler. See "Max Scheler on Personal Individuality," in my *Personalist Papers,* 145–73. I have myself tried to contribute to this subject in my *The Selfhood of the Human Person,* ch. 2.

kind, such as the human kind. This means that abstract thinking and notional apprehension are sure to bypass persons as persons. Martin Buber made a great point of this in his classic study *I and Thou.* He said that the openness to another person is always disrupted by classifying the properties and qualities of the other, by characterizing the other in general terms. For this approach always involves a distance to the other that interferes with an I-Thou encounter with the other and tends to degrade it to an I-It relation.[46] Buber would have recognized in Newman's real apprehension that openness to a concrete other that underlies a real encounter with the other as person.

Very interesting in this connection are Newman's reflections on the way we apply stereotypes to people, reading off of the stereotypes what must characterize certain people, but not directly consulting our experience of those people. We are prepared "without the trouble of direct inquiry, to draw the individual after the peculiarities of his type."[47] And in another place Newman complains of certain scientific ways of studying man: "'Man' is no longer what he really is, an individual presented to us by our senses.... He is attenuated into an aspect, or relegated to his place in a classification.... If I might use a harsh metaphor, I should say that he is made the logarithm of his true self, and in that shape is worked with the ease and satisfaction of logarithms."[48] A harsh metaphor, and a striking metaphor, very expressive for capturing that contraction of experience that comes from relating to persons through stereotypes. This contraction of experience has the effect of filtering out the concrete person, leaving us with only some conspicuous qualities and properties which the person may or may not have.

Newman discerns a species of this depersonalization in the traditional hagiography. He says that it often happens that the

46. *I and Thou,* trans. Walter Kaufmann (New York: Charles Scribner's Sons, 1970), 57–58, 80–81.

47. GA, 32.

48. GA, 31.

biographers of the saints "do not manifest a Saint, they mince him into spiritual lessons," "they chop up a Saint into chapters of faith, hope, charity, and the cardinal virtues."[49] "From such works I do but learn to pay devotion to an abstract and typical perfection under a certain particular name; I do not know more of the real Saint who bore it than before."[50] In other words, the saints become in the pages of their biographers mere instances or specimens of the virtues and do not appear in their individuality as this or that distinct person. We can appropriate what was just quoted from the *Grammar* and can say that the kind of hagiography to which Newman objects gives us a saint who "is attenuated into an aspect, or relegated to his place in a classification." And how, according to Newman, do we encounter the saints as living individuals, so as to gain a real apprehension of them? We do this by hearing them speak in their own name. Only the first-person self-disclosure gives us the individual person; the third-person description of the biographer speaks in universals that tend to obscure the individual person. "When a Saint converses with me, I am conscious of the presence of one active principle of thought, one individual character, flowing on and into the various matters which he discusses."[51] It is just this encounter with the first-person disclosure of the inner life of the saint that lets me pass from a notional apprehension of his virtues to a real apprehension of the saint himself or herself. With this I gain "that personal knowledge of the Saints which seems to me so desirable."[52]

And so it is not surprising that when Newman tries to convert notional into real apprehension, he commonly turns from something universal to something personal. Recall the line quoted above: "Persons influence us, voices melt us, looks subdue us, deeds inflame us." I almost want to say that the chief object of real apprehension is the personal. We will see in the final chapter that, when Newman tries to gain a real apprehension

49. HS II, 229.

50. HS II, 228.

51. HS II, 227.

52. HS II, 225.

of the being of God, he turns from the traditional demonstrations of God to the eminently personal encounter with God in conscience. Only God as personal can satisfy Newman's search for a concrete, imaginative, experiential apprehension of God.

As for notional apprehension, one might think that, whatever its merits, it has no personalist significance of its own; that it is only real apprehension that has personalist significance. But if we read closely in chapter 6 of the *Grammar of Assent* we find Newman acknowledging a certain kind of notional apprehension that has a distinctly personalist significance. Newman distinguishes there between simple and complex assent, saying that the latter involves something that the former lacks, namely a critical testing of the truth of the proposition assented to. The immediacy of simple assent is replaced by a moment of reflection in complex assent. As a result, a complex assent is a certain compound of real and notional; the critical reflection that makes for complex assent establishes a certain distance to the reality assented to; it is the distance of the notional. The immediacy of simple assent is blunted by the distance of a notional element. Now Newman argues that, despite the loss of immediacy, something of great existential importance is gained in those complex assents that he calls certitudes. Such a complex assent, through its moment of critical reflection, has a solidity and permanence that simple assents lack, a solidity without which a lasting commitment is impossible. "Without certitude in religious faith there may be much decency of profession and of observance, but there can be no habit of prayer, no directness of devotion, no intercourse with the unseen, no generosity of self-sacrifice. Certitude then is essential to the Christian."[53] Even though the reflective element in certitude blunts the experiential and imaginative force of the assent, making it less real and more notional, we do not, Newman says, only suffer an existential loss: we also acquire an existential gain, a personalist gain.

53. GA, 220.

Consistent with Newman's Theocentric Religion?

By way of concluding this chapter let us ask whether Newman's concern with personal experience has any tendency to compromise his theocentric religion. We know from the previous chapter that Newman is no friend of religious subjectivism. But one might wonder whether, contrary to his intention, a religious subjectivism creeps back into his thought through his concern with personal experience. Would it not cohere better with his theocentric religion, one might ask, for him to insist on revealed truth alone and not to worry about the believer's subjective experience of truth? Would we not expect Newman to say that the important thing is *to be* in the truth, and that it does not matter how much or how little we *feel* our being in the truth? Would we not expect him to treat notional assent as quite sufficient for religion, and to treat real assent as a religious luxury more than a religious necessity?

There might have been some such subjectivism of experience in Newman's thought if he had played off real against notional apprehension. But as we saw, he does not play them off against each other; he acknowledges that notional apprehension brings with it an indispensable work of thinking. And if we develop his concept of notional apprehension as I attempted to develop it above, enlarging it beyond his letter but still in his spirit, then his thought is secured all the more against any suspicion of subjectivism.

Newman may have been vulnerable to another kind of subjectivism if he had made a point of *directly* cultivating experiential fullness and being affectively "pierced." We will see in the next chapter how fundamentally Newman was opposed to any direct working on our subjectivity and affectivity. In fact, he thought that he had himself fallen into some such subjectivism in his early twenties as an Evangelical, and that he had to struggle to free himself from it. From his late twenties on he opposed this subjectivism very self-consciously, and nowhere more impressively than in his *Lectures on Justification,* lecture 13, where he says, among other things, "The true preaching of the Gospel is to preach Christ. But the fashion of the day has been, instead of this, to preach conversion; to attempt to convert by insisting on conversion ... to lead them to stir up and work up their minds, instead of impressing on them the thought of Him who can savingly work in them."[54] Newman's work of reviving real apprehension in his listeners began and ended with "the thought of Him who can savingly work in them." His real apprehension was based on exactly the kind of turning-outward that defeats this subjectivism. More on this subject in the next chapter.

Or one might think that the Kierkegaardian theme that I introduced by way of interpreting Newman opens the door to subjectivism. Kierkegaard is concerned, as we saw, with what is true *for me,* and this existential preoccupation may seem to divert the believer away from the theocentric focus of Newman's religion. Kierkegaard's way of speaking may even seem to be situated in what we have called the environment. But a moment's reflection shows that nothing prevents a strong existential concern from informing a strong theocentric commitment. Newman might have said that the existence of God is not just abstractly true but true *for him* when he encounters God in conscience; this would just have been another way of saying that he gains a real apprehension of God in conscience. Real existential concern of the kind that Kierkegaard expresses is, in fact, essentially world-open. The *tua res agitur* typically involves some ultimate concern.[55]

54. Newman, *Lectures on the Doctrine of Justification* (London: Longmans, Green, 1908), 325–26. Hereafter, LJ.

55. Among the twentieth-century personalists, Dietrich von Hildebrand is one who admirably clarifies this point. In a chapter entitled "Subjectivity and Transcendence" in his treatise *On the Nature of Love,* he says on 206: "A moral call is addressed to a person to intervene in a certain situation; perhaps another is in danger, or perhaps some injustice has to be prevented.... He grasps the morally relevant value, he understands its call, he is aware of the moral obligation, which appeals to his conscience. On the one hand, we have here a high-point of tran-

I proceed now to a more positive response to the objection. Let us recall this point of contrast between notional and real: by notional apprehension we apprehend something mainly with the intellect, by real apprehension we apprehend it with our whole being. And also this closely related point of contrast: by notional apprehension we are spectators of reality, by real apprehension we are participants in reality. A Newman-like response to the objection would say that *we venerate revealed truth more when we are present as a whole human being in the apprehending of it and in the assenting to it than when we apprehend it and assent to it merely intellectually.* Such a response would say that *we venerate truth more when we abandon the detachment of a spectator and encounter it with the engagement of a participant.* This means that *we take truth more seriously by striving to apprehend it with real apprehension and to assent to it with real assent. We commit ourselves to it more completely; we put ourselves in a position to live by it.* Considered in this way, Newman's concern with personal experience is not just a preoccupation with subjective feeling, but is constitutive of his theocentric religion, and imparts to it a depth and breadth that it would otherwise lack.

scendence in the pure commitment to the morally relevant value. But on the other hand, this call, insofar as it is morally obligatory, pre-eminently contains the element of *tua res agitur* (your personal concern is at stake). In a certain sense this call is my most intimate and personal concern, in which I experience the uniqueness of my self. Supreme objectivity and supreme subjectivity interpenetrate here."

3

"Heart Speaks to Heart"

Well known is the motto that Newman formulated for himself as cardinal and placed in his cardinal's coat of arms: *cor ad cor loquitur.* With this motto Newman seems to say that he has always wanted to speak from the heart, and has always wanted to reach the hearts of those whom he addressed. We should understand the talk of "heart" as forming a contrast with the mind or intellect. Newman means that he does not want to speak only out of his intellect and does not want to address people only intellectually. Of course, the author of the *Grammar of Assent* and the *Essay on the Development of Christian Doctrine* and many other works obviously does not neglect high-level intellectual communication. But he always sought to communicate at a deeper-than-intellectual level: heart to heart. Let us now examine this affective dimension of Newman and try to understand the personalism that is expressed in it.

Personalism and Affectivity

One of the great themes in the phenomenological personalism of Max Scheler and Dietrich von Hildebrand is the rehabilitation of the heart in our understanding of the human person. They want to overcome the traditional view that intellect and will represent the two main powers of the human person. If I rejoice in the birth of my child, my joy is something other than knowing and willing. Sometimes one has tried to place such joy among the body feelings and bodily appetites, but it clearly does not belong there, for this joy is as properly personal as knowing and willing are, and is just as little bodily as they are. Scheler and von Hildebrand argue that it shares a basic personal structure with knowing and willing: it shares with them what the phenomenologists called "intentionality." An act is intentional in their sense if it is "about" something, if it is born of understanding something. Now these two personalists observe that some affective acts are intentional, such as my joy over the birth of the child; my joy is about the birth, it is motivated by the birth. If I do not know about the birth and understand what it means, I cannot rejoice in it. Admittedly not all affective experiences are intentional; some, like a drug-induced euphoria, are not about anything, are not motivated; they have indeed causes, but causes of which I need not be aware in order to have the experience. All such non-intentional affective experiences cannot claim a central place in the human person, for we undergo them rather than perform them. But the intentional affective acts share a personal structure that makes them comparable in personal dignity to knowing and willing.

Scheler and von Hildebrand discern another personal excellence in some affective acts; some of them are motivated by something good in its own right. I need not take delight in the birth of the child because I gain some advantage from the birth, but I can take delight because the existence of the newborn child is something good in its own right. My delight is then a value-response, which we explained above. I thus achieve a self-transcendence in this joy, acting as a world-open being, and this too, along with intentionality, makes the joy eminently personal, and no less properly personal than the most significant acts of knowing and willing. Thus Scheler and von Hildebrand enlarge our image of the human person; they grant to the heart a more central place in the makeup of the person than almost all previous philosophers had granted it.[1]

And there is something else that they bring to light: the heart represents the "real self" of a person. Thus if I help a needy person by dint of a resolute and dutiful will but with no felt compassion for him, I am not really present to him, I hold something back from him, and he for his part perceives me, for all my active beneficence, as somehow uninvolved, as keeping him at a distance, as benefitting him without really giving myself to him. In helping with heartfelt compassion I am much more fully "in" the act of helping, am much more "present" to the needy person. It is just because of the special way that a person lives in the responses of his heart—lives in them as he does not live even in the choices of his will—that the rehabilitation of the heart along the lines of these phenomenologists represents an eminently personalist development.

Newman as a Forerunner of the Retrieval of Affectivity

This development is entirely congenial to Newman. Many of the elements of Scheler's account of the heart can be found in Newman. Newman would have welcomed this side of Scheler and would have felt that it articulates and raises to the level of philosophical reflection what he (Newman) himself had long thought.

1. Max Scheler, *Formalism in Ethics*, trans. Manfred Frings and Roger Funk (Evanston, Ill.: Northwestern University Press, 1973), 253–64; 328–44. Dietrich von Hildebrand, *Ethics* (Chicago: Franciscan Herald Press, 1972), 202–14; *The Heart* (South Bend, Ind.: St. Augustine Press, 2007), part 1.

Let us look into Newman's sermon "The Thought of God, the Stay of the Soul," where he develops with Augustinian grandeur the idea that each human person is *capax Dei,* that is, able to be happy only in God. The title of the sermon—the *thought* of God—might seem to suggest that the human intellect has an infinite capacity that only the knowledge of God can fulfill, but Newman does not go in this intellectualist direction at all. Instead he says:

> I say, then, that the happiness of the soul consists in the exercise of the affections; not in sensual pleasures, not in activity, not in excitement, not in self esteem, not in the consciousness of power, not in knowledge; in none of these things lies our happiness, but in our affections being elicited, employed, supplied. As hunger and thirst, as taste, sound, and smell, are the channels through which this bodily frame receives pleasure, so the affections are the instruments by which the soul has pleasure. When they are exercised duly, it is happy; when they are undeveloped, restrained, or thwarted, it is not happy. This is our real and true bliss, not to know, or to affect, or to pursue; but to love, to hope, to joy, to admire, to revere, to adore. Our real and true bliss lies in the possession of those objects on which our hearts may rest and be satisfied.[2]

Newman frees himself here entirely from the traditional idea that man is distinguished mainly by his intellect and his will, which would imply that he is happy only when he is intellectually and volitionally fulfilled. The primary fulfillment of the human person is an affective fulfillment. Newman reinforces this idea by considering the misery of those who are affectively dead:

> What a truly wretched state is that coldness and dryness of soul, in which so many live and die, high and low, learned and unlearned. Many a great man, many a peasant, many a busy man, lives and dies with closed heart, with affections undeveloped, unexercised. You see the poor man, passing day after day, Sunday after Sunday, year after year, without a thought in his mind, to appearance almost like a stone. You see the educated man, full of thought, full of intelligence, full of

2. PPS V, 315–16.

action, but still with a stone heart, as cold and dead as regards his affections, as if he were the poor ignorant countryman.[3]

When he says that the man who is "full of thought, full of intelligence, full of action" may have "a stone heart," he is saying in effect that it is not enough to be engaged intellectually and volitionally if one is not also alive affectively.

Newman develops the further idea that only in relation to God can the human heart be fully alive, as we will see in chapter 6. For the present I simply point out that, if the heart, that is, the center of affective life in human persons, were merely a matter of body feelings, then it would hardly require God for its full life; only because the heart is eminently personal, just as properly personal as intellect and will, can it be ordered to God for its fulfillment. Indeed, nothing shows so clearly the dignity of the heart as the fact that "He who is infinite can alone be its [the heart's] measure; He alone can answer to the mysterious assemblage of feelings and thoughts which it has within it."[4]

We recognize Newman's theocentric religion in this affirmation of the place of the heart in the human person. It is important for understanding Newman's personalism that the abundance of affective life coheres entirely with that spirit of adoration that lies at the center of his religious existence.

Affective Pathologies

There is a difficulty in the fact that Newman often seems to "rebuke" the heart, to warn against its excesses, to admonish us to steel ourselves against its promptings. He saw a great deal of affective excess in the "evangelical" Christians of his time, and so he often speaks, perhaps with them in mind, as if our task were to control and subdue the heart. Consider this poem from 1833, "Flowers without Fruit":

3. PPS V, 325.
4. PPS V, 319.

Prune thou thy words, the thoughts control
    That o'er thee swell and throng;
They will condense within thy soul,
    And change to purpose strong.

But he who lets his feelings run
    In soft luxurious flow,
Shrinks when hard service must be done,
    And faints at every woe.

Faith's meanest deed more favour bears,
    Where hearts and wills are weigh'd,
Than brightest transports, choicest prayers,
    Which bloom their hour and fade.[5]

Newman seems to be singing the praises of the affectively dead will, and to be warning against strong affections as a hindrance to the resolute will. But in reality he is not withdrawing here any of his appreciation of the heart.

He has in mind the case where strong feelings should lead on to action. Suppose I feel great compassion for a needy person, and am in a position to help that person; surely the compassion is not genuine if it does not lead to some helping action toward the needy person. But it happens all the time that my compassion spends itself as a feeling while I remain idle and find excuses for not acting; my compassion replaces action rather than awakens it. This is the case censured by Newman. We can understand better the grounds for his censure if we consider his reservations about reading novels; he says in an early sermon:

> Now the danger of an elegant and polite education is, that it separates feeling and acting; it teaches us to think, speak, and be affected aright, without forcing us to practise what is right. I will take an illustration of this, though somewhat a familiar one, from the effect produced upon the mind by reading what is commonly called a romance or novel....

5. *Verses on Various Occasions* (London: Longmans, Green, 1903), 169.

> Such works contain many good sentiments (I am taking the better sort of them): characters too are introduced, virtuous, noble, patient under suffering, and triumphing at length over misfortune. The great truths of religion are upheld, we will suppose, and enforced; and our affections excited and interested in what is good and true. But it is all fiction; it does not exist out of a book.... We have nothing to do; we read, are affected, softened or roused, and that is all; we cool again,—nothing comes of it. Now observe the effect of this. God has made us feel in order that we may go on to act in consequence of feeling; if then we allow our feelings to be excited without acting upon them, we do mischief to the moral system within us, just as we might spoil a watch ... by playing with the wheels of it.[6]

Newman must have later modified his view about reading novels, seeing as he wrote two himself, and read quite a few; but he certainly never modified his view that we suffer a certain *dissipation* when we feel strongly but fail to follow up with the action that goes with the feeling.[7] Such feeling is well described as a "flower without fruit." We can easily put this sermon together with the one quoted in the previous section, and then we get the result that the best action is born of strong feeling, and that the affectively dead action is not the ideal, it is just better, or less bad, than the volitionally inert feeling.

But there is something else that Newman rebukes in the affective life of believers. He rebukes "evangelical" Christians for trying to stir up their religious feelings by acting directly on them (we remarked on this in the last chapter). The most careful and differentiated statement of this rebuke is found in the masterful lecture 13 of Newman's *Lectures on Justification.* He says:

> The true preaching of the Gospel is to preach Christ. But the fashion of the day has been, instead of this, to preach conversion; to attempt to convert by insisting on conversion; to exhort men to undergo a change; to tell them to be sure they look at Christ, instead of simply

6. PPS II, 371.
7. PPS II, 377.

> holding up Christ to them; to tell them to have faith, rather than to supply its Object; to lead them to stir up and work up their minds, instead of impressing on them the thought of Him who can savingly work in them.... And thus faith and (what is called) spiritual-mindedness are dwelt on as ends, and obstruct the view of Christ, just as the Law was perverted by the Jews.[8]

Newman's idea is that you awaken a religious feeling not by focusing directly on the feeling but by focusing on the motivating object of the feeling. "We do not affect people by *telling* them to weep or laugh."[9] Newman is simply taking account of what Scheler and the phenomenologists called the intentionality of personal feeling, which means, as we saw, that personal feeling is always motivated by some object. It follows that if you want a feeling you have to start not with the feeling but with its motivating object. Here is Newman's clearest statement of the point: "Men who are acted upon by news good or bad, or sights beautiful or fearful, admire, rejoice, weep, or are pained, but are moved spontaneously, not with a direct consciousness of their emotion.... So it is with faith and other Christian graces. Bystanders see our minds; but our minds, if healthy, see but the objects which possess them. As God's grace elicits our faith, so His holiness stirs our fear, and His glory kindles our love. Others may say of us 'here is faith,' and 'there is conscientiousness,' and 'there is love'; but we can only say, 'this is God's grace,' and 'that is His holiness,' and 'that is His glory.'"[10]

Newman makes a keen observation on what happens when one fails to respect the intentionality of personal feeling and tries directly to induce feeling: "For the most part it [the feeling] will be produced by sympathy, and will consist in imitation. Men will feel this and that, because they are told to feel it, because they think they ought to feel it, because others say they feel it themselves; not spontaneously, *as the consequence of the objects presented to them.*"[11]

8. LJ, 325–26.
9. LJ, 327.
10. LJ, 337.
11. LJ, 328, my italics.

Newman had another reason for resisting this sentimentality of the Evangelicals. Not only do they get entangled in disordered affectivity, but they tend to let the religious feelings that they cultivate keep them from the moral struggle that makes for real Christian holiness. Thus for example they rest in a strong feeling of being converted instead of "working out their salvation" over a lifetime of continual conversion. Newman said that they make too much of faith, or rather the feeling of faith, and too little of obedience. Whenever, then, Newman seems to censure the affective life of believers, and to insist on obedience while he disparages feelings, he is in fact censuring certain affective disorders, and these he censures for the sake of a healthy, ardent affective life in which heart speaks to heart, and also for the sake of a serious Christian existence in which the believer becomes really transformed into a new creature.

Newman's account of these affective pathologies throws a new light on the religious subjectivism that he combats (we discussed this in chapter 1). One understands now how it happens that deep religious feeling, instead of connecting us with God, can come between us and Him, or can interfere with the reception of revealed doctrine. One also understands the antidote—not to cultivate an affective deadness, but to respect the intentionality of religious feeling, which means that the believer turns from the affection to its motive, so that the personal structure of religious feeling can fully unfold. In this way Newman can preserve religious feeling in all its ardor even as he affirms his theocentrism. He knows, as Pascal knew, that the heart has its own rationality, that reason has its own affective dimension. He knows that theocentric religion engages not only the intellect and the will, but also the heart.

Newman's Power of Speaking from *the Heart*

So far we have been speaking about the "heart" in "heart speaks to heart"; now we will speak about the interpersonal encounter that is expressed in Newman's motto. Personalist philosophers like Martin Buber and Gabriel Marcel have explored the ancient theme of the "social nature" of man in terms of interpersonal relation, intersubjectivity, shame, reciprocity, co-experiencing, empathy, sympathy. Let us see what we can draw out of Newman's motto for our understanding of these subjects.

Newman means to say through his motto that in addressing others he has always wanted to speak from his heart and to touch their hearts. As we saw, he means that he has not only wanted to speak to them at the level of ideas and arguments, but also at the deeper level of the heart. He once said of Paley's argument for the existence of God, "If I am asked to convert others by it, I say plainly I do not care to overcome their reason without touching their hearts."[12] I propose now to consider first Newman's ability to speak *from* his own heart, and then to consider his ability *to* speak to the heart of his listeners and readers.

For understanding the first part, namely, Newman's uncanny ability to make himself present in his words, I propose to introduce a concept taken from scholastic philosophy, the concept of *knowledge by connaturality*. St. Thomas gives the following example of such knowledge.[13] Consider two ways of knowing about the virtue of chastity. You can recognize it in others, you can study it in moral philosophy and moral theology, and in this way you can take hold of chastity as an object of knowledge, *per modum cognitionis,* as St. Thomas says, and so can teach about the virtue correctly even though you may not fully possess the virtue. But if you *possess* the virtue of chastity, you have another way of knowing what this virtue is. You *are* chaste and on this basis you know from within what chastity is. You do not know it by making an object of *your* chastity; no, you remain focused

12. GA, 425.

13. St. Thomas Aquinas, *Summa Theologica,* II–II, q. 45 c. Cf. the essay by Jacques Maritain, "On Knowledge through Connaturality," in *The Range of Reason* (London: Geoffrey Bles, 1953).

on what chastity is, but your knowing passes through your spontaneous chaste promptings of heart, it is a knowing *per modum inclinationis,* as St. Thomas says. You have knowledge of chastity by connaturality; you know what chastity is on the basis of being chaste. In the same passage St. Thomas gives another striking example of knowledge by connaturality. He contrasts the knowledge of God had by the well-trained theologian with the knowledge had by the mystic, who according to Dionysius "non solum discens, sed et patiens divina," that is, who does not just learn about divine things but "suffers" them in himself.

I find that the kind of knowing expressed in Newman's sermons is often a knowing by connaturality. I referred to this already in the Introduction. When, for example, Newman speaks about "unreal words" in the famous sermon that we quoted in the first and the second chapter, and when he admonishes us to be "real" in our speech, we immediately sense that his own words are eminently real, that unreal talk is as foreign to him as anything could be. He knows about real and unreal speech by connaturality. He speaks about it out of his own religious existence. When he speaks in other sermons about reverence or zeal, we feel in the sermons the presence of his own reverence and zeal. When he speaks of "the infinite abyss of existence" in each person (in chapter 6 we will unpack this idea in Newman), we hear him speaking out of his own strong sense of his own incommunicable existence. He is of course not consciously reflecting on himself, on his own speech and its being real, on his own reverence or zeal; he is not consciously projecting his sense of himself into the content of the sermon; but his knowing passes through the medium, as it were, of his own realness of speech, of his own reverence, of his own sense of incommunicable existence. This is what it means to say that he speaks out of a knowledge by connaturality: what he knows and proclaims is somehow based on what he is. As a result he is personally present in his words in an extraordinary way. Newman is not just talking about Christian holiness, but bearing witness to it.

He speaks with an ardor that already shares in the holiness to which he calls his listeners.

Perhaps we can clarify this knowledge by connaturality if we go back to Newman's distinction between real and notional apprehension. We said that what is notionally apprehended is kept at a certain distance, whereas what is really apprehended is experienced with a certain lived immediacy. I suggest that we think of this lived immediacy as being akin to what I just called knowledge by connaturality, and I suggest that we think of the distance of notional apprehension as being akin to a purely intellectual or cognitive relation to an object. Recall the two different ways of apprehending my coming death, as discussed in chapter 2. I apprehend it in a real way by experiencing my mortality in my bones, by feeling in myself that ebbing away of vital energy that is completed in death; in other words, the real apprehension of my coming death is an apprehension through the medium of my lived experience of my mortality. The notional apprehension of my coming death is by contrast more intellectual, based as it is on subsuming my death under the universal mortality of all living things. Remember Kierkegaard's contrast between the knowledge had by a spectator and the knowledge had by a full participant, a contrast that we appropriated to Newman's contrast between notional and real apprehension. Well, through his knowledge by connaturality Newman is a participant in and not just a spectator of the truth he proclaims, and he is for this reason so personally present in his words.

This knowledge by connaturality clearly has an affective dimension. Maritain says of it, "In this knowledge through union or inclination, connaturality or congeniality, the intellect is at play not alone, but *together with affective inclinations* and the dispositions of the will, and is guided and directed by them."[14] It is by speaking out of this knowledge by connaturality that New-

14. Maritain, "On Knowledge through Connaturality," 23 (my italics).

man makes himself present in his words and able to speak from the heart in an altogether exceptional way.

But our account of Newman's power of speaking from the heart is not quite complete. For consider: even though Newman were ever so holy a person, and possessed the deepest religious knowledge by connaturality, he may still have lacked the power to express this knowledge. It is entirely conceivable, and it has often happened, that someone possessing knowledge by connaturality expresses himself or herself mainly *per modum cognitionis.* For instance, St. Thomas Aquinas, when he spoke about virtue and grace and union with God, must have had a great deal of knowledge by connaturality, but he does not speak out of this knowledge like Newman does. It does not impress the reader as knowledge from the heart, as in Newman. The heart of St. Thomas remains hidden behind the severe objectivity of his discourse. It would not occur to anyone to inscribe over his *Summa* the motto *cor ad cor loquitur.* It does not fit him like it fits Newman. And so the question arises, how does Newman manage to express his knowledge by connaturality so as to make himself personally present in the sermons and so to speak from the heart?

I think that Newman himself gives us the materials for the answer in his paper "Literature," which is found in *The Idea of a University.* Here he makes a distinction between objective truth and subjective truth, or rather a distinction between the use of language to express objective truth and the use of language to express subjective truth. In expressing objective truth, language simply refers to things, it is entirely object-centered; it refers to what is there in the world whether we experience it or not. In expressing subjective truth, language refers indeed to things, but to things as experienced by the speaker. Newman thinks that literature and poetry involve this latter use of language. He thinks that the exuberance of literary and poetical language is not just superfluous ornamentation, as if a sober truth-loving person should have no use for it; he thinks that this exuberance is often really just the expression of the subjectivity of the speaker, a very legitimate function of language. Of particular interest for our purpose in this chapter is the strongly personalist way in which Newman describes the language used in expressing subjective truth. He says that it "must certainly belong to some one person or other, and is the expression of that one person's ideas and feelings,—ideas and feelings personal to himself ... proper to himself, in the same sense as his voice, his air, his countenance, his carriage, and his action, are personal."[15] And a little later: "Literature is the personal use or exercise of language."[16] It follows that a literary master has a special ability to be personally present in his words.

Now Newman was a master of the literary and personal use of language. A contemporary literary critic wrote of his sermons: "To call these sermons eloquent would be no word for them; high poems they rather were, as of an inspired singer, or the outpourings as of a prophet, rapt yet self-possessed."[17] In fact, this critic calls Newman one of the great "prose poets" of the English language. Newman expresses in his writings in an unforgettable way his religious and spiritual experiencing, not indeed in the way of direct autobiography, but in his way of speaking about things of faith. Of course, he takes with ultimate seriousness the objective truth and reality of faith, and he was known for his uncompromising defense of the truth of the creed, as we saw in examining his theocentrism. But at the same time he gives expression to his experience of living this truth, of longing for it, of falling short of it, of being nourished by it. When he proclaims Christian truth, he proclaims it in such a way as to express his religious seriousness, his reverence, his zeal, his sense of his incommunicable selfhood—in a word, in such a way as to express his religious subjectivity. It is, then, by a special literary gift of self-expression that Newman is able in his writings to connect with his knowledge by connaturality, to

15. Idea, 273.

16. Idea, 275.

17. Shairp, *John Keble,* 16.

speak out of it, and thus to be present in his words, so present as to speak from the heart.

Of course, my account of Newman's speaking from the heart remains very incomplete. There is something in Newman that still escapes the analysis so far offered by me. After all, St. Augustine, too, possessed knowledge by connaturality, and he possessed a rare literary power, but he does not speak heart to heart as Newman does, and he does not convey sympathy like Newman does. Perhaps we could approach the thing we seek by saying that the heart that speaks to us in Newman is a singularly *vulnerable* heart. One contemporary who heard him preach in Oxford discerned in his sermons "the grasp of a strong man's hand, combined with the trembling tenderness of a woman's heart."[18] This contemporary also spoke of the sermons as "quivering with suppressed but piercing emotion," and as sometimes giving expression to "a very tender heart that has a burden of its own, unrevealed to man."[19] Newman does not hide his vulnerability behind masks; in that sense he speaks from the heart, and does so in a way that is all his own.

One can approach this vulnerability by making use of a distinction drawn by Dietrich von Hildebrand in his philosophy of affectivity. There is "energized affectivity," as typified in anger, laughter, or cheering at a sports event, and there is "tender affectivity," which goes much deeper and is the real core of human affectivity. It is typified by heartfelt gratitude, by deep grief, by being deeply touched by, say, the kindness of a person. Von Hildebrand observes that we tend to hide from public view our tender affectivity, which stirs up something intimate in ourselves; we are rightly distressed when our intimate affective life is publicly exposed. The energized affectivity, by contrast, does not shrink from exposure, for it lacks the intimacy of tender affectivity. When von Hildebrand speaks of the heart as the "real self" of a person, he is referring to tender affectivity. Newman

18. Shairp, *Aspects of Poetry,* 443.
19. Ibid., 60, 254.

too aims at tender affectivity when he says, as we heard above, "Our real and true bliss lies in the possession of those objects on which our hearts may rest and be satisfied." Now I would say that the vulnerability of which I spoke lies in an abundance of tender affectivity in Newman. The sermons are charged with tender affectivity and this is part of their power to speak to us.

In a sermon already cited we read: "After the fever of life; after wearinesses and sicknesses; fightings and despondings; languor and fretfulness; struggling and failing, struggling and succeeding; after all the changes and chances of this troubled unhealthy state, at length comes death, at length the White Throne of God, at length the Beatific Vision. After restlessness comes rest, peace, joy;—our eternal portion, if we be worthy."[20] Whoever reads these sentences within the whole of the sermon, and the sermon within the whole of Newman's preaching, knows that the lament about the "fever of life" is spoken out of the deepest knowledge of connaturality. Newman felt in his bones this unhealthy fever of life; he constantly suffered from it. Whoever reads these sentences feels the tender affectivity of Newman's longing. Newman does not cramp up at his strongly felt suffering and his longing, but despite the intimacy of his feeling he lets it out in his way of speaking, so that we feel it. When he expresses his overcoming faith, as he does here, there is something deeply moving about the fact that he overcomes even as his heart remains vulnerable to "this troubled unhealthy state." He overcomes without repressing anything human, without claiming a certainty that he does not have. Even as we experience in Newman the "grasp of a strong man's hand," we continue to experience in him "the trembling tenderness of a woman's heart." With this polarity of masculine and feminine we gesture, I think, toward the mystery of Newman's heart.

20. PPS V, 369–70.

Newman's Power of Speaking to *the Heart*

We have so far dealt with Newman's speaking *from the heart;* we now want to say something about his way of speaking *to the hearts* of others. For this too is included in the motto "heart speaks to heart."

Many who heard Newman preach marveled at his power of sympathy, of sympathizing with his listener or reader. One of them said: "Persons look into Mr. Newman's sermons and see their own thoughts in them."[21] Another said: "He laid his finger how gently, yet how powerfully, on some inner place in the hearer's heart, and told him things about himself he had never known till then."[22] Many of us who know the sermons only by reading them feel the same thing; in fact, Newman's power of sympathy is, I suspect, experienced no less by us than by those who heard him in the 1830s and 40s. Newman himself seems to have been aware of this power; in the last lines of his last sermon as an Anglican, "The Parting of Friends," he says, speaking of himself in the third person, "And, O my brethren, O kind and affectionate hearts, O loving friends, should you know any one ... [who] has ever told you what you knew about yourselves, or what you did not know; has read to you your wants or feelings, and comforted you by the very reading ... remember such a one in time to come, though you hear him not."[23]

Now it is possible to read to others their wants or feelings yet without engendering deep sympathy with them. A writer may have a keen intellectual grasp of, for example, some struggle in the moral life, so that certain readers can readily recognize themselves in what he writes about the struggle, and be grateful for the clarification that they derive thereby: but there may be no special sympathy conveyed between the writer and

21. James Mozley, as quoted by Richard Church, *The Oxford Movement* (London: Macmillan, 1922), 141.

22. Shairp, *John Keble,* 15.

23. SD, 409.

his readers. In his classic work *Transformation in Christ,* Dietrich von Hildebrand characterizes in a masterful way many different deficient attitudes; his characterizations are so well drawn and so close to life that most readers recognize themselves in many of these deficient attitudes. But von Hildebrand does not communicate sympathy like Newman does; one would not express one's admiration for von Hildebrand's analyses by saying "heart speaks to heart."

It is not difficult to see that knowledge by connaturality plays a large role in sympathizing with others. When I recognize the joy or grief that another experiences, my recognition may be accurate but devoid of sympathy with the other, as we just said. What turns my recognition into real sympathy is apprehending the other's joy or grief *on the basis of my own experience of joy or grief.* I understand the other not through a pure act of objective cognition but through the medium of my own similar experiencing.[24] For example, it is possible to cognize objectively the special difficulties and needs of foreigners living in our midst, but real empathy and sympathy with them we achieve only when Moses reminds us that we were ourselves once foreigners in Egypt (Ex 23:9). The Letter to the Hebrews says that Christ is able to understand our sufferings on the basis of what He Himself suffered (4:15 and 5:2). Perhaps we can even say that God became man so that He might understand us by way of connaturality.

One contemporary who heard Newman preach and was deeply influenced by him wrote:

> He was intimately acquainted with his own heart, and he so read the hearts of his fellow-men, that he seemed to know their inmost secrets. In his own words he could tell them what they knew about themselves,

24. I have argued for this position in my study "The Empathetic Understanding of Other Persons," in my *Personalist Papers* (Washington D.C.: The Catholic University of America Press, 2004). This study takes the form of a debate with Max Scheler, who denied that the empathetic understanding of others necessarily goes through my own experiencing.

> and what they did not know, till they were startled by the truth of his revelations.... He took what he found within him, as the first of all knowledge, as the thing he was most absolutely certain of. The feelings, desires, aspirations, needs, which he felt in his own heart, the intimations of conscience, sense of sin, longing for deliverance, these were his closest knowledge.[25]

It is only natural to call such connatural understanding "heart-knowledge," and to contrast it with a more purely intellectual knowledge.

But one might ask if a person so absorbed in his own experiencing is really in a good position to enter with sympathy into the experiencing of others and to make others feel understood by him. It may seem that he first has to get out of his own experiencing before he can communicate sympathy to another. In his sermon "St. Paul's Characteristic Gift," Newman gives us what we need to respond to this difficulty, and he does so by supplying the middle term that connects knowing one's own heart with sympathy.

> Human nature, the common nature of the whole race of Adam, spoke in him, acted in him, with an energetical presence, with a sort of bodily fulness, always under the sovereign command of divine grace, but losing none of its real freedom and power because of its subordination. And the consequence is, that, having the nature of man so strong within him, he is able to enter into human nature, and to sympathize with it, with a gift peculiarly his own.[26]

The middle term is our common human nature. By experiencing that human nature powerfully in himself, and speaking out of it, Newman, as St. Paul before him, is enabled to say what is intelligible to every child of Adam. Newman continues with some very strong statements about St. Paul's union with others through the medium of his own human nature:

25. Shairp, *Aspects of Poetry*, 451–52.

26. Newman, *Sermons Preached on Various Occasions* (London: Longmans, Green, 1908), 95–96. Hereafter, SVO.

St. Paul felt all his neighbours, all the whole race of Adam, to be existing in himself. He knew himself to be possessed of a nature, he was conscious of possessing a nature, which was capable of running into all the multiplicity of emotions, of devices, of purposes, and of sins, into which it had actually run in the wide world and in the multitude of men; and in that sense he bore the sins of all men, and associated himself with them, and spoke of them and himself as one.[27]

This sermon is immediately followed by one entitled "St. Paul's Gift of Sympathy." Newman develops further the idea that St. Paul communicated sympathy to people through the medium of the human nature that he shares with them. And this is exactly how Newman communicated sympathy in the sense of *cor ad cor loquitur.* The knowledge you have by connaturality extends effortlessly to all who are "co-natured" to you, that is, to all who are one with you in human nature.

It is remarkable that Newman's understanding of St. Paul's sympathy is itself a knowledge by connaturality. Newman understands St. Paul's sympathy through the medium of his own sympathy.

One may raise a question about Newman's ability to sympathize with things that are foreign to him. It may seem that he would have to know these things in himself in order to understand by connaturality those who are oppressed by them. His power of sympathizing with unbelievers is well known. One of the Oxford men who heard Newman in the pulpit at St. Mary's wrote: "Nay, he enters deeply into what even scepticism has to say for itself; he puts himself into the infidel's state of mind, in which the world, as a great fact, seems to give the lie to all religions, converting them into phenomena which counterbalance and negative each other, and he goes down into that lowest abyss and bottom of things, at which the intellect undercuts spiritual truth altogether."[28] How does Newman enter with sympathy and connaturality into religious skepticism without being

27. SVO, 96.
28. James Mozley, as quoted in Church, *The Oxford Movement,* 140.

a skeptic himself? The answer is right at hand: it is clear that human nature, in its present state of fallenness, is vulnerable to unbelief; Newman can experience this vulnerability in himself even if he is a deeply committed believer. Newman states the point in principle when he says in a sermon entitled "Christian Sympathy":

> Any man of tolerably correct life, whatever his positive advancement in grace, will seldom read accounts of notoriously bad men, in which their ways and feelings are described, without being shocked to find that these more or less cast a meaning upon his own heart, and bring out into light and colour lines and shapes of thought within him, which, till then, were almost invisible. Now this does not show that bad and good men are on a level, but it shows this, that they are of the same nature. It shows that the one has within him in tendency, what the other has brought out into actual existence; so that the good has nothing to boast of over the bad.[29]

Newman preserves a certain solidarity with all human beings, even unbelievers and sinners; he never indulges in the perfectionism of trying to occupy a position outside of or above the human condition.[30]

In fact, he warns against a certain hollowness that corrupts our religious existence as soon as we resist this solidarity with unbelievers and sinners. He says in the same sermon, showing deep insight into human things:

> Perhaps the reason why the standard of holiness among us is so low, why our attainments are so poor, our view of the truth so dim, our belief so unreal, our general notions so artificial and external is this, that we dare not trust each other with the secret of our hearts. We have

29. PPS V, 125–26.

30. This solidarity is connected with another great theme of personalist thought. In resisting that individualism whereby *Gemeinschaft* is dissolved into *Gesellschaft,* many personalists such as Scheler and Mounier have tried to recover the deeper solidarity in which we are all established prior to making agreements and entering into contracts with each other. Newman's thought on the unifying power of our common human nature is a rich resource for making the personalist critique of individualism, even if Newman does not develop it in this direction.

each the same secret, and we keep it to ourselves, and we fear that, as a cause of estrangement, which really would be a bond of union. We do not probe the wounds of our nature thoroughly; we do not lay the foundation of our religious profession in the ground of our inner man; we make clean the outside of things; we are amiable and friendly to each other in words and deeds, but our love is not enlarged, our bowels of affection are straitened, and we fear to let the intercourse begin at the root; and, in consequence, our religion, viewed as a social system, is hollow. The presence of Christ is not in it.[31]

People who hide from each other instead of living their solidarity with each other do not speak heart to heart; their talk is corrupted by a falseness that deadens the heart and causes artificial distance. By always striving to know his fellow human beings by connaturality, the sinners as well as the saints, Newman lives by a humble truthfulness that keeps his heart open to them and lets his sympathy extend to all of them, according to the Latin saying that he often quoted: *homo sum, humani nihil a me alienum puto* ("I am a man and nothing that is human is foreign to me"). The humble truthfulness is clearly akin to the vulnerability of heart of which I spoke just above; both here and there we find that Newman does not wear masks, but that he is *real* in his way of speaking to us, and in that sense speaks to us heart to heart.

When, then, we examine the *encounter between persons* expressed in Newman's motto, we are led not exactly to a personalist teaching, but to a personalist way of being, or more exactly, to a personalist way of speaking. There is a mysterious affective tenderness in Newman's words, a power to pierce the heart of those whom he addresses, a power to sympathize with them. Of course, there is also something severe and extremely challenging and demanding about Newman's preaching, as we indicated in chapter 1, but that falls somewhat outside the scope of the present chapter, in which we have tried to unpack his motto, "heart speaks to heart."

31. PPS V, 126–27.

4

Personal Influence

In the course of explaining the origins of the Oxford Movement, Newman complains in his *Apologia* of his friend, William Palmer, an ally in the movement: "Nor had he any insight into the force of personal influence and congeniality of thought in carrying out a religious theory." For Palmer the "*beau ideal* in ecclesiastical action was a board of safe, sound, sensible men." But Newman was of the opinion that "living movements do not come of committees." And he said, "I, on the other hand, had out of my own head begun the Tracts; and these, as representing the antagonist principle of personality, were looked upon by Mr. Palmer's friends with considerable alarm."[1] We cannot even begin to understand Newman and to receive his rich personalist legacy if we do not understand his "principle of personality" and in particular his teaching on personal influence.

1. Apol., 39–41.

Dissolving Stereotypes by Personal Encounter

I turn to Newman's *Lectures on the Present Position of Catholics in England,* written in 1851 in response to an outburst of anti-Catholic agitation that had been set off by the act of Pope Pius IX restoring the Catholic hierarchy in England. In this work Newman gives a great deal of attention to the many absurd stereotypes that controlled the thinking of English Protestants about Catholics.

Toward the end of the first lecture Newman does a delightful satire on these stereotypes. He imagines a Russian count who fears English ways and wants to discredit them so as to keep them out of Russia. He imagines this count addressing an assembly in Moscow on the wickedness of English law. The count quotes from an English law book principles such as "the king can do no wrong," and expresses his horror at this idolatrous veneration of the English king. The count does not understand the narrow legal sense of this principle—it just expresses the legal immunity of the king—but supposes instead that it expresses a shocking impiety. With one gross misunderstanding of English law after the other, the count whips up the assembly into a frenzy of anti-English fury. Newman wants to say that Protestant thinking about English Catholics in 1851 was no less absurd and far-fetched.

So Newman in this work proceeds to advise his fellow Catholics on how to deal with the Protestant stereotypes of Catholics. We are struck by the fact that he does not suggest that Catholics protest against the stereotypes, and try to challenge their correctness. He gives a very different counsel. He draws a distinction between "metropolitan opinion" about Catholics, centered in London, and "local opinion" about Catholics, centered in the neighborhoods where they live. He admonishes his listeners to forget about the former: "Do not dream of converting the public opinion of London; you cannot, and you need not."[2]

2. Newman, *Lectures on the Present Position of Catholics in England* (London: Longmans, Green, 1908), 385. Hereafter, PPC.

Catholics should instead be concerned exclusively with affecting local opinion about themselves. "There is no such thing as local opinion in the metropolis; mutual personal knowledge, there is none; neighbourhood, good fame, bad repute, there is none; no house knows the next door. You cannot make an impression on such an ocean of units; it [metropolitan opinion] has no disposition, no connexion of parts. The great instrument of propagating moral truth is personal knowledge. A man finds himself in a definite place; he grows up in it and into it; he draws persons around him; they know him, he knows them; thus it is that ideas are born which are to live, that works begin which are to last. It is this personal knowledge of each other which is true public opinion; local opinion is real public opinion; but there is not, there cannot be, such in London."[3] Newman tells his listeners that at the level of local opinion Catholics can overcome Protestant prejudice, if only they "force upon others a personal knowledge of you, by your standing before your enemies face to face."[4]

We can also explain Newman's strategy in terms of notional and real apprehension, a subject that we studied in chapter 2. In the same lecture Newman supposes that a Protestant author writes an article against Catholicism, and then Newman asks, "What is Catholicism? can you touch it? point to it? no; it is an idea before his mind. He clothes it with certain attributes, and forthwith it goes all over the country that a certain idea or vision, called Catholicism, has certain other ideas, bad ones, connected with it. You see, it is all a matter of ideas, and abstractions, and conceptions."[5] In other words, it is all a matter of notional apprehension. Newman wants to say that the best antidote to this notional muddle is the encounter with the most concrete thing there is, with persons.

There immediately follows in this lecture a piece of vintage Newmanian satire. He imagines the division of mind that is

3. PPC, 380–81.

4. PPC, 380.

5. PPC, 381–82.

bound to arise in Protestants who have become personally acquainted with individual Catholics but who have not yet given up their anti-Catholic stereotypes. "The Birmingham people will say, 'Catholics are, doubtless, an infamous set, and not to be trusted, for the *Times* says so, and Exeter Hall, and the Prime Minister, and the Bishops of the Establishment; and such good authorities cannot be wrong; but somehow an exception must certainly be made for the Catholics of Birmingham.... Priests in general are perfect monsters; but here they are certainly unblemished in their lives, and take great pains with their people. Bishops are tyrants, and, as Maria Monk says, cut-throats, always excepting the Bishop of Birmingham, who affects no state or pomp, is simple and unassuming, and always in his work.'" Newman takes his satire to another level when he proceeds to imagine what the Protestants of Manchester will say about the Catholics in Birmingham: "Oh, certainly, Popery is horrible, and must be kept down. Still, let us give the devil his due, they are a remarkably excellent body of men here [in Manchester], and we will take care no one does them any harm. It is very different at Birmingham; there they have a Bishop, and that makes all the difference; he is a Wolsey all over; and the priests, too, in Birmingham are at least one in twelve infidels. We do not recollect who ascertained this, but ..."[6] Newman looks forward to the day when the personal influence exercised by Catholics will eventually eliminate this comical situation by destroying altogether the Protestant stereotypes; then the dividedness of the Protestant mind will give way to an understanding of Catholicism based entirely on the personal acquaintance with individual Catholics. The personalism of Newman shows itself in the fact that the stereotypes are not to be broken down at the level of intellectual argument, but at the level of personal encounter.

6. PPC, 387.

Personal Influence in Education

Newman's writings on education introduce us to another aspect of his teaching on personal influence. They also show us personal influence as it exists among friends and not, as above, as it overcomes enemies. I quote here from a paper entitled "What Is a University?" which Newman published in the *University Gazette,* a magazine he founded in the course of establishing a Catholic university in Dublin in the early 1850s. Newman begins in this paper by discussing the *litera scripta,* or written word, which has become available in his time, he says, in an unheard-of abundance. He acknowledges that "the inestimable benefit of the *litera scripta* is that of being a record of truth, and an authority of appeal and an instrument of teaching in the hands of a teacher." And then he continues, "but ... if we wish to become exact and fully furnished in any branch of knowledge which is diversified and complicated, we must consult the living man and listen to his living voice." He says that people really serious about education "avail themselves ... of the rival method [rival to reading the printed word], the ancient method, of oral instruction, of present communication between man and man ... of the personal influence of a master, and the humble initiation of a disciple."[7] In fact, real education is possible without the support of books at all. In his paper entitled "Athens," Newman says, "I doubt whether Athens had a library till the reign of Hadrian. It was what the student gazed on, what he heard, what he caught by the magic of sympathy, not what he read, which was the education furnished by Athens."[8]

Newman asks why it is that this ancient method of oral instruction plays so large a role in all real education, and he answers tentatively:

> Perhaps we may suggest, that no books can get through the number of minute questions which it is possible to ask on any extended subject, or

7. HS III, 8.

8. HS III, 40.

can hit upon the very difficulties which are severally felt by each reader in succession. Or again, that no book can convey the special spirit and delicate peculiarities of its subject with that rapidity and certainty which attend on the sympathy of mind with mind, through the eyes, the look, the accent, and the manner, in casual expressions thrown off at the moment, and the unstudied turns of familiar conversation.[9]

This coheres entirely with Newman's teaching in the *Grammar of Assent,* where he says, as we will see in the next chapter, that in our reasonings in concrete matters our minds work with far more strands of thought than can be formulated in propositions. In the passage just quoted Newman seems to suggest that much of this inner richness, though it escapes propositional formulation, can be intimated in non-propositional ways—through the eyes, the look, the accent, and the manner. Here, then, is something that the living teacher can bring to education: a medium for expressing thought that is more subtle and more versatile than the *litera scripta.*

We might think that when Newman comes to religious education, he would make more of the *litera scripta,* which for him is nothing less than the Bible. But consider what he says of religious education:

Its great instrument, or rather organ, has ever been that which nature prescribes in all education, the personal presence of a teacher, or, in theological language, Oral Tradition. It is the living voice, the breathing form, the expressive countenance, which preaches, which catechises. Truth, a subtle, invisible, manifold spirit, is poured into the mind of the scholar by his eyes and ears, through his affections, imagination, and reason ... by propounding and repeating it, by questioning and re-questioning, by correcting and explaining, by progressing and then recurring to first principles.[10]

Newman did not think that the understanding of sacred scripture could dispense with the personal element that is present in what he calls here oral tradition.

9. HS III, 8–9.

10. HS III, 14–15.

Newman contrasts his ideal of personal influence, not only with the written word and the reading of books, but also with the organization and juridical structure of a university. In another paper in his *Gazette,* "Discipline and Influence," he constructs a dialogue with a critic who says, "I cannot help thinking that your *Gazette* makes more of *persons* than is just, and does not lay stress enough upon order, system, and rule, in conducting a University."[11] In response Newman acknowledges that order, system, and rule are indeed indispensable for the *integrity* of a university, but he says that teaching and learning by way of personal influence constitute the *essence* of the life of a university, and in this way he asserts the primacy of personal influence. "I say, then, that the personal influence of the teacher is able in some sort to dispense with an academical system, but that the system cannot in any sort dispense with personal influence. With influence there is life, without it there is none."[12]

In a memorable passage from *The Idea of a University* Newman states this last idea in a still more radical way, saying that personal influence can be separated not only from "an academical system" but even from teachers; the personal influence that students exercise on each other can constitute a kind of education, and in fact an education more worthy of the name than one based only on reading books and passing examinations. "How is this to be explained? I suppose as follows: When a multitude of young men, keen, open-hearted, sympathetic, and observant, as young men are, come together and freely mix with each other, they are sure to learn one from another, even if there be no one to teach them; the conversation of all is a series of lectures to each, and they gain for themselves new ideas and views, fresh matter of thought, and distinct principles for judging and acting, day by day."[13] Newman says that in such unstructured interactions among students there will be more real formation and enlargement of mind than in a university "which

11. HS III, 70.
12. HS III, 74.
13. Idea, 146.

exacted of its members an acquaintance with every science under the sun."[14] A contemporary phenomenologist might say it like this: the intersubjective world constituted by learners is the medium in which minds are formed and enlarged; educational structures that do not build on this intersubjectivity cannot provide for the same formation of mind. Just as for the purpose of learning a language there is no substitute for living among the native speakers of the language, so for the purpose of acquiring the formation of mind that makes for an educated person, there is no substitute for living in this intersubjective world. And just as language labs and dictionaries and textbooks cannot substitute for immersing oneself in the spoken language, so required courses and reading lists and examinations cannot substitute for living and moving in the intersubjective world of learners.

Some years ago I became embroiled in a debate at my university about a proposal to offer university degrees by means of "distance education." Courses were to be put on audiotape, and some limited e-mail contact between teacher and student was envisioned. It was only when I went back to these papers of Newman that I realized why I was so strenuously opposed to it. Distance education in the form then proposed, but also in the more sophisticated online forms available today, would largely block the flow of personal influence. The living presence of a teacher who is responsive to his students, as well as the interpersonal medium constituted by a community of learners, would be largely filtered out. The electronically facilitated transmission of information is not education, at least not in the same sense in which teaching and learning on the basis of personal influence is education; it can never enable influence to flow between persons as happens when teachers and learners see each other in the flesh and live in community with each other.

One sees how Newman implies something about the rich personalist theme of the embodiment of persons. He helps us

14. Idea, 145.

to understand why it is that one of the curses of the digital age is the highly disembodied way in which persons communicate with one another.

Newman's Athenian Principle

After being received into the Catholic Church in 1845 Newman surveyed the various religious communities in the church, looking for the one in which he would be at home. He eventually joined the Oratory of St. Philip Neri, and in fact brought the Oratory to England for the first time. In talks given to his brother Oratorians Newman tried to articulate the genius of religious community as lived in the spirit of St. Philip, and in doing this he brings out yet another aspect of his thought on personal influence. In one of these talks Newman goes back to the funeral oration of Pericles, as reported in Thucydides, and in particular to the famous passage in which Pericles contrasts the Athenian and the Spartan. Newman wants to say that the genius of Athens, once it is baptized and made the principle of a religious community, yields the spirit of the Oratory. "The point of the Orator's [Pericles's] praise of the Athenians is this, that they, unlike the Spartans, have no need of laws, but perform from the force of inward character those great actions which others do from compulsion. Here the Oratorian stands for the Athenian, and the Spartan for the Jesuit."[15]

This means for Newman that in the Oratory, as in Athens, personal influence has a natural home. "Obedience to the official Superior is the prominent principle of the Jesuit; personal influence is that of the Oratorian."[16] And again: "Jesuit Fathers are part of a whole, but each Oratorian stands by himself and is a whole, promoting and effecting by his own proper acts the wellbeing of the community."[17] Newman explains what he

15. Placid Murray, OSB, ed., *Newman the Oratorian: His Unpublished Oratory Papers* (Dublin: Gill and Macmillan, 1969), 210.

16. Ibid., 211–12.

17. Ibid., 210.

means by "his own proper acts": "It is the common sense, the delicacy, the sharp observation, the tact of each which keeps the whole in harmony. It is a living principle, call it (in human language) judgment or wisdom or discretion or sense of propriety or moral perception, which takes the place of formal enactment" and of commands and prohibitions.[18] Newman returns here again to the contrast with the Jesuit, who is of course deliberately made into a stereotype for the sake of sharpening the contrast: "An Oratorian as I have said is in a great measure a law to himself, and is almost the reverse of a regular, for instance a Jesuit."[19]

We find everywhere in Newman this aversion to the Spartan spirit, as found in those who slavishly follow and apply rules that remain external to them, and everywhere this admiration for the Athenian spirit, as found in those who have so internalized rules and laws as to be eminently free in living by them and imaginative and resourceful in connecting them with concrete situations. These latter are alive as persons, they engage others as persons, they give and receive personal influence, while the former tend to act in a passive and mechanical way.

Personal Influence in Transmitting Revelation

Let us now enter into a deeper dimension of Newman's teaching on and practice of personal influence. In an early sermon entitled "Personal Influence, the Means of Propagating the Truth," Newman asks how revealed truth has made its way and held its ground in the world. He is especially concerned to avoid rationalistic explanations of the propagation of Christian revelation. In particular he wants to avoid the idea that Christian truth is understood in its inner reasonableness by people and in this way gets accepted by more and more of them, much as certain basic rights of persons have become widely accepted

18. Ibid., 208.
19. Ibid., 208.

in our time. For example, people understand today that coercion in matters of religious faith is inappropriate, or that persons must not be subject to arbitrary arrest but must be told the crimes they are charged with and be given the chance to defend themselves. These rights are better and more widely understood today than they were several hundred years ago. It is a question of elementary moral truths making their way in the consciences of the people of our time. Newman thinks that if we were to apply this pattern of diffusion of truth to Christian revelation, we would make ourselves guilty of an un-Christian intellectualism. Christian revelation does not appeal in exactly this way to the intellect, and does not become diffused among many believers primarily by being intellectually understood as self-evidently true. It rather appeals to the heart and not just to the understanding. And so he protests against the idea that "it [Christian revelation] is, after a time, on mature reflection, accepted by the world in general from a real understanding and conviction of its excellence; that it is in its nature level to the comprehension of men, considered merely as rational beings, without reference to their moral character, whether good or bad."[20] In fact, when in this sermon Newman considers believers who try to exercise religious influence on others by intellectual argument alone, he goes surprisingly far in granting that unbelievers have many intellectual advantages over them.

Newman also flags the anonymity that characterizes the transmitting of propositions: "The exhibitions of Reason, being complete in themselves, and having nothing of a personal nature, are capable almost of an omnipresence by an indefinite multiplication and circulation, through the medium of composition." One cannot help noticing that this omnipresence of propositions takes on an entirely new meaning in the age of digital technology. Newman continues in the same personalist vein, "Being in their operation separable from the person furnishing them, [the exhibitions of Reason] possess little or no

20. OUS, 78.

responsibility. To be anonymous is almost their characteristic."[21]

There is another way of trying to transmit revealed truth, and Newman takes an even dimmer view of it. Sometimes Christians have tried to uphold revelation by means of the legal establishment of Christianity, that is, by making Christianity the law of the land, which typically means, among other things, that those who have some important function in society must profess the Christian faith and receive the Christian sacraments. It seemed to many to be a great boon for the dissemination of Christianity when in the fourth century it became the official religion of the Roman Empire. The Church of England in which Newman grew up was such an established church, and many thought that the propagation of Christianity in England depended on this establishment. Newman not only did not expect much from establishment, he even thought that it worked at odds with the propagation of Christianity. In a letter to a friend written in 1863 Newman said: "I am not at all sure that it would not be better for the Catholic religion every where, if it had no very different status from that which it has in England. There is so much corruption, so much deadness, so much hypocrisy, so much infidelity, when a dogmatic faith is imposed on a nation by law, that I like freedom better. I think Italy will be more religious, that is, there will be more true religion in it, when the Church has to fight for its supremacy, than when that supremacy depends on the provisions of courts, and police, and territorial claims."[22] Writing to the same friend a year later he expands on the advantage for the Church of precisely not enjoying the privileges of being established: "The presence of Protestantism, where it is tolerated, stirs up Catholics and keeps them from sinking into a low carnal state, into tyranny, superstition, and immorality. It is a *sort of persecution* against Catholics; and a very profitable one."[23] It is not difficult to see the person-

21. OUS, 91.

22. LD XX, 477.

23. LD XXI, 43. See the very able discussion of these passages in Ian Ker, *John Henry Newman: A Biography* (Oxford: Clarendon Press, 1988), 538–39.

alist impulse in Newman's statement, "The age is such, that we must go by reason, not by force."[24] Perhaps we can discern here once again his aversion to the Spartan principle.

And so the question becomes urgent: how then *do* believers exercise influence and propagate the truth of Christian revelation? Newman answers that revelation "has been upheld in the world not as a system, not by books, not by arguments, nor by temporal power, but by the personal influence of such [holy] men as have already been described, who are at once the teachers and the patterns of [Christian truth]."[25] And he explains: "Men persuade themselves, with little difficulty, to scoff at principles, to ridicule books, to make sport of the names of good men; but they cannot bear their presence: it is holiness embodied in personal form which they cannot steadily confront and bear down: so that the silent conduct of a conscientious man secures for him from beholders a feeling different in kind from any which is created by the mere versatile and garrulous Reason."[26] He explains a little this difference in kind when he goes on to say, "The attraction, exerted by unconscious holiness, is of an urgent and irresistible nature; it persuades the weak, the timid, the wavering, and the inquiring; it draws forth the affections and loyalty of all who are in a measure like-minded."[27] It is personal influence that accomplishes what rational arguments alone cannot accomplish and what legal coercion cannot accomplish.

First-Person Self-Disclosure

Newman introduces his study of St. John Chrysostom with an examination of two different ways of presenting the lives of the saints, only one of which lets the saint exercise personal influence. A writer can present a saint in the saint's own words expressing his own self-understanding (the writer will typically

24. LD XX, 477.
25. OUS, 91–92.
26. OUS, 92
27. OUS, 95.

draw on the letters of the saint), or the writer can present the saint without the help of the saint's self-expression and can thus take the saint entirely in the third person and give a narrative of the saint's life as a series of events seen from the outside. Newman says that only in the first kind of hagiography does the saint appear as *this individual person;* in the second kind of hagiography the personal individuality of the saint disappears and the writer is led to reduce the saint to an instance or specimen of certain virtues. Newman is referring to the second approach when he complains of books which "chop up a saint into chapters of faith, hope, charity, and the cardinal virtues." He says that these virtues are presented abstractly and "put under the patronage" of a saint, but they are not taken in such a way as to reveal the saint in his personal individuality.[28] We have already encountered this thought in chapter 2: in place of the living saint we get idealized images of holiness and spiritual stereotypes. The saint has to disclose himself in the first person in order to become present to us as *this individual.* Newman explains that only the first-person self-disclosure lets us into the *interior life* of the saint. Personalist philosophers would speak of the *subjectivity* of the saint and would say that this center of the individual person becomes accessible to us only when the saint speaks in the first person.[29] They would agree with Newman when he says that a person who is known through his self-disclosure is related to a person known only from without, as an original is related to a copy.[30]

One sees the bearing on our subject of personal influence. The saint known only in the third person is shrouded in ab-

28. HS II, 229.

29. Again we refer to Wojtyla's seminal essay "Subjectivity and the Irreducible in the Human Being," where this all-important connection of subjectivity and personhood is affirmed and explained. He also distinguishes between a "cosmological" view of the human being and a "personalist" view of him: the former takes him "from without" and the latter, based on first-person self-disclosure, takes him "from within."

30. HS II, 224.

straction and is apprehended notionally, whereas the saint known through his self-disclosure is present to us in his living personal individuality, and is far better able to establish himself in our imagination and to move us affectively. When Newman speaks in his sermon of personal influence as the means of propagating the truth, he is speaking of the influence exercised by a saint in this latter way.

Legitimate and Illegitimate Personal Influence

Now there are all kinds of influence that people exercise on each other, and not all of them are respectful of the person influenced. For instance, the influence based on what is called "emotional contagion" is a sub-personal kind of influence; if I feel anger because people around me feel it, because the emotional charge of their anger works on my emotional system, then I do not really own as a person the anger with which I have been infected; my anger is too much of an offshoot of the anger of others. No less sub-personal is the influence exercised by a dynamic person on a weak and suggestible personality, or by a crowd on an individual who gets swept up in its dynamism (this is the kind of depersonalized social life that Kierkegaard is always warning against). And then there are the different forms of manipulation, where we find something deliberate in the depersonalizing influence. Personalists are very keen on identifying that influence that takes people seriously as persons, and empowers them as persons rather than subjects them to the control of others.

The personal influence of which Newman speaks is eminently personal in the sense that the person influenced is in no way manipulated but is fully respected. This becomes clear when we consider the kind of personal influence that Newman had on others, for this influence of his is just the kind of personal influence of which he speaks in this early sermon. He speaks in this sermon out of a knowledge by connaturality. He did not, of course, intend to speak about himself in that sermon, but in the case of connatural knowledge his own being and ethos interpret for us and concretize for us his teaching.

In studying the Oxford Movement one finds that Newman exercised an influence on people that was experienced as something extraordinary, an influence that far exceeded the reasons and arguments that Newman offered in his writings and lectures. Thus William Gladstone, four-time prime minister of England, reminiscing in Oxford in 1877 about Newman during the Oxford Movement, said, "When the history of Oxford during that time comes to be written, the historian will have to record the extraordinary, the unexampled career of that distinguished man in the University. He will have to tell, as I believe, that Dr. Newman exercised for a period of about ten years after 1833 an amount of influence, of absorbing influence, over the highest intellects ... of this University, for which perhaps, there is no parallel in the academical history of Europe, unless you go back to the twelfth century or to the University of Paris." The next sentence expresses the thought that particularly concerns us in this chapter and that rules out any suspicion of depersonalizing influence: "We know how his influence was sustained by his extraordinary purity of character and the holiness of his life."[31] The influence of which Gladstone speaks is not the kind of influence that typically contains manipulative elements, or elements that tend to dominate the influenced persons; it is rather a kind of influence that is quiet and deep, and is readily resisted by those who do not appreciate the "purity of character" and the "holiness of life" of the witness.

I venture to say that it is not too much to think of Newman's influence as being like the influence of Socrates on Alcibiades, as reported by Plato in the *Symposium*. The case of Alcibiades is instructive not only as showing us an influence of almost preternatural power, but also as showing us an influence that seems

31. Quoted in LD XXVIII, 351.

to be entirely free of suspicious psychodynamics. Socrates's influence lacks any hint of depersonalizing pressure, since by it Alcibiades experiences himself as being led by Socrates back to his real self. In the *Symposium* Alcibiades says of Socrates, "For the moment I hear him speak I am smitten with a kind of sacred rage ... and my heart jumps into my mouth and the tears start into my eyes—oh, and not only me, but lots of other men. Yes, I've heard Pericles and all the other great orators, and very eloquent I thought they were, but they never affected me like that; they never turned my whole soul upside down and left me feeling ... I simply couldn't go on living the way I did."[32] This is exactly how Newman affected many young men in Oxford, such as William Lockhart, who as we saw spoke of Newman "turning our souls inside out." Newman continued to exercise this power throughout his life. One German visitor to Newman in 1878 spoke in exactly the same vein as those who remembered Newman in Oxford during the Oxford Movement; he said, "Newman's personality made a lasting impression on me.... I was cut to the quick in my soul by his venerable features, cast as it were in bronze, so infinitely earnest and yet so gentle, and by his wonderful and noble looking at me; he seemed to ask me, 'Why, my son, do you not give your heart totally to your God?' To this day I shudder at what I saw in him."[33] Newman seems to have affected him in the same radical way that Socrates affected Alcibiades, but with the difference that this German visitor did not run away from Newman's influence like Alcibiades ran away from Socrates's influence. What concerns us is that Newman's influence on his German visitor was powerful and piercing and yet gentle and silent, indeed it was so gentle that many another visitor might have overlooked entirely the penetrating presence of Newman.

32. Plato, *Symposium,* 215b–16a. Translated by Michael Joyce in *The Collected Dialogues of Plato,* edited by Edith Hamilton and Huntington Cairns (New York: The Bollingen Foundation, 1961), 567.

33. Quoted in LD XXVIII, 350. The visitor was the German historian Franz Xaver Kraus.

And there is something else in the Alcibiades passage that throws light on Newman's influence. Alcibiades says, "I don't know whether anybody else has ever opened him up when he's been being serious, and seen the little images inside, but I saw them once, and they looked so godlike, so golden, so beautiful, and so utterly amazing that there was nothing for it but to do exactly what he told me."[34] In the following we hear a contemporary of Newman speaking of him just like Alcibiades speaks of Socrates: "Nothing could be more alien to Dr. Newman's whole nature, than to withdraw the veil, and indulge in those exhibitions of himself, which are now-a-days so common and offensive. It is but a mere indirect hint he gives—a few indirect words, dropped as it were unawares, which many might read without notice, but which, rightly understood, seem breathed from some very inward experience. It is ... as though he suddenly opened a book and gave you a glimpse for a moment of wonderful secrets, and then quickly closed it. But the glance you have had, the words you have caught, haunt you ever after with an interest in him who uttered them, which is indescribable."[35] To be moved by such a glimpse of unearthly beauty is to be deeply influenced, it is perhaps even, as Plato says in the *Phaedrus,* to be taken over by a certain madness of love, but yet in such a manner as to be never so much yourself as when you are thus "beside yourself."

This influence of Newman during the Oxford Movement was, then, based not in the first place on his literary accomplishments or his philosophical and theological contributions; it was based on a mysterious personal radiance of Newman's holiness. Or perhaps it would be better to say that it was based on his literary work insofar as he disclosed through it something of his inner life. And the influence of Newman was not an enchantment which swept people away against their better judgment

34. *Symposium,* 216e–17a.

35. Schairp, *Aspects of Poetry* 454–55.

(though some called him "the great enchanter"), but was an influence in which people "came to themselves," in which they underwent an "awakening." John Coleridge, Lord Chief Justice of England, heard Newman preach at Oxford, and spoke many years later about him, remembering "that great penetrating influence, that waking up of the soul, that revelation of hopes, desires, motives, duties not of this world ... which came to us week by week from the pulpit of St. Mary's."[36]

When Newman died in 1890 there was an extraordinary outpouring in the English press of testimonials to his personal influence. Typical of many of these was one in the *Times* of London, in which a Protestant editorialist said, "Of one thing we may be sure, that the memory of his pure and noble life, untouched by worldliness, unsoured by any trace of fanaticism, will endure, and that whether Rome canonizes him or not he will be canonized in the thoughts of pious people of many creeds in England."[37] This writer is remembering not Newman's arguments, not his literary accomplishments, not his contributions to philosophy and theology, but "his pure and noble life," his freedom from worldliness and fanaticism. In the English magazine *Spectator* a Protestant writer made this point explicit: "It is as the saint, not as the profound scholar ... that Newman has kept and will keep hold on our imaginations.... In this busy, material, striving and crying age, Newman revived in his beautiful personality and serenely-ordered life what seemed a dead and gone ideal.... The simplicity of the man's life, the solemnity of his tones, his marvelous spiritual history, his wondrous influence over his contemporaries of an earlier day, all helped to bring to life again the old notions of saintship."[38] This con-

36. Quoted in the "Note on Cardinal Newman's Preaching and Influence at Oxford," in an appendix to Newman, *My Campaign in Ireland* (Aberdeen: A. King, 1896), 16.

37. Quoted by Philip Boyce, OCD, in "Newman as Seen by His Contemporaries at the Time of His Death," in Katherina Strolz and Margarete Binder, eds., *John Henry Newman: Lover of Truth* (Rome: Urbaniana University Press, 1991), 113.

38. Ibid., 112.

firms exactly what Newman meant in saying in the sermon on personal influence that "holiness embodied in personal form" is the secret of personal influence. The same writer also makes a point of saying that Newman's influence was often exercised wordlessly: "The mere knowledge that he was living in the quiet Oratory at Edgbaston helped men to realise that the spiritual world is even more real than the material world."[39] As we saw, Newman wrote in this sermon, "The attraction, exerted by unconscious holiness, is of an urgent and irresistible nature": well, much of England, Protestant no less than Catholic, felt this urgent and irresistible attraction in the case of Newman. Even though Newman had dealt the Church of England a tremendous blow, and even though most members of that church strongly disagreed with Newman's turn to Rome, many of them nevertheless felt this irresistible attraction, and they could not not revere and venerate Newman. And yet his influence, though in a sense irresistible, was not intrusive or overwhelming; it was an influence that worked *fortiter* and at the same time *suaviter.* He exercised throughout his life exactly the personal influence that he had written about in this early sermon.

Final Remarks on Personal Influence

One may find it strange that Newman's influence was often strongly felt by people who could not follow him to his doctrinal conclusions. All of those just quoted as remembering him at his death were Protestants; most of those quoted earlier as remembering his preaching in Oxford remained Protestants. What Newman says in this sermon is not that personal influence is always successful in fully transmitting revealed truth, but only that truth cannot be transmitted in any other way. Just as my illative sense cannot compel your illative sense and cannot produce unanimity among all who exercise their illative

39. Ibid., 110.

sense on a subject, so faith that is personally embodied does not compel the faith of others. We are after all speaking here of an *encounter between persons.* And yet Newman's witness was not without influence even on those who remained Protestant, for he renewed the Christian faith of many Protestants, so that thousands of them felt a deep spiritual indebtedness to him. He transmitted something of faith to them, even if it was not the full faith that Newman himself embraced. And he transmitted it with a mysterious power because of the way it lived in him.

But what about Newman's influence on us—on us who did not know him in Oxford and were not his contemporaries in England? We live in a later century and, having no direct personal acquaintance with him, we know him mainly through his writings. It might seem that Newman was able to exercise personal influence only on those who knew him personally, and that on us who come later he exercises mainly the intellectual influence that he contrasts with personal influence. So it seems—until we consult our experience of Newman. And then we find to our surprise that his personal influence reaches us too. I would even venture to say that many who have read deeply into Newman's sermons and letters can be influenced by him *almost as much as the Oxford undergraduates who heard him preach were influenced by him. Personal influence can dispense with actual personal acquaintance and can reach across many centuries.* The same writings of Newman in which he gives his reasons and makes his arguments are instruments of personal influence. In virtue of the things we examined in the previous chapter, namely, his ability to express his subjectivity and to speak in the first person, his vast connatural knowledge, and what we called his humble truthfulness, he was able to make himself present in his writings in such a way as to exercise personal influence on us *almost as much as* on his contemporaries.

I might add here a word on Newman and Kierkegaard.

Since I have often stressed the deep kinship of spirit that unites them, I should mention that they diverge on the subject of personal influence. Kierkegaard approaches with much suspicion the idea of one human being directly influencing another in the direction of faith. He thinks that all kinds of human-all-too-human methods of intimidation and manipulation are at work in such influence. He cannot stress enough that we are "alone before God" when we accept revealed truth. Thus he sometimes reflects on the reputed ugliness of Socrates, and says that every great teacher must have something repellent for his students, lest they acquire a slavish dependency on the teacher; by repelling them the teacher drives them back into the solitude where they find their way to truth as individuals existing before God.

Kierkegaard says many wise things on the "direct" and "indirect" communication of truth and he says much that resonates with Newman. Newman would certainly concur with the Kierkegaardian warning about the danger of being lost in admiration for a revered person, to the point that one fails to be challenged to become in one's own way like that person; Newman dealt severely with any and every kind of influence that tends to make us dreamy and passive. But in the end Newman seems to envision a believer playing a more positive role in transmitting faith than Kierkegaard would acknowledge. The personal influence of which Newman speaks involves not just a negative repelling but a positive attracting. Newman himself as religious teacher did not just repel but attracted. He is speaking of something entirely positive when he says that "the attraction, exerted by unconscious holiness, is of an urgent and irresistible nature; it persuades the weak, the timid, the wavering, and the inquiring." The best way to continue the dialogue between Kierkegaard and Newman would be to gather together all that Kierkegaard says about the interpersonal dangers that accompany the attempt to influence others in matters of faith, and to see whether Newman makes any concessions to them in his way of putting forward "personal influence as the true means of propagating the truth." Such an encounter between the two thinkers would, I think, serve to confirm the personalist credentials of Newman's teaching on personal influence. It would also confirm that the great personalist theme of intersubjectivity is much more developed in Newman than in Kierkegaard.

5

"You Must Consent to Think"

We have by now gotten acquainted with various facets of Newman's personalism. In chapter 2 we examined the experiential concreteness of Newman's thought, and why he is thereby particularly attuned to the personal. In chapter 3 we examined interpersonal encounter as expressed in his motto, "heart speaks to heart," and we brought to light the personalist import of the connatural knowledge by which he is connected with others. And in chapter 4 we found another dimension of his thought on intersubjectivity; we found something eminently personalist in his account of how religious truth is transmitted by personal influence. Now we come to one of the richest personalist themes in Newman; we will even hear Newman himself speaking in terms of "person" and "the personal." We come to his personalist account of thinking, of intellectual understanding, and of reasoning.

The Freshness of Newman as Thinker

Shortly after Newman entered the Catholic Church in 1845 he was asked by someone to publish a brief account of his reasons for taking this step; he responded by refusing to undertake such a work, and he gave a very significant reason for refusing. He shows his deep spiritual kinship with Kierkegaard when he says in answer: "I do not know how to do justice to my reasons for becoming a Catholic in ever so many words—but if I attempted to do so in few, and that in print, I should wantonly expose myself and my cause to the hasty and prejudiced criticisms of opponents. This I will not do. People shall not say, 'We have now got his reasons, and know their worth.' No, you have not got them, you cannot get them, except at the cost of some portion of the trouble I have been at myself. You cannot buy them for a crown piece.... You must consent to *think*.... Moral proofs are grown into, not learnt by heart."[1] Newman wants to challenge people to exert themselves as persons and not to hide behind a show of reasons and arguments that is really an escape from thinking. He says that he would interfere with their thinking—their thinking as responsible persons—if he were to fulfill their request for clearly formulated reasons. He would make them overrate such reasons and he would inhibit the exercise of their personal judgment, which is what they have to employ in order to think fruitfully about the Catholic claims. He wants to "lead them on by their own independent action, not by any syllogistic compulsion."[2] One can already discern in this letter of Newman something of the distinctly personal character of what he here calls "thinking."

Before we examine Newman's personalist teaching on thinking, let us take notice of his practice of it. No one who reads Newman seriously can fail to be struck by the extraordinary freshness and originality of his thought. In Newman's

1. Letter of February 8, 1846, in LD XI, 110.
2. GA, 309.

writing there is very little "boilerplate," very little "party line," very little that is painfully predictable, very little that is hackneyed, very little that is dominated by conventional strands of thought. All these things are obstructions to real thinking; they are like mechanical intrusions into what should be living and personal. They are very little present in Newman because of the way in which he is really thinking when he speaks. It is eminently *he* who speaks, it is not some pattern or structure speaking through him. What he writes is extraordinarily *interesting*, indeed he is interesting as hardly anyone else is interesting. Open any one of the thirty-two volumes of his letters and diaries, start reading at any page: most of what you read will light up with an exceptional human interest. This comes, at least in part, from his being present as a living intelligence in his words. We spoke in chapter 3 about the connatural knowledge by which Newman makes himself present in his words, so as to speak to us heart to heart. But he also makes himself present in his words by the way in which he "consents to think." He speaks from the heart, but also from a living intelligence. He becomes present to us in a particularly personal way by "consenting to think" when he speaks.

Of course, no one can be absolutely original in his or her thinking. No one can fail to rely on inherited patterns of thought. The very act of living within a tradition means that we take our bearings from the canonical writers in that tradition and work on the presumption that they are trustworthy.[3] Nor can any writer

3. For example, Newman never really studied St. Thomas Aquinas, and did not feel any particular affinity with what he knew of St. Thomas. So he is speaking not so much in his own name as in the name of the Catholic tradition when he writes: "It was the Dominican and Franciscan doctors, the greatest of them being St. Thomas, who in those medieval Universities fought the battle of Revelation with the weapons of heathenism.... With the jawbone of an ass, with the skeleton philosophy of pagan Greece, did the Samson of the schools put to flight his thousand Philistines" (Idea, 470). I do not mean that Newman was not really thinking at all when he wrote this, or that he did not really believe what he said, or that he did anything blameworthy, but I mean that the thinking that imparts such a freshness and originality to his writing is not particularly on display in these sentences.

fail to fall back on what he has previously thought or written on a subject, when he addresses that subject again. It is neither possible nor desirable to go back to the very beginning in every one of one's utterances. But if we speak of a proportion between what one takes over from others, and what one owns with one's own insight, or of a proportion between passing on a tradition and bringing new things out of the tradition (and to the tradition), then we have to say that in Newman the proportion favors the latter over the former to an extraordinary degree.[4]

Notice that the thinking of which we speak here is exercised by Newman not only in matters of "natural reason," but also in matters of faith. Thus when Newman admonishes the recipient of this letter to "consent to think," he means "think about the truth of the Catholic claims." The freshness and originality of Newman is found everywhere in his religious and theological writings. The energy of his thinking is found on both sides of the line between "natural reason" and "supernatural faith."

We now turn from Newman's practice of thinking to his teachings on thinking. Since these teachings correspond to his practice, since they are sprung from his own intellectual virtue, we will recognize in them yet another level of Newman's knowledge by connaturality.

I begin with his teaching on thinking as developed in the *Grammar of Assent;* later in this chapter I will draw on *The Idea of a University* in exploring certain pathologies of thinking.

The Limits of Formal Inference

Consider the motto Newman chose for the *Grammar;* it is perfectly chosen, and catches the spirit of the work as well as

4. It is interesting to see that in one place he blames himself for not sufficiently favoring the latter over the former. "I was angry with the Anglican divines. I thought they had taken me in; I had read the Fathers with their eyes. . . . I had used words or made statements, which by right I ought rigidly to have examined myself. I had thought myself safe, while I had their warrant for what I said. I had exercised more faith than criticism in the matter" (Apol., 203).

any motto could. It is from St. Ambrose: *Non in dialectica complacuit Deo salvum facere populum suum* ("God has not wanted to save His people by means of formal logic"). We see here in 1870 the same wariness of proof and demonstration that we see in the letter of 1846. Newman argues in the *Grammar* that there is another kind of reasoning, different from formal logic, and that this one does play a large role in our salvation. Newman calls it "informal inference" and he calls the power in us that carries out informal inference by the name of "the illative sense" (from the Latin *illatio,* reasoning). We want to understand the deep personalist meaning that the illative sense had for Newman.

Let us first examine what Newman calls formal inference, and then we can advance, by way of contrast, to the informal inference that mainly interests him. We all encountered formal inference when we studied mathematics. The steps by which you prove a theorem in geometry are based on formal inference. Given any square, you form a new square exactly double the area of the given square by using the diagonal of the given square. This is not self-evident, but starting with self-evident axioms, and some already proved theorems, you can advance rigorously and relentlessly to the conclusion. Such formal reasoning is at work in algebra as well. Aristotle's syllogism is a thing of formal logic. We see that formal inference has an impressive precision and exactness. It also has the power to bring minds together, for in formal inference we trace out the way in which *any* reasonable person thinks. Thus no reasonable person could think that you produce a new square that is double the area of a given square from any other length than the diagonal of the given square. People of course make mistakes in their formal reasoning, but the mistakes are such that, once pointed out, no one can persist in making them. Disputes that are amenable to formal inference are disputes that can be settled once and for all. Newman calls particular attention to the fact that formal inference appeals solely to the intellect, and not at all to the will and the heart; it is only by sharpness of intellect, not goodness of will and of heart, that you reason well, and only by weakness of intellect, not weakness of will and of heart, that you go astray. It does not matter what condition your heart is in; your intellect is always able to follow a formal argument.

Newman thinks that formal inference, for all its excellences, encounters difficulties when employed in matters of historical fact; indeed, he thinks that if we use formal inference alone we cannot make our way to truth in such matters. Let us consider with Newman Hume's famous attempt to discredit the occurrence of miracles by means of a simple formal inference. He says that whenever a person alleges a miracle, it is always more likely that that person is deceived or is lying than that the miracle has really occurred; for it is a very common occurrence for people to be deceived or to tell lies about miracles, whereas the real occurrence of miracles is by definition very rare. With this single stroke of formal inference Hume claims to prove that no alleged miracle is worthy of our belief, that we are almost certain to be wrong if we acknowledge it as a real miracle.

There is a well-known line of formal inference commonly used in Christian apologetics. One argues that Christ, who claimed to be the Son of God, must really have been the Son of God. For there are only three possibilities: in claiming divinity He must have been insane, or have been a liar, or must have really been the Son of God. But everything we know about him tells us that He was not insane, and that he was unconditionally committed to the truth and thus the opposite of a liar; there remains only the third possibility, namely, that He must really have been the divine person He said He was.

Now Newman took a dim view of formal inference in matters of historical fact, and he even took a dim view of formal inference as sometimes used in Christian apologetics. Or more exactly: he denied that the reasoning we do in matters of historical fact, and in Christian apologetics, is for the most part done by formal inference. We cannot make our way by formal inference alone. And his reason was this: formal inference picks out only one aspect of reality, and shows what follows logically from this one aspect. But concrete reality has innumerable aspects, and if in our reasoning we do not take account of many of these aspects, we are liable to come to a wrong conclusion.

Let us look at Newman's response to Hume and see how he challenges him by thinking more concretely than Hume ever did about the alleged Christian miracles, and more concretely than Hume ever could by using only formal inference. He begins: "Doubtless it is abstractedly more likely that men should lie than that the order of nature should be infringed." Note that Newman grants the main premise of Hume's formal inference; he contests Hume's reasoning not by contradicting his premise, but by showing how deficient Hume's reasoning is in terms of concreteness.

> Doubtless it is abstractedly more likely that men should lie than that the order of nature should be infringed; but what is abstract reasoning to a question of concrete fact? To arrive at the fact of any matter, we must eschew generalities, and take things as they stand, with all their circumstances. À priori, of course the acts of men are not so trustworthy as the order of nature, and the pretence of miracles is in fact more common than the occurrence. But the question is not about miracles in general, or men in general, but definitely, whether these particular miracles, ascribed to the particular Peter, James, and John, are more likely to have been or not.

And here Newman enters into some of the concrete aspects of these miracles; he asks of these miracles

> whether they are unlikely, supposing that there is a Power, external to the world, who can bring them about; supposing they are the only means by which He can reveal Himself to those who need a revelation; supposing He is likely to reveal Himself; that He has a great end in doing so; that the professed miracles in question are like His natural works, and such as He is likely to work, in case He wrought miracles; that great effects, otherwise unaccountable, in the event followed upon the acts said to be miraculous; that they were from the first accepted

as true by large numbers of men against their natural interests; that the reception of them as true has left its mark upon the world, as no other event ever did; that, viewed in their effects, they have—that is, the belief of them has—served to raise human nature to a high moral standard, otherwise unattainable: these and the like considerations are parts of a great complex argument, which so far can be put into propositions, but which, even between, and around, and behind these, still is implicit and secret, and cannot by any ingenuity be imprisoned in a formula, and packed into a nut-shell.[5]

Newman means that no series of formal inferences can capture and assess all of these considerations that enter into our reasoning about the apostolic miracles. If all of our reasoning is a matter of formal inference, we will not be able to think fruitfully about the occurrence of these miracles, or about any matter of concrete fact.

Newman thinks that the abstractness of Hume's argument cannot be helped in the sense that it is inseparable from formal inference as exercised in concrete historical subject matters. Newman is always contrasting the luxuriant abundance of concrete reality with the relative poverty and barrenness of those concepts that are needed for formal inference. In one place Newman describes vividly how logicians flee from the concrete to the abstract so as to make our language suitable for formal inference.

The concrete matter of propositions is a constant source of trouble to syllogistic reasoning, as marring the simplicity and perfection of its process.... In inferential exercises it is the very triumph of that clearness and hardness of head, which is the characteristic talent for the art, to have stripped them [words] of all these connatural senses, to have drained them of that depth and breadth of associations which constitute their poetry, their rhetoric, and their historical life, to have starved each term down till it has become the ghost of itself, and everywhere one and the same ... so that it may stand for just one unreal aspect of the concrete thing to which it properly belongs, for a relation, a generalization, or other abstraction, for a notion neatly turned out of the

5. GA, 306–7.

laboratory of the mind, and sufficiently tame and subdued, because existing only in a definition.

Newman concludes with a striking metaphor.

Thus it is that the logician for his own purposes, and most usefully as far as those purposes are concerned, turns rivers, full, winding, and beautiful, into navigable canals.[6]

The marvelous exactness and certainty of formal logic makes it ill-suited for concrete historical subject matters. We are liable to miss the mark with our formal inference, just as Hume did. We may reach a conclusion that indeed follows with logical rigor from "one unreal aspect of the concrete thing," only to have it cancelled by other aspects of the same concrete thing. And even if it is not cancelled by other aspects, even if it hits the truth, as in the example of apologetic reasoning that I gave above, Newman still says that our thinking is not adequate to the subject matter, and will become really fruitful thinking only if our formal inferences are completed by another kind of inference.

Informal Inference Contrasted with Formal

As I said, Newman speaks of informal inference as exercised by the illative sense; this is the alternative kind of inference that Newman seeks for concrete matters of fact. And in fact he gave us a good specimen of informal inference in his way of reasoning about the Christian miracles. Let us stay with that passage.

Newman says here that he is able to give no more than some specimens of the concrete considerations that accumulate in the mind of the believer in the Christian miracles, and that he is not able to give anything like an exhaustive account of these considerations. In saying that many of these considerations are "implicit and secret, and cannot by any ingenuity be imprisoned in a formula," he means that they are too numer-

6. GA, 267.

ous to be formulated in propositions. Hence he says that many of these considerations that support the Christian miracles are "between, and around, and behind" the propositions that he formulates. This is in sharp contrast to formal inference, where all that enters into our reasoning is formulated in definite propositions. Perhaps we can explain this contrast by referring to computers—an explanatory strategy that was not yet available to Newman. A formal inference could be entered into a computer in such a way that the computer could unfailingly determine whether the inference is valid; it could test the inference faster and more reliably than any human mind could. But an informal inference is altogether beyond the reach of the most powerful computer, for the simple reason that it cannot be completely entered into the computer; for as Newman says, there are always more considerations accumulating in the mind of the reasoning person than can be formulated in propositions. This is fundamental in Newman's thought: there is always more in our experience of concrete reality than can be captured in our propositions, and even if we are ever so articulate and elaborate in formulating them. Informal inference for him works with this "more": it works not only with our experience as formulated in propositions, but also with that "excess" of experience that cannot be propositionally formulated.

It follows that informal inference has a different relation to time than formal has. Informal inference is intimately embedded in time, whereas formal has something almost timeless about it. In the letter of 1846 cited above, Newman says that one "grows into" an informal inference. In the *Grammar* he says that certain informal inferences "distill like dew into our minds" (GA, 314). He thinks of informal inference in terms of organic growth, whereas formal inference has by contrast something almost mechanical about it. Formal inference does not grow mysteriously; it is not "as if a man were to scatter seed on the land and would sleep and rise night and day and the seed would sprout and grow, he knows not how." It is not averse to being rushed. It can after all be handed over to a computer, which, with sufficient input and with sufficient computing power, can test in an instant the most complex process of reasoning. In the *Apologia* Newman says: "All the logic in the world would not have made me move faster towards Rome than I did; as well might you say that I have arrived at the end of my journey, because I see the village church before me, as venture to assert that the miles, over which my soul had to pass before it got to Rome, could be annihilated, even though I had been in possession of some far clearer view than I then had, that Rome was my ultimate destination. Great acts take time."[7] But there is nothing like this on the side of formal inference; no one could reasonably see the conclusion of his reasoning and yet need some years to embrace the conclusion.

In developing the contrast between formal and informal inference we are led back to chapter 2 where we discussed real and notional apprehension (assent): formal inference is akin to notional apprehension, whereas informal inference is akin to real apprehension. Just as we can fail to do justice to a concrete person by relying too heavily on stereotypes, as we saw, so we can fail to do justice to some concrete matter of fact by relying too heavily on formal inference. The excess of experience over notional meaning that we found in real apprehension, we find again in informal inference.

But there is one point of contrast between formal and informal inference that seems to cast the latter in a questionable light. Formal inference seems to give expression to the universal validity of truth, and to lead to it, and to unite us with others in the one objective truth; but informal inference seems to be dangerously subjective, and to lead each person in a different direction. In one place Newman admits that informal inference can lead people to opposite conclusions. "From the sight of the same sky one may augur fine weather, another bad; from the signs of

7. Apol., 169.

the times one the coming in of good, another of evil; from the same actions of individuals one infers moral greatness, another depravity or perversity, one simplicity, another craft[iness].... The miracles of Christianity were in early time imputed by some to magic, others they converted; the union of its professors was ascribed to seditious and traitorous aims by some, while others it moved to say, 'See how these Christians love one another.' ... The downfall of the Roman Empire was to Pagans a refutation, to Christians an evidence, of Christianity."[8]

Thus informal inference seems to awaken the suspicion of subjectivism. But formal inference is free of any such suspicion; it seems to be a model of objectivity. One could think that authentic inference is formal, and that what Newman calls informal inference is a substandard form of inference, too subjective to count as the real thing of inference. Perhaps we can defeat the suspicion of subjectivism if we proceed to show that what looks like subjectivism is really the personalist character of informal inference.

Informal Inference as an Eminently Personal Act

So we come to the point that especially interests us in our study of Newman's personalism: the exercise of informal inference is an eminently personal act, and it is personal in a way in which formal inference is not. We just had a glimpse of this personal character when we saw that informal inference cannot be replaced by a computer, but can only be carried out by a living human mind. Insofar as formal inference is replaceable by a computer, it is somehow impersonal. Another way of seeing the personal character of informal inference is this: the mind has to estimate the force of the evidence with which it works, for it has no algorithm to apply to the evidence. We have no clear criteria to apply to the evidence for miracles, criteria that would let us "read off" the conclusion that follows from all the evi-

8. OUS, 210.

dence. With formal inference you have many such criteria; for instance, there is the rule for syllogistic reasoning that from two negative premises nothing follows, or the rule that in the second figure of the syllogism a valid argument must contain one positive premise and one negative one. Armed with enough of these rules you can quickly tell whether a syllogistic argument is valid or not. But with informal inference we have no such criteria to apply; we have nothing but our personal judgment about what the evidence proves. As Newman puts it, we *feel* the upshot of the evidence more than we see what it implies. And in thus feeling the evidence we are forced to think in a personal way. In the case of formal inference, we can mindlessly apply our rules and criteria in determining what follows from our premises and what does not; our mental activity can remain mechanical, and we need not really think about the argument. But with informal inference we take responsibility for our conclusion; we cannot "hide" behind rules and criteria. In one place Newman says that we arrive at the conclusions of informal inference "not *ex opere operato,* by a scientific necessity independent of ourselves,—but by the action of our own minds, by our own individual perception of the truth in question, under a sense of duty to those conclusions and with an intellectual conscientiousness."[9]

It is not difficult to discern in Newman's teaching on the illative sense different personalist aspects. Here is one of them: a person does not show himself as person by passively undergoing what befalls him, but by acting through himself. Now there is a certain passivity in following a formal inference, and Newman expresses this passivity in saying that we are "indolently carried into" the conclusion by the inference.[10] We expressed this passivity in speaking of the mechanical character of our thinking when we test a formal inference for validity. In one place Newman expresses the active element in the illative sense by speaking of "a living spontaneous energy within us," an ex-

9. GA, 318.
10. GA, 305.

pression he would never apply to the understanding of a formal inference.[11]

And here is another aspect of properly personal life: it stands in contrast with the anonymous. There is something anonymous about following a formal inference; every right-thinking person who turns his attention to it traces out exactly the same line of reasoning. I am present in the formal reasoning as *just another rational being.*[12] But I am in the informal reasoning as *this individual person,* for I carry out my informal inference in my own way. Even when people concur in the conclusion of their informal reasoning, they typically reach the conclusion each in his or her own way. My "living spontaneous energy of thought" leads me along a different path than yours leads you. In the following Newman gives a striking expression to the "personal originality" of each person's illative sense.

The mind ranges to and fro, and spreads out, and advances forward with a quickness which has become a proverb, and a subtlety and versatility which baffle investigation. It passes on from point to point, gaining one by some indication; another on a probability; then availing itself of an association; then falling back on some received law; next seizing on testimony; then committing itself to some popular impression, or some inward instinct, or some obscure memory; and thus it makes progress not unlike a clamberer on a steep cliff, who, by quick eye, prompt hand, and firm foot, ascends how he knows not himself; by personal endowments and by practice, rather than by rule, leaving no track behind him, and unable to teach another. It is not too much to say that the stepping by which great geniuses scale the mountains of truth is as unsafe and precarious to men in general, as the ascent of a skilful mountaineer up a literal crag. It is a way which they alone can take; and its justification lies in their success. And such mainly is the way in which all men, gifted or not gifted, commonly reason,—not by rule, but by an inward faculty.

11. OUS, 257.

12. This anonymity, however, should not be taken to mean "depersonalizing"; we mean only that in formal inference a person is hidden rather than revealed in his or her unique personal identity, but not that a person undergoes something unworthy of himself as person. What is unworthy of a person is to remain anonymous under circumstances in which one ought to be speaking in one's own name.

Reasoning, then, or the exercise of Reason, is a living spontaneous energy within us, not an art.[13]

In this passage we recognize both of the personalist elements that we just distinguished: we see how informal inference is not passive but active, and not anonymous but personal.

We are, then, not surprised to find Newman often using the word "personal" in connection with informal inference, but never in connection with formal. "But what logic cannot do, my own living personal reasoning ... does for me." Or again: "Such a living *organon* [as the illative sense is] is a personal gift, not a mere method or calculus." Or again: "Thus a proof, except in abstract demonstration, has always in it, more or less, an element of the personal." And particularly striking: "the personality (so to speak) of the parties reasoning is an important element in proving propositions in concrete matter."[14] This talk of "personal" seems to be especially natural in light of the role of the heart and of character in the illative sense, to which we now turn.

The Illative Sense Involves Heart and Character

We pointed out above that formal inference makes demands only on our intellectual abilities; informal inference, especially in religious questions, makes demands on the whole man, on his heart and will no less than on his intellect. Of course, some cases of informal inference make few demands on our moral nature, as in Newman's example of the informal inference involved in knowing that England is an island. But the person inquiring for instance into the Christian miracles needs to approach the question with a reverential awe of God, with an eagerness to see whether God has acted miraculously in the way that Christians claim, with a longing to encounter God acting in the world, with a strong sense of his need to find God,

13. OUS, 257.

14. GA, 300, 316, 317, 320.

and with a fear of missing some revelation that He may make of Himself. If the inquirer approaches Christianity with only academic curiosity, he will not be capable of fruitful informal inference. Thus Newman says in one of his Anglican sermons,

> For is not this the error, the common and fatal error, of the world, to think itself a judge of Religious Truth *without preparation of heart?* "I am the good Shepherd, and know My sheep, and am known of Mine." "He goeth before them, and the sheep follow Him, for they know His voice." "The pure in heart shall see God." ... Gross eyes see not; heavy ears hear not. But in the schools of the world the ways towards Truth are considered high roads open to all men, however [they may be] disposed, at all times. Truth is to be approached without homage. Every one is considered on a level with his neighbour; or rather the powers of the intellect, acuteness, sagacity, subtlety, and depth, are thought the guides into Truth.[15]

The powers of mind mentioned here by Newman may suffice for a formal inference, but they do not suffice for informal inference, especially on religious questions, for here there *is* a test of character. A well-prepared heart enables us to discern strands of evidence that are lost on the merely curious inquirer, and also able to be more resourceful than he is in weaving the strands together and making them reinforce each other. In addition, a well-prepared heart makes us willing to venture to believe while having less than perfect evidence. Newman contrasts such a heart with "that cold, sceptical, critical tone of mind, which has no inward sense of an overruling, ever-present Providence, no desire to approach its God, but sits at home waiting for the fearful clearness of His visible coming, whom it might seek and find in due measure amid the twilight of the present world."[16] Informal inference, then, has a personalist character that formal inference lacks, for it engages the whole man, including character and the heart, while formal inference engages only the intellect.[17]

15. OUS, 198. My italics.
16. OUS, 221.
17. For an excellent study of this aspect of Newman's personalist account of

Newman's idea is no novelty; it is present throughout Western philosophy from the beginning. Thus Plato in his *Seventh Letter* says: "Neither quickness of learning nor a good memory can make a man see when his nature is not akin to the object, for this knowledge never takes root in an alien nature; so that no man who is not naturally inclined and akin to justice and all other forms of excellence, even though he may be quick at learning and remembering ... will ever attain the truth ... about virtue."[18] We cannot fail to notice in these words of Plato the idea of knowledge by connaturality, which we discussed back in chapter 3. Plato speaks of a connatural knowledge of justice, which is not just a purely intellectual knowledge of justice *(per modum cognitionis).* Such knowledge is important for personalism because it is knowledge that is gained not just through the intellect but through the medium of one's whole being and character.

We can focus Newman's view of character and the heart by comparing it with the view of William James in his famous essay "The Will to Believe." There is much in this essay that is deeply akin to Newman. Like Newman, James resists the idea that we have to have conclusive demonstrative proof for our religious convictions, and that in the absence of conclusive proof we ought to suspend our convictions until we gain the proof. Like Newman, James sees no reason to ban our "passional nature" from the forming of our beliefs. Newman would have heartily agreed with this spirited sentence from James: "When I look at the religious question as it really puts itself to concrete men, and when I think of all the possibilities which both practically and theoretically it involves, then this command that we shall put a stopper on our heart, instincts, and courage, and *wait*—acting of course meanwhile more or less as if religion were *not* true—

inference see William Wainwright, *Reason and the Heart: a Prolegomenon to a Critique of Passional Reason* (Ithaca, N.Y.: Cornell University Press, 1995), chs. 2, 4, and 5.

18. *Plato's Epistles,* trans., with critical essays and notes, by Glenn R. Morrow (Indianapolis: Bobbs-Merrill, 1962), 240–41. Aristotle, too, is well known for teaching the same thing throughout his ethical writings.

till doomsday, or till such time as our intellect and senses working together may have raked in evidence enough—this command, I say, seems to me the queerest idol ever manufactured in the philosophic cave."[19] If we call by the name of rationalism the tendency to overrate proof and demonstration, and to portray the "passional nature" of human beings as having no place in responsible thinking, then we can say that James and Newman are often allies in the struggle against rationalism, and we can also say that to this extent they share a certain personalism.

But consider this from James's essay: "Our passional nature not only lawfully may, but must, decide an option between propositions, whenever it is a genuine option that cannot by its nature be decided on intellectual grounds."[20] Newman would keep a critical distance from this statement; he does not think that the heart shows itself in our religious beliefs by making us believe when we have no reasons; he thinks that it shows itself in our religious beliefs by disclosing reasons that are not available to an affectively dead person. A person exercising his illative sense with a purified heart really discovers more about, say, miracles than a rationalist discovers. He sees more in the experience of conscience than a psychologist who examines conscience with scientific objectivity. Newman (as Plato before him) thinks of our passional nature and our intellectual nature as intimately bound together, and in this they differ from James. The purified heart does not go wherever it wants in a rational vacuum; it rather sensitizes us to discern reasons that another person fails to discern, and in this way it keeps us from being in a rational vacuum. Thus when Newman says of informal inference that "the whole man moves," he is affirming a wholeness that James has lost; heart and intellect have broken apart in James, but they remain more integrated in Newman. The heart does not pick up where reason leaves off, but it empowers reason.

19. William James, "The Will to Believe," in *William James: Writings 1878–1899* (New York: The Library of America, 1992), 477–78.

20. Ibid., 464.

Newman acknowledges the role of heart and character not only in our inferring but also in acts of perceiving and understanding that would not count as acts of inferring. I am thinking of acts in which something is understood directly and immediately and without the mediation of premises. Here is an example taken from a sermon of Newman; it will help us clarify the role of heart and character in acts of inferring. "We think heaven must be a place of happiness to us, if we do but get there." Then Newman asks whether a person does not have to have a certain disposition of heart in order to perceive the glory of heaven. Here is the full passage: "We think heaven must be a place of happiness to us, if we do but get there; but the great probability is, if we can judge by what goes on here below, that a bad man, if brought to heaven, would not know He was in heaven;—I do not go to the further question, whether, on the contrary, the very fact of his being in heaven with all his unholiness upon him, would not be a literal torment to him, and light up the fires of hell within him.[21] This indeed would be a most dreadful way of finding out where he was. But let us suppose a lighter case: let us suppose he could remain in heaven unblasted, yet it would seem that at least he would not know that he was there. He would see nothing wonderful there."[22]

Newman proceeds to say that sinners taken into heaven "would walk close to the throne of God; they would stupidly gaze at it; they would touch it; they would meddle with the holiest things; they would go on intruding and prying, not meaning any thing wrong by it, but with a sort of brute curiosity, till the avenging lightnings destroyed them;—*all because they have no senses to guide them in the matter.*"[23] The problem for the reprobate is not that they are not in heaven, but that they lack the

21. Newman expressed a version of this thought already in his very first published sermon (1826): "If we wished to imagine a punishment for an unholy, reprobate soul, we perhaps could not fancy a greater than to *summon it to heaven*" (PPS I, 7).

22. PPS IV, 246.

23. PPS IV, 247 *(Emphasis mine).*

interior disposition that would let them perceive the glory of heaven. Newman uses a drastic simile to explain the predicament of the reprobate; he says that they are "like the cattle which are slaughtered at the shambles, yet touch and smell the very weapons which are to destroy them."[24] Only those with a pure heart and a good character can experience the beatific glory of heaven. When they experience this glory they are not indeed inferring to the glory, they rather immediately experience it through their well-disposed heart and character.

An open heart can empower us in a similar way in the exercise of the illative sense; it can enable us to discern realities by informal reasoning that are lost on persons who exercise their illative sense with nothing more than curiosity.[25]

Newman's Personalist Way of Saying "I"

Well known is Newman's statement that "egotism is true modesty."[26] He says this of the illative sense's exercising informal inference in moral and religious inquiries. The "egotism" that he approves of is really just an aspect of his personalism, and it is expressed by a certain way of saying "I."

The phenomenologist Robert Sokolowski distinguishes between the informative and the declarative way of saying I.[27] In the latter I express my agency in acting, I take responsibility for my acting. When St. Thomas More, in the play about his life and death, says, "I will not give in because I oppose it—I do—not my pride, not my spleen, nor any other of my appetites but *I* do—*I*,"

24. PPS IV, 248.

25. Among the phenomenologists no one studied this connection between moral character and moral understanding more closely than Dietrich von Hildebrand in his treatise "Sittlichkeit und ethische Werterkenntnis," in Husserl's *Jahrbuch für Philosophie und phänomenologische Forschung* V (1922), 463–602.

26. GA, 384.

27. Robert Sokolowski, *Phenomenology of the Human Person* (Washington D.C.: The Catholic University of America Press, 2008), ch. 1. In what follows I explain the distinction in my own way, not exactly as he explains it; but I am aiming at the same distinction that he explores.

he speaks with a strong declarative I.[28] He expresses his resolute commitment in such a way that he does not just describe it, as any other person looking in on More from the outside could describe it, but he lives it from within, he enacts it, as only he can enact it. In other words, with the declarative I there is a great difference between the first person and the third person, that is, between More declaring his commitment and someone else describing it. But with the informative I this difference shrinks from great to insignificant. When I say, "I had a headache yesterday," my utterance is no more informative than that of someone else who says of me "he had a headache yesterday." My report about my headache is in no way declarative; I am not enacting the headache, I am only reporting it. Sokolowski is surely right that, through the declarative I, we express ourselves as persons, and in some declaratives we express ourselves as persons in an eminent way. If we were to anticipate the theme of personal subjectivity, which comes up in the next chapter, we would add to Sokolowski that, with the declarative I, I speak out of my subjectivity, from within myself, taking myself as subject and not object, uttering what only I can utter.

Let us now look back at the "egotism" that Newman professes. He says in effect that we speak with a declarative I not only when we take a stance like St. Thomas More takes a stance, but also when we exercise our illative sense in matters of morality and religion. Let us hear some parts of the well-known passage that begins with "egotism is true modesty."

> In religious inquiry each of us can speak only for himself, and for himself he has a right to speak. His own experiences are enough for himself, but he cannot speak for others: he cannot lay down the law.... It causes no uneasiness to any one who honestly attempts to set down his own view of the Evidences of Religion, that at first sight he seems to be but one among many who are all in opposition to each other.... However that may be, he brings together his reasons, and relies on them,

28. Robert Bolt, *A Man for All Seasons* (New York: Vintage Books, 1990), 123–24.

> because they are his own, and this is his primary evidence; and he has a second ground of evidence, in the testimony of those who agree with him. But his best evidence is the former, which is derived from his own thoughts; and it is that which the world has a right to demand of him; and therefore his true sobriety and modesty consists, not in claiming for his conclusions an acceptance or a scientific approval which is not to be found anywhere, but in stating what are personally his own grounds for his belief in Natural and Revealed Religion.... His own business is to speak for himself. He uses the words of the Samaritans to their country-woman, when our Lord had remained with them for two days, "Now we believe, not for thy saying, for we have heard Him ourselves, and know that this is indeed the Saviour of the world."[29]

When Newman speaks here of "scientific approval," he is of course referring to formal inference and to the unanimity that it can command. He wants to express the special personal exertion that we have to make when nothing but informal inference is available to us. He also wants to express the special "ownership" of my convictions that I achieve by exercising my illative sense; I do not just think as part of a group, but I think in my own name. Thus it is an eminently declarative I that I speak when I profess these hard-won convictions. It is also an eminently personal I.

The Specter of Subjectivism

We mentioned above the plausible objection of subjectivism to which Newman's theory of informal inference is exposed. The objection seems to grow in plausibility when informal inference is contrasted with formal, which seems to be a model of objectivity. And it seems to be precisely the personal element in informal inference that awakens the suspicion of subjectivism, for this is what lets us differ from others when we should be concurring with them. This objection is particularly important within the context of this book, for if the objection has merit

29. GA, 384–86.

then Newman's personalism really is at odds with his theocentrism, and his thought, instead of displaying an extraordinary breadth, is in the end divided against itself.

Let us stay with the passage on egotism as modesty, just quoted, and let us consider some sentences that I left out. The person practicing "egotism" in taking responsibility for his convictions

> knows what has satisfied and satisfies himself; if it satisfies him, it is likely to satisfy others; if, as he believes and is sure, it is true, it will approve itself to others also, for there is but one truth. And doubtless he does find in fact, that, allowing for the difference of minds and of modes of speech, what convinces him, does convince others also. There will be very many exceptions, but these will admit of explanation. Great numbers of men refuse to inquire at all; they put the subject of religion aside altogether; others are not serious enough to care about questions of truth and duty and to entertain them; and to numbers, from their temper of mind, or the absence of doubt, or a dormant intellect, it does not occur to inquire why or what they believe; many, though they tried, would not be able to do so in any satisfactory way.[30]

Newman clearly affirms here the universality of the truth attained by the illative sense. He affirms it again when he goes on to say that this "egotist," whose reasons for believing are based on his illative sense, "thinks that others do hold them [these reasons] implicitly or in substance, or would hold them, if they inquired fairly, or will hold if they listen to him, or do not hold from impediments, invincible or not as it may be, into which he has no call to inquire."[31] Thus the highly personal character of informal inference does not prevent us from really attaining objective truth, the same for all; it does not lead to subjectivism. Newman's "egotist" does not think he has his own truth, he just thinks that he arrives at the one truth in his own personal way.

Perhaps we can unfold Newman's thought like this. For the very reason that heart and character are involved in informal inference but not in formal, informal inference can go wrong

30. GA, 385.
31. GA, 386.

in more ways than formal. Innumerable are the ways in which the human heart can be wayward and perverse, and innumerable are the ways in which the character of a person can be misshapen. Thus the consensus formed on the basis of informal inference will never comprehend as many people, and certainly not comprehend them as quickly and effortlessly, as the consensus based on formal inference. But there is no reason to think that the latter consensus expresses a greater objectivity of truth and that the former is infected by some kind of subjectivism. For consider that even within formal inference it happens that some truth, such as truth in advanced mathematics, is available only to a few highly trained people; and yet such truth is no less universally valid than is the multiplication table, which is available to everyone. It would be a ridiculous egalitarian prejudice to think that truth counts as objective and universal only when it is readily apparent to everyone, no matter how much or little prepared they are for receiving the truth. Max Scheler discerned a certain envy at work in this prejudice; people with modest intellectual ability try to discredit those with greater ability, and they do this by declaring that the truth accessible only to a few of special ability is deficient in objectivity. If, then, there are special conditions of heart and character required for the successful exercise of the illative sense in moral and religious matters, so that not everyone will quickly and effortlessly reach the same conclusion, this does not taint the illative sense with subjectivism, any more than the need for special training taints advanced mathematics with subjectivism. The particular investment of oneself as person that goes with the illative sense, along with the special act of taking responsibility, is simply the way in which the regions of moral and religious truth are accessed. This special mode of access, Newman claims, does not prevent people from coming together in one truth that is the same for all.

I might add that all who are indebted to Newman have experienced this coming together on the basis of informal inference. Though he almost always speaks in the personal manner proper to the illative sense, what he says finds a deep resonance in his readers. They feel that he has led them more deeply into the world of truth, and that they stand together with him in this truth. We conclude that both a principled consideration of truth and consensus, as well as our experience of Newman the teacher, converge in such a way as to show that his personalism as expressed in his theory of inference is free of subjectivism and is entirely coherent with the theocentrism of his fundamental religious stance.

Some Pathologies of Thinking

It is always fruitful to know a thing through its opposites. We saw this when just a few pages ago we contrasted what is personal with what is merely passive and then with what is anonymous. In a similar way it is fruitful to know a thing through its typical deformities. So let us consider now some forms of intellectual activity that fail to amount to real thinking; let us see what we can gather from Newman about typical pathologies of thinking. Of course, we have already encountered one such pathology, namely, the rationalism that overrates proof and demonstration. At the beginning of the chapter we also encountered the deficiency that comes from being dominated by conventional patterns of thinking. But from *The Idea of a University* we can learn about two other pathologies of thinking. The first is a conspicuous absence of thinking, and the second is a certain narrowness of thinking. In each case we are of course looking for the deficiency of personal life that comes to light in Newman's analysis.

1. *Passive mental life.* He explains the conspicuous absence of thinking by drawing a parallel with a conspicuous absence in our power of seeing. He imagines a person born blind who awakens from the surgery that has restored his sight.

Then the multitude of things, which present themselves to the sight under a multiplicity of shapes and hues, pour in upon him from the external world all at once, and are at first nothing else but lines and colors, without mutual connection, dependence, or contrast, without order or principle, without drift or meaning, and like the wrong side of a piece of tapestry or carpet. By degrees, by the sense of touch, by reaching out the hands, by walking into this maze of colors, by turning around in it, by accepting the principle of perspective, by the various slow teaching of experience, the first information of the sight is corrected, and what was an unintelligible wilderness becomes a landscape or a scene, and is understood to consist of space, and of bodies variously located in space.[32]

Newman says that the condition of our thinking is often like the condition of the blind man's vision on awakening from surgery. We do not know how to clarify the issue in a discussion; we do not know what is relevant to an argument and what is not; we do not know which science is competent to clarify a question and which is not; we have no sense of what is central and what is peripheral in a theory; we move in our thinking more by association than by the inner logic of an issue. In a word, our thinking is undisciplined, it lacks form and principle. The process of acquiring a liberal education, Newman says, is a process like the blind man learning to see things in space; it is a process of discerning the order of issues, of discriminating between more and less important, between relevant and irrelevant, of recognizing things that belong together and things that have nothing to do with each other, or recognizing parts and wholes. In a word, it is a process of acquiring a sense of space and perspective and proportion in the world of the mind. It is learning to think.

Newman describes in masterful, priceless detail this deficiency of thinking. In the following his description lays particular stress on the passivity of the mind incapable of really thinking.

Seafaring men, for example, range from one end of the earth to the other; but the multiplicity of external objects, which they have encoun-

32. Idea, 495.

tered, forms no symmetrical and consistent picture upon their imagination; they see the tapestry of human life, as it were on the wrong side, and it tells no story. They sleep, and they rise up, and they find themselves, now in Europe, now in Asia; they see visions of great cities and wild regions; they are in the marts of commerce, or amid the islands of the South; they gaze on Pompey's Pillar, or on the Andes; and nothing which meets them carries them forward or backward, to any idea beyond itself. Nothing has a drift or relation; nothing has a history or a promise. Every thing stands by itself, and comes and goes in its turn, like the shifting scenes of a show, which leave the spectator where he was. Perhaps you are near such a man on a particular occasion, and expect him to be shocked or perplexed at something which occurs; but one thing is much the same to him as another, or, if he is perplexed, it is as not knowing what to say, whether it is right to admire, or to ridicule, or to disapprove, while conscious that some expression of opinion is expected from him.[33]

The passivity of these seafaring men would be explained by contemporary personalists like this. These men simply passively endure a succession of impressions; they have no inner center of experiencing, no subjectivity, nothing which would let them preserve some unity in the midst of multiplicity; they take no distance to what they experience, they do not stand over against it, but are rather immersed in the multiplicity of impressions, taken over by them, lost in them. Their inner life is simply a passive reflection of them.[34]

Newman discerns this passivity not only in uneducated persons, but also in persons who devote their lives to study, acquiring vast learning but little real education, little real formation of mind. In their case the passivity takes the form of a vulnerability to mental mechanisms.

Derangement, I believe, has been considered as a loss of control over the sequence of ideas. The mind, once set in motion, is henceforth deprived of the power of initiation, and becomes the victim of a train

33. Idea, 136.

34. I have tried to describe and to analyze just this passivity of mind in my *The Selfhood of the Human Person*, 99–104.

> of associations, one thought suggesting another, in the way of cause and effect, as if by a mechanical process, or some physical necessity. No one, who has had experience of men of studious habits, but must recognize the existence of a parallel phenomenon in the case of those who have over-stimulated the Memory. In such persons Reason acts almost as feebly and as impotently as in the madman; once fairly started on any subject whatever, they have no power of self-control; they passively endure the succession of impulses which are evolved out of the original exciting cause; they are passed on from one idea to another and go steadily forward, plodding along one line of thought in spite of the amplest concessions of the hearer, or wandering from it in endless digression in spite of his remonstrances.[35]

These men of studious habits, for all their learning, are not really thinking; they are the prey of mechanisms of association. Their mental lives are unworthy of a person; they lack the self-possession that is the signature of personal selfhood.

When Newman proceeds to describe the working of a mind that by contrast really thinks, he describes the mind as acting and taking the initiative, not just passively undergoing, and in this way he brings out the personal character of thinking. Thus he speaks of the mind "leavening the dense mass of facts and events with the elastic force of reason," or of "the mind's energetic and simultaneous action upon and towards and among those new ideas, which are rushing in upon it," or of "the action of a formative power, reducing to order and meaning the matter of our acquirements," or of "making the objects of our knowledge subjectively our own."[36] One readily sees the analogy of this intellectual activity with the active looking and observing that lets the formerly blind person gradually discern in the chaos of his sensations foreground and background, three spatial dimensions, and individual things standing in spatial relations with other things.

Needless to say, this talk of the mind's energetic action upon its objects is not to be taken in the sense that the mind

35. Idea, 106–7.

36. Idea, 138, 134.

constructs its objects, or bends them to itself and its structures, so that what would result from our activity of knowing would be simply an expression of our cognitive powers and not a disclosure of what is really there. Newman preserves the fundamental receptivity of the mind energetically acting upon its objects; its energetic acting is in the service of discovering what they really are. We find here just what we found with the illative sense; its "living spontaneous energy," so expressive of the person, is in the service of discerning what is really there in the world.

2. *Narrowness of mind.* Newman also speaks of narrow-minded and bigoted persons, as displaying a certain deformation of thinking. Here too Newman's description is exactly right, almost perfect. Nor can anyone read it without seeing himself or herself in it. "They conceive that they profess just the truth which makes all things easy. They have their one idea or their favourite notion, which occurs to them on every occasion. They have their one or two topics, which they are continually obtruding, with a sort of pedantry, being unable to discuss, in a natural unconstrained way, or to let their thoughts take their course, in the confidence that they will come safe home at the last. Perhaps they have discovered, as they think, the leading idea, or simple view, or sum and substance of the Gospel."[37] Clearly there is more thinking going on in these persons than in the seafaring men or in the men of studious habits. Newman describes here not the conspicuous absence of thinking but a certain deformity of thinking. He proceeds to describe the crisis that is sure to arise in the narrow mind; he speaks of

> the helplessness which they exhibit, when new materials or fields of thought are opened upon them. True philosophy admits of being carried out to any extent; it is its very test, that no knowledge can be submitted to it with which it is not commensurate, and which it cannot annex to its territory. But the theory of the narrow or bigoted has already run out within short limits, and a vast and anxious region lies beyond,

37. OUS, 30

unoccupied and in rebellion. Their "bed is shorter than that a man can stretch himself on it; and the covering narrower, than that he can wrap himself in it." And then what is to be done with these unreclaimed wastes?—the exploring of them must in consequence be forbidden, or even the existence denied. Thus, in the present day, there are new sciences, especially physical, which we all look at with anxiety, feeling that our views, as we at present hold them, are unequal to them, yet feeling also that no truth can really exist external to Christianity.[38]

Newman means that Christians are really thinking only when they can encounter the new sciences, only when they know how to engage them in discussion. If the new sciences seem hopelessly foreign to Christians, if they are simply incommensurable with all that Christians understand, and seem threatening, that is a sure sign that the thinking of Christians has become too narrow, that they lack the breadth of true wisdom.

Newman keenly discerned that the belief of narrow-minded Christians is vulnerable to cracking and giving way to unbelief.

Persons of narrow views are often perplexed, and sometimes startled and unsettled, by the difficulties of their position. What they did not know, or what they knew but had not weighed, suddenly presses upon their notice. Then they become impatient that they cannot make their proofs clear, and try to make a forcible riddance of objections. They look about for new arguments, and put violence on Scripture or on history. They show a secret misgiving about the truth of their principles, by shrinking from the appearance of defeat or from occasional doubt within. They become alarmists … and sometimes, in this conflict between broad fact and narrow principle, the hard material breaks their tools; they are obliged to give up their principles. A state of uncertainty and distress follows, and, in the end, perhaps, bigotry is supplanted by general scepticism.[39]

The thinking that Newman defends against narrowness of mind involves a suppleness of mind, a "power of assimilation," an intellectual resourcefulness, a capacity for intellectual growth. A good example of the alarmism of which Newman speaks was

38. OUS, 309
39. OUS, 310

the reaction of some of his contemporaries to Darwin. They assumed that Darwin's teaching undermined Christianity and they inveighed mightily against it and made all kinds of attempts to refute it. Newman was different; he kept quiet in public on the subject; he was not sure whether every teaching of Darwin really had to be understood as contradicting Christian teaching.[40] He felt that the prudent thing was to wait and see, to sort out the issues, and to find out where exactly were the points of contact between the different Darwinian theses and Christian faith. After all, Newman had discovered a dimension of development in Christian doctrine (in his *Essay on the Development of Christian Doctrine,* 1845) that in the previous centuries had gone unnoticed by Christian theologians; perhaps, he may have mused, Darwin has made a similar discovery in biology. As Newman pondered these things in his heart he was *thinking* more than those over-zealous contemporaries of his were, though he had at first less to say than they did.

Here is another example of how the kind of narrow mind discerned by Newman has sometimes interfered with the development of important Christian responses to the modern world. This example concerns the very personalism which is serving in this book as our interpretive key to Newman. As everyone knows there is a great deal of subjectivism and relativism in modern thought. Many say that it originates in Kant and Hume, and gets radicalized in thinkers such as Nietzsche. Now personalism has as one of its great themes the subjectivity, or interiority of each person. In the next chapter, in fact, we will be speaking about this personalist theme in Newman. But with subjectivity comes conscious experiencing, self-presence, motivation, personal uniqueness, and the like, and when these ideas begin to take on a larger role in the understanding of the hu-

40. Cf. Newman's personal letter to Pusey of June 5, 1870, in LD XXV. Cf. also the entry of December 9, 1863, in his posthumously published "philosophical notebook": Edward Sillem and A. J. Boekraad, eds., *The Philosophical Notebook,* vol. 2 (Louvain: Nouwelaerts Publishing, 1970), 158. Cf. also the remarkable passage from 1841 in ECH II, 193–94, which we will cite and discuss in the next chapter.

man person than they had in the Aristotelian-Thomistic philosophy, it looks to some people as if subjectivism is breaking into Christian thought. They think that the only way to take a resolute stand against subjectivism is to keep clear of the modern interest in subjectivity altogether, and to recommit themselves to the pre-modern philosophy of Aristotle and St. Thomas. But to think like this would be to fall prey exactly to the narrowness of mind that Newman deprecates. The real challenge, Newman would say to us, is to discriminate between subjectivism and a new kind of interest in subjectivity; to work out a "reception" of personal subjectivity into the Christian intellectual tradition; to appropriate it so as to achieve a deeper understanding of man as person.[41] To meet this challenge Christian intellectuals "must consent to think." If they respond in the reactionary way, their thinking will be skewed by the narrowness of mind characterized by Newman.

There is yet another kind of narrowness of mind that is worth mentioning here; it too helps us understand by contrast the breadth of Newman's thinking. In public debate it often happens that one caricatures the position of one's opponent, and presents it tendentiously, passing over its strengths and accentuating its weaknesses. One speaks as if one's opponent incomprehensibly favors the greatest absurdities. Newman conducted himself very differently in public debate. He showed a most unusual ability to do justice to the point of view of unbelievers, to state it fully and fairly, to acknowledge any truth in it. Newman would sometimes state the case for unbelief so strongly as to shock his Catholic readers, who thought that he was conceding too much to the adversary.[42] Thus he acknowl-

41. This is what Karol Wojtyla attempts in his seminal paper "Subjectivity and the Irreducible in Man," 209–17.

42. He even managed to shock unbelievers, such as the agnostic Thomas Huxley, who famously declared that he could draw up a "primer of unbelief" from the writings of Newman. I have discussed Huxley's remark in my paper "A 'Primer of Infidelity' in Newman? A Study of the Rhetorical Strategy of Newman," *Newman Studies Journal* 8.1 (2011), 6–19.

edged the force of many of the objections that were made in the nineteenth century to the design argument for the existence of God. Even in his sermons Newman could go surprisingly far in feeling himself into the position of unbelief. Thus he once expressed in a sermon the distressing absence of God from the world like this:

> Indeed how far does the whole world come short in all respects of what it might be. It is not even possessed of created excellence in fulness. It is stamped with imperfection; everything indeed is good in its kind, for God could create nothing otherwise, but how much more fully might He have poured His glory and infused His grace into it, how much more beautiful and divine a world might He have made, than that which, after an eternal silence, He summoned into being.... Set man's wit and man's imagination to the work of devising a world, and you would see, my brethren, what a far more splendid design he would submit for it, than met the good pleasure of the Omnipotent and All-wise.... Pass from man's private fancies and ideas, and fastidious criticisms on the vast subject; come to facts which are before our eyes, and report what meets them. We see an universe, material for the most part and corruptible, fashioned indeed by laws of infinite skill, and betokening an All-wise Hand, but lifeless and senseless; huge globes hurled into space, and moving mechanically.... And, then, when at length we discover sense as well as life, what, I repeat, do we see but a greater mystery still? We behold the spectacle of brute nature; of impulses, feelings, propensities, passions, which in us are ruled or repressed by a superintending reason, but from which, when ungovernable, we shrink, as fearful and hateful, because in us they would be sin. Millions of irrational creatures surround us, and it would seem as though the Creator had left part of His work in its original chaos, so monstrous are these beings, which move and feel and act without reflection and without principle.... They live on each other's flesh by an original necessity of their being; their eyes, their teeth, their claws, their muscles, their voice, their walk, their structure within, all speak of violence and blood.[43]

43. DMC, 271–73. The reader will want to know the context of this passage. Newman is arguing that the church is divine in origin and he is responding to those who, though they believe in God, find her divine origin hard to discern in her history. He says to them, using a rhetorical strategy that is very characteristic for him: Look, you believe in God despite the fact that He is hidden in nature; is the

No unbeliever can state more forcefully the case for unbelief. When Newman proceeds to defend and affirm his faith in God, his faith stands out as all the more convincing for the very reason that he understands so well the appeal of unbelief. His thinking achieves a rare comprehensiveness as a result of being able to find a place for all that speaks in favor of unbelief. His religious faith does not force him to look the other way when the unbeliever makes his case. He consents to think, and so he finds the larger whole that contains indeed the reality of God's working in the world, but also contains a world in which God's active presence is surprisingly hidden. He strives to make theistic sense of this absence of God from the world, and in the end he lends far more support to theism than he would have lent to it by pretending that God is everywhere clearly present in the world.

We begin to see the antidote that Newman offers to narrowness of mind. In *The Idea of a University* he develops the idea that a liberally educated mind, confronted with some one truth, knows how to find the place of that truth within the whole of truth. Such a mind does not assert that truth at the expense of other truths, but also does not deprive other truths of the light cast on them by that truth. For the well-formed mind knows nothing so much as this, that one area of knowledge is not the whole of knowledge, and that one method, fruitful in an area, is not equally fruitful in all areas, and may be absurdly inappropriate in some. Such a mind, free from that narrowness of mind analyzed by Newman, "never views any part of the extended subject-matter of Knowledge without recollecting that it is but a part, or without the associations which spring from this recollection. It makes every thing in some sort lead to every thing else; it would communicate the image of the whole to every separate portion, till that whole becomes in imagination like a spirit, every where pervading and penetrating its component parts, and giving them one definite meaning.... [Such a mind]

divine origin of the church any more hidden in the history of the church than the existence of God is hidden in nature?

cannot but be patient, collected, and majestically calm, because it discerns the end in every beginning, the origin in every end, the law in every interruption, the limit in each delay; because it ever knows where it stands, and how its path lies from one point to another."[44] It is the thinking of such an "imperial intellect" that is Newman's antidote to narrowness of mind.

And what is distinctly personalist about such thinking? Surely it is the illative sense that "communicates the image of the whole to every separate portion." The narrow-minded person, by always taking some part for the whole ("they have their one idea or their favourite notion, which occurs to them on every occasion"), thinks too abstractly and evades that exertion of the living intelligence whereby the part is woven into the whole. I cannot fail to think here of the so significant line of Newman's that I have already cited: "But one aspect of Revelation must not be allowed to exclude or to obscure another; and Christianity is dogmatical, devotional, practical all at once; it is esoteric and exoteric; it is indulgent and strict; it is light and dark; it is love, and it is fear."[45] Newman has to summon all the powers of his illative sense to discern how these disparate aspects of Christianity cohere with and condition each other. He has to "consent to think" about the unity that they form.

Newman as a "Liberal Catholic"

In his Catholic period Newman was well acquainted with narrowness of mind in a particularly oppressive form. He thought

44. Idea, 137–38. When Newman speaks of having an image of the whole of knowledge, he does not mean to claim a systematic knowledge of the whole such as Hegel claimed. He rather means something like this: you may know a city very well in the sense that, wherever you are, you can always find your way to any other point in the city; but your sense of the city as a whole does not mean that you can draw a good map of the whole city.

45. DD, 36. Another impressive example of Newman's comprehending various aspects that are commonly thought to exclude each other is his discussion of the priestly, prophetical, and regal aspects of the church (introduction to the third edition of his *Via Media*).

that the English Ultramontanes, Nicholas Cardinal Wiseman and Henry Cardinal Manning, Frederick Faber and William George Ward, who were the dominant voices in the leadership of the Catholic Church in England, tended to reject the modern world so massively that they were not able to think sufficiently about the issues it raised; that they treated the modern world as "a vast and anxious region, unoccupied and in rebellion." He regretted that they were not looking for the elements of truth in nineteenth-century liberalism. He said that instead of carefully discriminating they were just reacting. He said that their policy was too military, that it had too much of the spirit of Sparta and too little of Athens. He held that they were trying "to make a forcible riddance of objections" instead of really thinking them through. He deplored the way the Ultramontanes ruled the church in England, for he saw that it tended to inhibit real thinking in Catholics, including Catholic theologians. Newman himself longed to engage the great questions of the modern world, and he knew that he could contribute something toward this engagement, but he was deeply pained to realize that his help was not wanted, indeed was held in suspicion by the dominant Ultramontane party. He deplored the fact that Catholic writers and theologians were expected to work "under the lash."[46] He was keenly aware of the danger that the rigid Ultramontane stance against the modern

46. In the *Apologia* Newman wrote: "He [any Catholic theologian] would not dare to do this [test out his ideas in discussion and debate], if he knew an authority, which was supreme and final, was watching every word he said, and made signs of assent or dissent to each sentence, as he uttered it. Then indeed he would be fighting, as the Persian soldiers, under the lash, and the freedom of his intellect might truly be said to be beaten out of him" (Apol., 267–68). Here Newman speaks conditionally about an excessive ecclesiastical surveillance of theologians, but he thought, and elsewhere often says, that this disorder in fact existed as a serious problem in the English church in the nineteenth century, and we know that he personally suffered greatly under it. When in the 1870s a committee was formed to consider establishing a Catholic college at Oxford, Newman declined to participate on the grounds that "our present rulers [of the Catholic Church in England] would never give us a real one." He explains: "I dread a minute and jealous supervision on the part of authority which will hamper every act of the heads of the University." Letter of April 9, 1872, in LD XXVI, 61.

world would eventually crack and expose some Catholics to complete loss of faith.

In the second half of the nineteenth century no voice in England was more powerful than Newman's in pleading for the importance of Christians' really thinking about their faith as they encountered the modern world. He wrote in his personal diary in 1863, "Now from first to last, education, in this large sense of the word, has been my line." He explains what he means by "this large sense of the word": he aimed "at improving the condition, the status, of the Catholic body, by a careful survey of their argumentative basis, of their position relatively to the philosophy and the character of the day, by giving them juster views, by enlarging & refining their minds, in one word, by education."[47] Sometimes his Ultramontane superiors complained that Newman was doing too little to "make converts." Newman acknowledged that his concern with education led him to spend his energy in a different place than making as many converts as possible, but he was sure that it was as important to have thinking converts as to have many of them.

Newman explained the "elbow room" that Christians need who appropriate their faith by really thinking about it and by thinking about its relation to the science and culture of the day. He uses the analogy of a ship that moves not by going straight to its destination but by tacking back and forth, and sometimes seeming to go far off course. He acknowledges that a Christian who tries to think will make mistakes and will have to correct those mistakes, but that he will be "confident, from the impulse of a generous faith, that, however his line of investigation may swerve now and then, and vary to and from in its course, or

47. John Henry Newman, *Autobiographical Writings*, ed. Henry Tristram (New York: Sheed and Ward, 1957), 259. On the same page Newman mentions the journal *The Rambler*, which he edited for a short time; he says that this journal aimed "to raise the status of Catholics, first by education, secondly by a philosophical basis of argument." *The Rambler* was a center of controversy in the English Catholic Church; the bishops felt it to be provocative and eventually shut it down, and Newman was for a long time "under a cloud" because of his association with it.

threaten momentary collision or embarrassment with any other department of knowledge, theological or not, yet, if he lets it alone, it will be sure to home, because truth never can really be contrary to truth."[48] People with no understanding of the intellectual life will think that this tacking and swerving is a mischief for the life of the church, that it serves only to complicate needlessly the simple faith of believers, that it weakens the witness of the church against the world. But Newman sees an inestimable good for the church in having believers who really think about the Christian faith in relation to the surrounding culture, even as he sees great harm for the church in having only narrow-minded believers. "Instead of being irritated at the momentary triumph of the foes of Revelation, if such a feeling of triumph there be, and of hurrying on a forcible solution of the difficulty, which may in the event only reduce the inquiry to an inextricable tangle ... he [the Christian who thinks] will commit the matter to reason, reflection, sober judgment, common sense; to Time, the great interpreter of so many secrets."[49]

It is not hard to discern the deep personalist significance of Newman's commitment to the education of thinking Christians. You *own* your Christian faith in a more personal way when you are able to think about it in its relation to the rest of human knowledge and human activity; you have not only faith but also wisdom.[50] You achieve a certain freedom when you "discern the end in every beginning, the origin in every end, the law in every interruption, the limit in each delay,"[51] and you are not similarly free when you anxiously "make a forcible riddance of objections," and are too defensive really to think. And there is a personalist issue all its own when we consider the exercise of authority in the church. When the persons exercising authority suffer from what Newman calls narrowness of mind,

48. Idea, 357.
49. Idea, 467.
50. On this wisdom, see OUS, sermon 14.
51. OUS, 310.

so that those subject to authority are working "under the lash," then these latter persons are clearly de-personalized, degraded to mere extensions of those exercising authority; whereas when they are granted the space they need to think, and the time they need to work things out, then they are being treated with the respect due to them as persons.[52]

We touch here on the basis for Newman's reputation as a "liberal Catholic," and one may at first wonder whether this side of Newman's mind is at odds with his resolute anti-liberalism, which we examined in chapter 1. But a moment's reflection shows that his being a "liberal Catholic" in the sense explained involves no compromise with his "dogmatical principle," and that it is simply a way of holding the dogmatical principle; he *thinks about* this principle and he tries to understand revealed truth in relation to other kinds of truth. Consider how Newman, in explaining the "freedom of movement" that is required for thinking, is led by the logic of his subject to a strong affirmation of the "sovereignty of Truth," which is the very thing that stands at the center of his dogmatical principle. "Error may flourish for a time, but Truth will prevail in the end. The only effect of error ultimately is to promote Truth. Theories, speculations, hypotheses, are started; perhaps they are to die, still not before they have suggested ideas better than themselves."[53] Thus the freedom of thought for which he pleads provides the very setting in which Truth can make its way; it is the setting in which "Time, the great interpreter of so many secrets," can let Truth come to light, and come to light in a way that lasts.[54]

We can say here by way of conclusion what we said at the end

52. Needless to say, one would make oneself guilty of the most unhistorical kind of thinking if one took it for granted that the excessive ecclesiastical surveillance over Catholic intellectuals which concerned Newman in the nineteenth century is repeating itself in every exercise of the magisterium of the church in the twenty-first century. Whoever really venerates the name of Newman will abstain from this kind of partisan use of him.

53. Idea, 478.

54. Idea, 467.

of chapter 2 when we were harmonizing Newman's concern for real apprehension with his commitment to theocentric religion. We said then that one venerates revealed truth more by apprehending it with one's whole being than by apprehending it just with one's intellect; we can now say that one venerates revealed truth more by a thinking faith than by a narrow-minded faith. The final confirmation of this harmony is the living witness of Newman, whose religion was radically theocentric and whose faith is expressed with the freshness and originality of one who really thinks. The two things cohere in Newman and reinforce each other; neither interferes with the other.

6

"An Infinite Abyss of Existence"

Lost in the Cosmos?

There is a depersonalizing way of viewing our place in society and in the cosmos that comes very naturally to us. I refer to the way we are easily awed by the immensity of our social world—there are after all over seven billion of us alive on the earth at present—and by the immensity of the cosmos. We feel ourselves to be mere specks in these vast totalities. Each of us is only one seven-billionth of humanity, and each is an even smaller fractional part of the cosmos. There is also temporal immensity; it too annihilates our sense of being something important and reduces us to feeling like a negligible quantity, whether we see ourselves within the untold number of human generations, or within the eons of geological history, or within the 13.5 billions of years that make up cosmic history. Set within such bewildering immensities each one of us seems to be inconceivably small and insignificant. Our fleeting moment of existence within these immensities seems to make no difference to them.

Now I want to say that in thus experiencing our inconceivable smallness we run the risk of losing all sense of ourselves as persons. It is not as if there were no truth in this experience. Our profound awe in the face of the quantitative immensity of things registers a certain truth, namely, the truth that lies in the analogy between this quantitative immensity and the immensity of God. But what concerns us here is that you cannot easily experience yourself as person and at the same time experience yourself as just one among innumerably many, or as a speck so small that there is virtually no difference between a world with you in it and a world without you in it. This blow to your sense of being a person is surprising when we consider that it is our world-openness as persons that makes it possible for us to feel this blow at all. An environment-bound being does not have that sense of the whole that leads to this experience of smallness. The primates give no sign of being oppressed by the fact that they are just a few beings among the innumerably many beings of nature; they cannot set themselves in relation to these innumerably many beings so as to be unsettled by a sense of ultimate insignificance.

A truly personalist philosophy insists that our inconceivable smallness is not the last word, but that in some important respect we are not entirely encompassed by these totalities and that as persons we have a significance that cannot be swallowed up by them. Thus we see a certain personalist impulse at work in Kant when he famously contrasts the starry sky above us and the moral law within us. He says that in standing under the starry sky, we feel indeed annihilated in our importance as animal creatures, but that in experiencing the moral law in our conscience we encounter ourselves as persons "in which the moral law reveals a life independent of all animality and even of the whole world of sense." This significance revealed in moral consciousness is, Kant says, "not restricted to the conditions and limits of this life but reaches into the infinite."[1] Note how Kant

1. Immanuel Kant, *Critique of Practical Reason*, trans. Lewis Beck (New York: Bobbs-Merrill, 1956), 166.

distinguishes between man as animal and man as person, and how he insists that it is as person that man is no longer vulnerable to the annihilating effect of the immensity of space-time.

Now I find that Newman grasps with great intuitive power the fact that man as person is not completely contained in this immensity; he achieves a deep real apprehension of it, and in such a way as to deepen the personalism of his thought.

Let us look at Newman's sermon "The Individuality of the Soul," in which he begins by considering how natural it is for us to let individual human beings be completely absorbed in the social wholes to which they belong, that is, how natural it is for us to yield to that depersonalizing perspective just mentioned.

> Nothing is more difficult than to realize that every man has a distinct soul, that every one of all the millions who live or have lived, is as whole and independent a being in himself, as if there were no one else in the whole world but he. To explain what I mean: do you think that a commander of an army realizes it, when he sends a body of men on some dangerous service? I am not speaking as if he were wrong in so sending them; I only ask in matter of fact, does he, think you, commonly understand that each of those poor men has a soul, a soul as dear to himself, as precious in its nature, as his own? Or does he not rather look on the body of men collectively, as one mass, as parts of a whole, as but the wheels or springs of some great machine, to which he assigns the individuality, not to each soul that goes to make it up? ...
>
> We do not understand the doctrine of the distinct individuality of the human soul. We class men in masses, as we might connect the stones of a building.... When this one dies and that one dies, we forget that it is the passage of separate immortal beings into an unseen state, that the whole which appears is but appearance, and that the component parts are the realities. No, we think nothing of this; but though fresh and fresh men die, and fresh and fresh men are born, so that the whole is ever shifting, yet we forget all that drop away, and are insensible to all that are added; and we still think that this whole which we call the nation, is one and the same, and that the individuals who come and go, exist only in it and for it, and are but as the grains of a heap or the leaves of a tree.[2]

2. PPS IV, 80–81.

As Newman says here, it is a question of parts and wholes. Where are the real wholes and what are their parts? Newman says that we all strongly incline to take some social group or to take society itself as the real whole, with the individual human beings serving as mere parts of that whole.

Newman challenges us to look more closely and to realize that the real whole is first of all the individual person. When persons live together in some social group, they can never be so encompassed by the group as to exist as *mere* parts of it. We should instead say, using a felicitous expression of Maritain, that they exist as "wholes within a whole." In this same sermon Newman goes on to give forceful expression to the wholeness of the individual person. After evoking again the sense of swarming crowds ("survey some populous town: crowds are pouring through the streets; some on foot, some in carriages; while the shops are full, and the houses too, could we see into them") he asks, "But what is the truth? why, that every being in that great concourse is his own centre and all things about him are but shades, but a 'vain shadow,' in which he 'walketh and disquieteth himself in vain.' He has his own hopes and fears, desires, judgments, and aims; he is everything to himself, and no one else is really any thing. No one outside of him can really touch him, can touch his soul.... He has a depth within him unfathomable, an infinite abyss of existence; and the [social] scene in which he bears part for the moment is but like a gleam of sunshine upon its surface."[3]

Notice that Newman does not just say that each person *feels himself* from the inside to be something vaster and more real than the surrounding social world. One could after all take this feeling to be a natural optical illusion, a natural egocentrism through which we lose our grip on the modest significance that each of us in fact has. No, Newman thinks that in this feeling we experience real metaphysical truth from within, namely, the

3. PPS IV, 82–83.

truth that each of us really lives out of an infinite abyss of existence. What looks like megalomania is really the very truth of our being as personal subject. In experiencing this truth we are experiencing our incommensurability with all the wholes in which we are situated.

It is remarkable how in this passage Newman completely reverses our natural way of thinking about persons in society. The social whole is no longer the dominant reality; it is instead reduced to "a gleam of sunshine" upon the surface of the individual person. The social whole does not itself have "a depth unfathomable," does not have "an infinite abyss of existence." Since the individual person experiences within himself "an infinite abyss of existence," he knows himself as a being far too real and powerful to be completely contained as a mere part in any social group. As person he is incommensurable with any social group. The smallness that he may have qua replaceable member of the group is in a way reversed when he is considered qua person.

One might object that Newman cannot be right in asserting that the social world is "like a gleam of sunshine on the surface" of my consciousness, because the social world after all comprises other persons, each of whom has, no less than I have, an infinite abyss of existence in himself or herself. So I would after all be living in a kind of natural self-centeredness by speaking of the social world as a "gleam of sunshine on the surface" of my consciousness. The truth of my being is that I am, seen within any social group, just one of many. Let me try to explain Newman's intuition in a way that frees him from this objection.

I turn to a mathematical analogy. It is not found in Newman, but it helps to unfold his thought. Consider the strange behavior of "infinitely many" as considered in mathematics. You cannot add to infinitely many. If you take the infinitely many odd numbers, and add to it an even number, the sum is the same as the infinitely many odd numbers taken alone, for what should be more than infinitely many? Indeed, if you add to the infinitely many odd numbers the infinitely many even numbers, you still have no more than the infinitely many odd numbers taken alone, for here too we have to ask, what should be more than infinitely many of the odd numbers? This strange behavior of infinitely many is in contrast to the behavior of finite numbers. Whenever you add to a finite number, you always get more. If you add enough to a finite number, you get a large sum of which that finite number is a small fractional part. Now we are in a position to clarify why I am threatened when set in relation to billions of other human persons. I am subject to the logic of finite numbers; I am a very small fractional part of the whole of humanity. But what if each person has a kind of infinity in himself or herself? Then he is subject to the logic of infinitely many, and that means that he in a sense cannot be added to. Even if he is set in the midst of billions of others, they will not be able to make him small, because in some sense he and all those billions are not any more than he alone. In other words, each person exists *as if* the only one. When, then, Newman speaks of the social world as a gleam of sunshine on the surface of his consciousness, he need not mean anything else than that all the others cannot overwhelm him in a quantitative way, that he exists in their midst as if the only one. He is just drawing the consequence of the infinite abyss of existence that he has discerned in each person. Since he recognizes this infinite abyss *in every person,* there is no suspicion of any environment-bound egocentrism. Of course, I realize that the infinite abyss of existence in each of us is not a mathematical infinity, subject to operations like addition and subtraction; I say only that there may be enough of an analogy between mathematical infinity and personal infinity to help us understand why persons are not made small when set within quantitatively immense frames of reference, including frames of reference that include other persons.

We have been speaking of human persons set within a large social world. If we turn from a social to a cosmic setting, we get the same result. The infinitesimally short duration of my life when compared with the 13.5-billion-year duration of the universe, and the infinitesimally small space that I occupy in the universe, and the uncountable number of beings in the midst of which I find myself, do not have the effect of reducing me to insignificance. As person I have "an infinite abyss of existence" that the universe, for all its spatio-temporal immensity, does not have. Perhaps Newman would have said that the whole cosmos is but a gleam of sunshine on the surface of my being, and he would have thereby made a profound personalist utterance, and would have spoken as a world-open spirit.

Newman's understanding of the moral existence of persons plays a large role in supporting and confirming this intuition. In this respect Newman is close to Kant, who as we saw thinks that man is lifted above the immensity of space-time by his relation to the moral law; by being subject to the moral law he shows himself as person, and his life acquires a significance that transcends the limits of earthly existence. In a sermon Newman says: "There is something in moral truth and goodness, in faith, in firmness, in heavenly-mindedness, in meekness, in courage, in loving-kindness, to which this world's circumstances are quite unequal, for which the longest life is insufficient, which makes the highest opportunities of this world disappointing, which must burst the prison of this world to have its appropriate range."[4] This latter expression, "burst the prison of this world to have its appropriate range," expresses well what we have called the incommensurability of a human person with the spatio-temporal frame of reference of earthly existence. If we were to proceed now to bring in Newman's thought on conscience, on the sense of right and wrong, on the experience of obligation and of personal responsibility, we would find other aspects of our moral existence that serve to reinforce this sense of incommensurability. But instead of proceeding further in this direction let us turn to an objection that has probably already occurred to the reader.

4. PPS IV, 212.

A Monadic View of the Person?

One might object that what emerges in Newman is a view of each person as a self-enclosed monad. The talk of the incommensurability of the person with the spatio-temporal world reinforces this concern. Thus Newman seems to save persons from being lost in the cosmos only by detaching them from the cosmos in a problematic manner, or only by falling into what is called an "acosmic" view of the human person.[5]

We will find a way to deal with this objection if we return to the world-openness of human persons, as discussed at the end of chapter 1 in the course of trying to understand Newman's theocentric religion. I have said that persons are not bound to an environment but exist in openness to the world. By this I meant, first, that persons can take an interest in what things are in their own right and do not have to connect things with some human need as the condition for taking an interest in them, and I meant, secondly, that taking such an "objective" interest in things involves situating them within the whole of reality. The "partiality" of the environment, which is merely that segment of my surroundings that has some bearing on my needs, gives way to the "wholeness" of the world, which is a whole that is not a mere region in some larger whole but is an "unsurpassable" whole. Now a human person, by being open to the whole and to the place of things within the whole, is the very opposite of a self-enclosed monad; a person is a being that exists in radical openness to all that is. So if the line of thought about persons and the "infinite abyss of existence" in each has a monadic tendency, the line of thought about the world-openness of the person has the opposite tendency. We have now to try to harmonize these apparent opposites. To this end we have to de-

5. In my *The Selfhood of the Human Person*, 54–58, I dealt with another version of this objection, the version which says that Newman's sense of selfhood, as expressed in "the infinite abyss of existence" in each person, undermines interpersonal relation and estranges us from life in community.

velop the intuitions of Newman, interpreting them by the work of personalist philosophers.

What harmonizes the apparent opposites is the subjectivity of persons, or as I could as well say, the interiority of persons. It is personal subjectivity that makes sense both of the infinite abyss of existence in each person, and the world-openness of each, binding them together in a relation of polarity.

Let us first explain what we mean by subjectivity. A human person exists as a subject of acting and not just as an object that other people act on. Each person lives out of an inner center and is aware of himself not just as object in front of himself in the same way that other persons are in front of him, but is aware of himself from within himself as subject, experiencing himself as only he can experience himself. No other person can experience me as subject in the manner in which I experience myself as subject; the other would have *to be* me in order to experience me as subject in this way. Newman had a keen grasp of this subjectivity of persons. In one of his posthumously published papers he makes his own the Cartesian idea that I have an incomparably greater certainty regarding my own conscious being than I have regarding the external world. He understands the reason for this difference: while I experience myself from within myself as subject, and so experience myself with an intimate inwardness, I cannot achieve this same inwardness of experience with respect to other persons or to things in the world, because I can experience them only as objects, not as subjects. The point is not exactly that I have to be uncertain about things other than myself, but rather that I am incomparably certain about the conscious being that I live from within. Thus Newman writes in this paper: "Surely I am indefinitely more sure, or sure in a way different in kind, that I am, than that other things are."[6]

6. This posthumously published paper is contained in A. J. Boekraad and Henry Tristram, eds., *The Argument from Conscience to the Existence of God according to J. H. Newman* (Louvain: Editions Nauwelaerts, 1961), 103–25. I have quoted from 123.

Now it is clear that the "infinite abyss of existence" in each person is found within; it is nothing other than the depth of our subjectivity. And it is just as clear that the immensity that we have been discussing in this chapter is an immensity of objects; insofar as I exist as object, I really am just one of innumerably many, existing in the midst of them. It is through my subjectivity that I become incommensurable with these immensities; as subject I have an interior existence such that all objects are outside of me, over against me. We just heard Newman say, after evoking our sense of being lost amidst many, "But what is the truth? why, that every being in that great concourse is his own centre.... He has his own hopes and fears, desires, judgments, and aims." Newman is here evoking our subjectivity, which in turn leads him to the "infinite abyss of existence" in each of us, which is what saves us from being just "one among many" and keeps us from disappearing in those threatening immensities.

But subjectivity does not just yield up the infinite abyss of existence in each person; the world-openness of persons begins to come here into view as well. Through my subjectivity I gain a world of objects that are over against me. Being gathered into my subjectivity sets me indeed at a distance to things, but a distance that establishes me in a conscious relation to them, that lets them present themselves as objects in front of me; it is like the distance that vision presupposes. In fact, the subjectivity proper to persons has often been characterized as that inner principle that is so strong as to open me to the whole of reality; in other words, subjectivity has been characterized precisely in terms of "world-openness." This means that the world-openness that we brought into the discussion back in chapter 1 is really a piece of a larger whole, which includes the subjectivity and interiority of persons. Despite their appearing as opposites, the infinite abyss of existence in each person is woven together with world-openness in the makeup of the person. Newman supplies one piece of this whole when he affirms his theocentric religion, and he supplies another piece of it when he is led into the infinite abyss of existence in each person. These pieces are just being brought into a larger unity by personalist philosophers when they follow Norris Clarke in speaking of the "dyadic" structure of the person, by which Clarke means that the more deeply a person lives within himself (interiority or subjectivity), the greater his capacity to reach beyond himself as a world-open being.[7] We can sum it up in Greek: the appearance of a monadic distortion of the person gives way, in a balanced interpretation of the whole Newman, to the fuller vision of the person as dyadic.

In the next section we will find confirmation of this dyadic vision in the fact that for Newman the abyss of existence in each person awakens not in solitude but vis-s-vis the living God.

The Encounter with God

We naturally want to know in what way a person awakens to the "infinite abyss of existence" in himself. For it is at first natural for us to experience ourselves as entirely embedded in the social and natural worlds that we inhabit. Thus Newman says in another sermon: "To a child this world is every thing: he seems to himself a part of this world,—a part of this world, in the same sense in which a branch is part of a tree; he has little notion of his own separate and independent existence. He views himself merely in his connexion with this world, which is his all."[8] How does Newman see the child awakening to a sense of its true stature as person?

We already have from the previous discussion a partial answer to the question. The child snugly fitting into its surroundings is living mainly in its environment. Whenever its subjectivity begins to stir, whenever it begins to open to the world, it disengages itself from its snug fit, and begins to come to itself as person. We also saw above that this process of disengagement takes

7. In my book *The Selfhood of the Human Person,* 85–86,167–70, I discuss this significant dialectic of being centered in myself and reaching beyond myself.

8. PPS I, 18–19.

place in a particular way, according to Newman (and Kant), as the moral consciousness of the child awakens. But for Newman the deepest source of the experience of the infinite abyss of existence in each person is the relation of each person to God. It is only before God that each person really comes to himself. Let us revisit his great sermon "The Thought of God, the Stay of the Soul," in which he brings out the religious transcendence that goes with the infinite abyss of existence in each person.

He opens with a deep reflection on human happiness, saying that "the happiness of the soul consists in the exercise of the affections; not in sensual pleasures, not in activity, not in excitement, not in self esteem, not in the consciousness of power, not in knowledge; in none of these things lies our happiness, but in our affections being elicited, employed, supplied.... Our real and true bliss lies in the possession of those objects on which our hearts may rest and be satisfied."[9] Newman proceeds to say that only in relation to God can all of the affections of which we are capable awaken. In relation to finite things the human heart can indeed stir, but it cannot come fully alive; if we lived only in relation to finite things we would never know how vast our heart is, nor suspect the infinite abyss of existence in it. He says in a memorable passage:

> We may indeed love things created with great intenseness, but such affection, when disjoined from the love of the Creator, is like a stream running in a narrow channel, impetuous, vehement, turbid. The heart runs out, as it were, only at one door; it is not an expanding of the whole man. Created natures cannot open us, or elicit the ten thousand mental senses which belong to us, and through which we really live. None but the presence of our Maker can enter us; for to none besides can the whole heart in all its thoughts and feelings be unlocked and subjected.... We know that even our nearest friends enter into us but partially; ... whereas the consciousness of a perfect and enduring Presence, and it alone, keeps the heart open. Withdraw the Object on which it rests, and it will relapse again into its state of confinement

9. PPS V, 315–16.

and constraint; and in proportion as it is limited, either to certain seasons or to certain affections, the heart is straitened and distressed. If it be not over bold to say it, He who is infinite can alone be its measure; He alone can answer to the mysterious assemblage of feelings and thoughts which it has within it.[10]

In a living relation to God, if only in the form of yearning for God, we experience ourselves as *capax Dei,* as having a capacity for God, as therefore having an infinite capacity, an infinite abyss of existence. Without this relation to God we would not know ourselves, would never suspect our infinite capacity, and so we would underestimate ourselves, and would remain vulnerable to being intimidated by the immensity of space-time, and to being depersonalized. We would not know the meaning of the ineradicable restlessness that drives us. But once we encounter God as the measure of our heart, we come to ourselves, we experience "the ten thousand senses by which we really live," and are freed for good from thinking of ourselves as mere cosmic specks.

But we have to articulate something that has so far remained only implicit. This encounter with God in which we are revealed to ourselves is for Newman an eminently personal encounter. If it were not a personal encounter it would not save us from being intimidated by the immense totalities in which we find ourselves. For consider: if we think that the whole world is the primary object of divine attention, each individual man or woman being seen by Him only as a part of the whole, but not being seen in his or her own right, then the encounter with God would not save us from depersonalization. The cosmic smallness that I spoke of would not be overcome but would, on the contrary, be ratified by the encounter with God. The encounter with God enables us to find ourselves as persons only if it is an encounter face-to-face, in which I am called by name. Newman takes this for granted in this sermon, but affirms it

10. PPS V, 318–19.

more explicitly in another sermon. So I turn now to that sermon, "A Particular Providence as Revealed in the Gospel," a rich source of Newman's personalism.

Newman explains here well the difficulty we have of realizing that God deals personally with each of us. "Men talk in a general way of the goodness of God, His benevolence, compassion, and long-suffering; but they think of it as of a flood pouring itself out all through the world, as the light of the sun, not as the continually repeated action of an intelligent and living Mind, contemplating whom it visits and intending what it effects. Accordingly, when they come into trouble, they can but say, 'It is all for the best—God is good,' and the like; and this does but fall as cold comfort upon them, and does not lessen their sorrow, because they have not accustomed their minds to feel that He is a merciful God, regarding them individually, and not a mere universal Providence acting by general laws."[11] Newman even recognizes that we incline to think that a "particular providence" is somehow unworthy of God. "How shall He who is Most Holy direct His love to this man or that for the sake of each, contemplating us one by one, without infringing on His own perfections?"[12]

He finds a way to the particular providence of God by listening to the human heart. He says, "Men of keener hearts would be overpowered by despondency, and would even loathe existence, did they suppose themselves under the mere operation of fixed laws, powerless to excite the pity or the attention of Him who has appointed them."[13] In spite of all the dignity of universal laws and necessary truths, indeed in spite of the divine character of universality and necessity, we are oppressed by a God who could only be understood in terms of them. We have a profound need for "God living and seeing." Newman goes so far as to say that we would "loathe existence" if God were only some universal law with which no interpersonal relation were possible.

11. PPS IV, 117–18.

12. PPS IV, 119.

13. PPS IV, 124.

Newman's personalism is apparent here. I cannot be lost in the cosmos if God knows me as the individual person I am; if I appear before Him as if the only one, then I cannot be reduced to insignificance by the immensity of space-time. I am such that God takes me individually, in a way that He does not take every grain of sand. My smallness within that immensity is not also an absolute smallness, a smallness simply speaking. Something of the immensity of God is somehow imparted to me when He sees me individually and deals with me individually, indeed it is already imparted to me when I yearn for a personal encounter with Him. And there is another aspect of Newman's personalism that appears in this great sermon. We have so far been considering the person in contrast to the quantitative immensity of space-time. And this contrast indeed brings out one dimension of personal being. But there is another contrast that brings out another dimension of personal being, and that is the contrast with universality and with necessary law. This other dimension emerges in Newman's idea that religion is fundamentally interpersonal, that God deals with individual persons, taking each as if he or she were the only person. Especially personalist is the idea that each of us has an elementary need to be known by God not through the lens of some universal but as individual person, and to be called by name.

Participants, Not Spectators

It may sound strange if I proceed to say that Newman not only leads us to the encounter with God, but also in a certain way restricts this encounter, and it may sound even stranger if I also say that it is precisely his personalism that leads him to restrict it. But if I explain what I mean, we will understand still better the personalism that surrounds Newman's talk of the infinite abyss of existence in each person.

Newman was convinced that authentic religion energizes us, that it appeals to our deepest freedom, and challenges us and empowers us to act in our own name; he abhorred any kind of religion that tends to make us passive, that puts us in a position of waiting for God to do for us what is ours to do. He was so opposed to the "evangelical" Christianity of his time just because it cultivated religious feelings at the expense of "working out one's salvation with fear and trembling," as we saw in chapter 3. The Evangelicals sought a one-time conversion experience at the expense of a lifetime of continual conversion. Newman also put it like this: they sought justification at the expense of sanctification. They concentrated on what God has done for them and neglected what they have to become in response to Him. Newman vehemently rejected Luther's teaching that God's grace covers our sins like snow covers animal feces; he was certain that God's grace aims at making us clean on the inside and not just on the outside. One readily sees the personalist character of this stance of Newman's; he did not want religion to interfere with our sense of responsibility before God, but to intensify it. He did not want Christ just to stand between us and the Father, but he held that Christ wants to us to become "sons in the Son," and this by an inner transformation that engages our deepest freedom. Newman's resistance to religious passivity is a significant sign of his personalism.

As a result of this personalism Newman lay great stress in his preaching on our part in the work of our salvation, and he tended to hold back the doctrines about God's initiative in this work. This is in part why his preaching took on the severe and demanding character that it has. Newman's friend Samuel Wilberforce told him that the first volume of Newman's *Parochial and Plain Sermons* (first published in 1834) "on the whole induces fear, and depression," as Newman renders Wilberforce's complaint. Newman astonishes us with his answer to Wilberforce: "*I grant it.* It was meant to do so. *We require the 'Law's stern fires.'* We need a continual Ash-Wednesday."[14] In another letter

14. LD V, 39–40.

to Wilberforce Newman says, explaining further his sense of what was pastorally needed in his day: "*We require the Law* not the Gospel in this age—we want [that is, need] rousing—we want [that is, need] the claims of duty and the details of obedience set before us strongly. And this is what has led me to enlarge on our part of the work not on the Spirit's."[15] What Newman grants about this first volume of his sermons is, it seems to me, true of almost all of his sermons: they are all meant to be unsettling, rousing, challenging. Christian teachings on the mercy of God, on Christ's doing for us what we cannot do for ourselves, on the Spirit's pleading for us with unutterable cries, on His power to write straight with crooked lines, on our appearing on the last day before God with empty hands and relying only on His mercy, on God's loving us first so that we can love Him in return, are sometimes deliberately left by Newman in the background. We will not understand this emphasis in Newman if we do not connect it with his personalism. He is not severe, harsh, merciless; if he sometimes seems this way it is because he sees our danger of becoming mere spectators of our salvation. He challenges us to see to it that we are participants in it. He tells those who think they stand secure to take care lest they fall. Newman's sermons have a certain bracing and reinvigorating power that comes in part from the personalist appeal to us to be real participants in our salvation.

So it is that the same Newman who shows how we come to ourselves as persons in the encounter with God, how the "ten thousand senses by which we really live" awaken in Him, how the "infinite abyss of existence" in us resonates with the God who calls us by name, this same Newman also "restricts" this encounter in the sense that he throws us back on ourselves, he stirs up our religious subjectivity, he says to us, *tua res agitur.* We

15. LD V, 22. In the same letter Newman says: "Do not we own that our *body* is sustained by Him in whom we live etc. Yet who therefore thinks a medical man deficient who is not every minute speaking of the sustaining power, the need for God's blessing etc etc?"

are reminded of Kierkegaard's profound meditations on the hiddenness of God in the world. Kierkegaard thought that if we registered God's existence as an obvious fact, we would relate to Him too passively; it is good for our religious subjectivity, for our *existence,* that we have to search Him out where He is hidden, and strain with the "passion of the infinite" to discern Him within the twilight of the present world. In a similar vein is Kierkegaard's comment on the ugliness of Socrates; this was a divine gift for Socrates, since it kept his disciples from becoming slavishly attached to him, and made each of them stand alone in the truth.[16] In a somewhat similar way, it is according to Newman good for our religious subjectivity to be confronted with the demands of religious obedience, and with the consequences of disobedience, and so thrown back on ourselves, before we let ourselves be lifted up and consoled by the redeeming work of Christ.

We will in the next chapter examine Newman's thought on conscience, which is for him *the* fundamental bond between each person and God. Newman was so drawn to conscience just because it does not let us lose ourselves in contemplating God (as may happen when we take our idea of God simply from the order found in nature), but presents God to us as demanding something of us, stirring us up in our inmost parts. Conscience is a primary source for experiencing the "infinite abyss of existence" in ourselves; it connects us with God without any danger of putting us into a spectator attitude toward Him.

Does Newman Depreciate the Material World?

Critics of Newman have said that his acute sense of the interiority of persons is strongly conditioned by his psychological makeup. They have said that his introversion—Bremond even speaks of his "autism"—disposed him to register his inner

16. Søren Kierkegaard, *Concluding Unscientific Postscript,* trans. David Swenson (Princeton, N.J.: Princeton University Press, 1941), 217–24.

world of experiencing more strongly than the external world of matter. Others have discerned a certain philosophical tendency in his thought to play off his sense of interiority against the reality of matter. Indeed, he sometimes spoke of matter almost like Bishop Berkeley had spoken of it. Thus he wrote in his first book: "What are the phenomena of the external world, but a divine mode of conveying to the mind the realities of existence, individuality, and the influence of being on being, the best possible, *though beguiling the imaginations of most men with a harmless but unfounded belief in matter as distinct from the impression on their senses?*"[17] When asked about this passage he said that he does recognize a distinction between our impressions and material things themselves, but does not think the distinction important. He said: "It seems to me, while a man holds the moral governance *of God as existing in and through his conscience,* it matters not whether he believes his senses or not. For at least he will hold the external world as a *divine* intimation, a scene of trial, (whether a reality or not)."[18] And he had another reason for thinking the distinction to be of little importance, namely, his idea that our experience of matter does not disclose anything about matter itself. "What do I know of substance or matter? Just as much as the greatest philosophers, and that is nothing at all; —so much is this the case, that there is a rising school of philosophy now, which considers phenomena to constitute the whole of our knowledge of physics."[19] And so one might well think that Newman's sense of personal interiority is somewhat suspect if it bears the mark of an introverted psychological makeup, and especially if it depends on a failure to do justice to

17. Arians, 75; my italics. This idealism about the material world, by the way, has been proposed before by personalist philosophers; the American personalists, or Boston personalists, thought that they were vindicating the absolute primacy of persons in the world by holding this idealism, that is, by holding that the world is nothing but persons and their impressions and that matter does not belong to the world as something irreducible to our impressions of it. See Rufus Burrow Jr., *Personalism: A Critical Introduction* (St. Louis, Mo.: Chalice Press, 1999), 18–23.

18. LD IV, 253 (letter of 1834).

19. Apol., 239–40.

the reality of the material.[20] One might wonder if, once we do greater justice to the reality of the material world as a realm of being all its own, Newman's way of speaking of the infinite abyss of existence in each person does not have to be modified.

I grant that Newman had an unusual awareness of his inner life, and I grant that almost all of his statements about the material world stand in a worrisome proximity to idealism à la Berkeley. Even when he later tried to establish a little distance from this idealism, he never spoke about the reality of the material world as certain other Christian philosophers have spoken about it.[21] Here, for instance, is Romano Guardini, an important personalist voice in twentieth-century thought, speaking about it: "In all our admiration for the greatness, the unity and the fervor of the medieval concept of the world we must not forget that it contained, at all points, a religious short circuit. The absolute was so strongly felt that the finite world and its own meaning were not given proper and proportionate consideration.... The modern age decided to accept the world as reality and not to thin it out by an immediate transition to the absolute."[22] In this passage Guardini explains that the material world was tak-

20. When I speak of Newman's "failure to do justice to the reality of the material world," I do *not* include in this deficiency the point of his convergence with Descartes mentioned above, that is, I do not include Newman's view that "surely I am indefinitely more sure, or sure in a way different in kind, that I am, than that other things are" (n. 6). For this view of his seems to me undeniably true and to be entirely coherent with all the truth that is to be affirmed about matter and the material world, and also about our power of sense perception.

21. In his study *Clear Heads and Holy Hearts: the Religious and Theological Ideal of John Henry Newman* (Louvain: Peeters Press, 1993), 32, Terrence Merrigan rightly points out that by the time of the *Grammar of Assent* (1870) Newman had to affirm the reality of the material world in order to complete his analysis of conscience. For in that work Newman argued (we will discuss this in the next chapter) that just as we discern material things through our sensations, so we discern God through our experience of moral obligation. Just as God is an "objective reality" that is irreducible to our experience of moral obligation, so material things too have an "objective reality" that is irreducible to our perceiving them—if the parallel between conscience and sense perception is going to hold.

22. Romano Guardini, *The World and the Person* (Chicago: Regnery, 1965), 15–16.

en in the Middle Ages too much as a symbol of divine things and not sufficiently acknowledged as something in its own right. Newman is very vulnerable to being included in this censure of Guardini. Guardini continues: "Objects are not merely the concepts of God's consciousness. The world does not exist as the play of the imagination of an infinite Being. The Hindu idea that the world is Maya, the unreal play of divine phantasy, is very superficial. It takes from the world that very character from which its true depth results, namely, the seriousness of reality. Whatever God creates He creates absolutely in its entirety. He releases what He has created and grants it its own nature, position, and activity."[23] Of course, Newman would be averse to seeing *other persons* in light of the Hindu idea of Maya, for they incontestably have a being of their own. But when he speaks of the material world as "floating before our eyes merely as some idle veil," he is perhaps not so far from this idea, and in any case he falls far short of Guardini's affirmation of the being of the material world.[24]

Newman also falls short of an ancient Christian idea about the place of man within the material cosmos. Certain Christian thinkers have said that we human beings are not waiting to escape from the threatening immensity of the cosmos, but that we have a very definite place in it, and not just a temporary place. Some have spoken of the "priestly" position of man in the universe, by which they mean that man, existing as he does at the border of matter and spirit, has the task of mediating between matter and spirit—of spiritualizing matter and of embodying spirit.[25] Sometimes one develops this idea by making the bold statement that in the human person the universe becomes conscious of itself, and that the human person is there-

23. Ibid., 22–23.

24. PPS I, 20.

25. On this priestly function of the human person in creation see Norris Clarke, SJ, "Living on the Edge: Man as 'Frontier Being' and Microcosm," in his *The Creative Retrieval of St. Thomas Aquinas* (New York: Fordham University Press, 2008), 132–51, esp. 139–40.

fore sufficiently united with the material universe to be able to give voice to its praise of God. This means that we do not just offer praise to God in the midst of an alien world, but that we take this world into our praise, giving it the voice that it does not have on its own. On this view the human person is no alien in the world, but performs a unique work of cosmic integration and exercises a unique kind of "cosmic leadership." In vain do we look in Newman for this perspective; in order to perceive the priestly function of man in the world one would have to take the being of matter more seriously than Newman does.[26]

All of this I grant to Newman's critics. I even grant them that his personalism suffers from these deficiencies in his understanding of the material world. But I do not think that Newman's insight into personal interiority and subjectivity is thereby undermined. It is not undermined because it never in the first place rested only on his estimation of the material world; it rests most of all on the truth about the human person as *capax Dei.* Even when you restore a more adequate view of the reality of matter, it remains true that our being *capax Dei* reveals an infinite abyss of existence in each person.

It is worth mentioning here that there is one theme in Newman that tends to draw him to a more adequate understanding of the material world, something that strongly inclines him to think of human persons as rooted in the material world and not as incommensurable with the world in such a way as to be aliens in it. I refer to Newman's deep sense of and respect for time and history, which in my view tends to counteract somewhat the idealist tendencies in his thought about matter. If we look into his most seminal theological treatise, his *Essay on the Development of Christian Doctrine,* we find a highly original account of the historical existence of Christians. He explains that the articulated understanding that Christians have of revela-

26. We can suppose that Newman was not unfamiliar with this conception of man as pontifex within creation, since it is a conception found in some of those Greek fathers of the church to whom he was so indebted.

tion is not complete all at once, is not exactly the same in every generation, but unfolds in history, new aspects of revelation coming to light in response to the new challenges of each era. He compares this unfolding with the unfolding of a plant. This historical existence does not just characterize believers; it is for Newman the human condition. We can add that it follows from existing in space and time and matter. He often says that some good thing is not possible in the present generation, but will be possible in a generation or two; that every good thing has its time, and great harm can be done if one tries to force the good thing into existence before its time.[27] Newman even applied his historical sense to his own work; he thought that some of his own ideas were not yet able to be "received" and would come into their own only in some future time that he would not live to see.[28] Newman's keen sense of our temporality, of our dwelling in the rhythms of history, has the effect of keeping human persons, for all the infinite abyss of existence in each of them, rooted on the earth and in their bodies. In other words, when Newman articulates the new sense of historical consciousness that he gained for theology, he is forced to take our material existence more seriously than he otherwise tends to take it.

Let us conclude like this. Once we have avoided all Berkleyan idealism regarding matter, and have restored the ancient understanding of man as microcosm and as having a priestly function in material creation, we do not undermine in any way Newman's profound insights into personal subjectivity and interiority. It is true that we can no longer speak of the incom-

27. Cf. Apol., 259–60.

28. This is why Newman was sometimes slow to defend himself against critics. Well known is his response to an editor who invited him to respond to a paper critical of Newman's thought on the nature of belief. Newman declined the invitation with these words: "I shall cheerfully leave it to Time to do for me what Time has so often done in the last 40 or 50 years. Time has been my best friend and champion: and to the future I lovingly commit myself with much resignation to its award." Letter of November 20, 1877, in LD XXVIII, 270. Recall the expression of Newman that we encountered in the last chapter: "Time, the great interpreter of so many secrets" (Idea, 467).

mensurability of the human person and the cosmos in the tone of voice that we used at the beginning of this chapter. For we find in the idea of the "priestly" role of man in the cosmos a resource for understanding how it is that man is not lost but profoundly at home in the cosmos. But this being at home implies a kind of headship of man in the cosmos, not an absorption into the cosmos as a mere part of it.

Some Particular Aspects of Interiority

Once we are alerted to the issue of subjectivity and interiority in Newman we can discern it in many places in his writings. Here is a striking instance of Newman's sensitivity to subjectivity. In his sermon "The Mental Sufferings of Our Lord in His Passion" he prepares his meditation on the mental sufferings of Christ by considering why it is that a human person can suffer more than a conscious animal. There is no neurological reason why a human person would suffer more than, say, a chimp, but there is a difference in subjectivity that explains it. When persons suffer they exercise a certain kind of memory that raises their experience of pain to a higher power, making for a difference of kind between their pain and animal pain. In a masterful piece of phenomenological analysis Newman says:

> Consider, then, that hardly any one stroke of pain is intolerable; it is intolerable when it continues. You cry out perhaps that you cannot bear more; patients feel as if they could stop the surgeon's hand, simply because he continues to pain them. Their feeling is that they have borne as much as they can bear; as if the continuance and not the intenseness was what made it too much for them. What does this mean, but that the memory of the foregoing moments of pain acts upon and (as it were) edges the pain that succeeds? If the third or fourth or twentieth moment of pain could be taken by itself, if the succession of the moments that preceded it could be forgotten, it would be no more than the first moment, as bearable as the first (taking away the shock which accompanies the first); but what makes it unbearable is, that it is the twentieth; that the first, the second, the third, on to the nineteenth

moment of pain, are all concentrated in the twentieth; so that every additional moment of pain has all the force, the ever-increasing force, of all that has preceded it.

Newman here anticipates an original idea that Edmund Husserl brought to light in his *Lectures on the Phenomenology of Internal Time Consciousness.* The "memory" of which Newman speaks is the Husserlian "retention," in which just-past moments do not fall completely into the past but remain in a way continuous with the present moment. Newman captures this continuity with a felicitous expression when he speaks of the just-past moments "edging" our experience of the present moment. When the experience is an experience of pain, the edging has the effect of heightening the pain, of concentrating all the moments of the pain into the present moment. This retention of the just-past moments is clearly very different from remembering some long-past pain, such as a sharp intestinal pain experienced last year. Even if I am experiencing sharp intestinal pain again right now, my remembrance of last year's similar pain does not coalesce with my present pain so as to edge it and sharpen it. The mind through its power of retention can have one experiencing that lasts throughout a stretch of time; the mind's experiencing is not dissolved into discrete, discontinuous moments of experience that succeed each other. He goes on to describe this discontinuity of experience, which he takes to characterize animal consciousness.

Hence, I repeat, it is that brute animals would seem to feel so little pain, because, that is, they have not the power of reflection or of consciousness. They do not know they exist; they do not contemplate themselves; they do not look backwards or forwards; every moment as it succeeds is their all; they wander over the face of the earth, and see this thing and that, and feel pleasure and pain, but still they take everything as it comes, and then let it go again, as men do in dreams. They have memory, but not the memory of an intellectual being; they put together nothing, they make nothing properly one and individual to themselves out of the particular sensations which they receive; nothing

> is to them a reality, or has a substance, beyond those sensations; they are but sensible of a number of successive impressions. And hence, as their other feelings, so their feeling of pain is but faint and dull, in spite of their outward manifestations of it. It is the intellectual comprehension of pain, *as a whole diffused through successive moments,* which gives it its special power and keenness, and it is the soul only, which a brute has not, which is capable of that comprehension.[29]

Of course, the talk of "memory" is imprecise, since it can express not only retention but also remembrance of things long past; but Newman is clearly aiming at retention. Earlier in this passage Newman had mentioned the efforts we make at distracting ourselves when we are in pain; our intention is to disrupt our pain as "a whole diffused through successive moments" and to replace this whole with discontinuous successive moments, each its own whole, thus turning our personal pain consciousness as far as possible into animal pain sensation.[30]

Newman proceeds to argue that the strength of subjectivity that distinguishes persons from animals is surely raised to a higher power in the God-man, so that we have to assume that His sufferings in His passion far surpass what we would have experienced in being subjected to the same treatment. What interests us in the present chapter is the highly original exploration of subjectivity and interiority that Newman brings to his reflection. Had he been less attuned to subjectivity he would either not have noticed the difference between the pain con-

29. DMC, 327–28; my italics.

30. Newman makes the same analysis in a somewhat different connection; discussing the suffering of the damned, he remarks that the endlessness of their suffering does not necessarily make their suffering intense. "For what we know, the suffering of one moment may in itself have no bearing, or but a partial bearing, on the suffering of the next; and thus, as far as its intensity is concerned, it may vary with every lost soul. This may be so, unless we assume that the suffering is necessarily attended by a consciousness of duration and succession, by a present imagination of its past and its future, by a sustained power of realizing its continuity." (GA, 422) Newman entertains the possibility that God shows His mercy to the damned by mitigating their suffering as a result of His interfering with their "present imagination of its [their suffering's] past and future." Newman pursues this thought in note III appended by him to the *Grammar.*

sciousness of animals and that of persons, or he would have tried to explain it in purely neurological terms. But the thinker who was so sensitive to the "infinite abyss of existence" in each person was sure to be alive to the internal time consciousness of persons. Indeed, the very experience of an "infinite abyss of existence" in a person would seem to require Husserlian retention; just as this retention makes the intensity of pain intelligible, so it makes the intensity of personal existence intelligible.

This is the place to mention another passage on time-consciousness where Newman probes deeply the subjectivity of persons. At the beginning of his sermon "The Greatness and Littleness of Human Life," Newman is marveling at the fact that "it matters not, when time is gone, what length it has been.... When life is past, it is all one whether it has lasted two hundred years or fifty." He also marvels at the fact that "the year passes quick though the hours tarry, and time bygone is as a dream, though we thought it would never go while it was going." He proceeds to venture an explanation: "And the reason seems to be this; that, when we contemplate human life in itself, in however small a portion of it, we see implied in it the presence of a soul, the energy of a spiritual existence, of an accountable being; consciousness tells us this concerning it every moment. But when we look back on it in memory, we view it but externally, as a mere lapse of time, as a mere earthly history. And the longest duration of this external world is as dust and weighs nothing, against one moment's life of the world within. Thus we are ever expecting great things from life, from our internal consciousness every moment of our having souls; and we are ever being disappointed, on considering what we have gained from time past, and can hope from time to come."[31] Perhaps we can interpret Newman's thought in terms of subject and object. When I experience myself as subject from within myself, I experience "the energy of a spiritual existence," a certain abundance

31. PPS IV, 215–16.

of life; and I experience this always only in the present.[32] But when I look back on my past self as an object, I no longer find the same abundance of life; I find instead a shell, a shadow, "a mere earthly history." The objectification of myself in the past removes from view a certain subjective fullness. This is why my past life, and even if it contains many years, seems "as dust" to me, this is why it pales in comparison with "one moment's life of the world within." Once again Newman shows unusual sensitivity with regard to subjectivity and time-consciousness.

Just one more thought of Newman on subjectivity, or interiority. In the last chapter of the *Grammar of Assent* Newman is speaking to those who say that the Christian God is too severe in His dealings with human beings, and who say this mainly with reference to His severity in dealing with *others.* Newman admonishes them to look into their own experience; he says, "When we are about to pass judgment on the dealings of Providence with other men, we shall do well to consider first His dealings with ourselves. We cannot know about others, about ourselves we do know something; and we know that He has ever been good to us, and not severe."[33] Perhaps we can interpret Newman like this. The sufferings of others are often only an object for us. Recall that Ivan Karamazov made his case against God on the basis of *newspaper reports* about other people's sufferings—Dostoevsky's way of underlining the fact that Ivan is taking human suffering as an object. Real subjective knowledge about human suffering, that is, knowledge of it from within, is available to me primarily in myself and not in others. Newman suggests that this more reliable experience that I have of myself tells a different tale. In my own life the suffering I know from within, while it is very real, is not always the dominant thing that suffering seems to be as presented in the newspapers. I know from within, Newman seems to say, about suffering

32. The "present" that is here meant is the present as "extended" by retention and protention.

33. GA, 421.

mitigated, about suffering turned to good, about suffering that wakes me up and challenges me just as I need to be awakened and challenged. The subjectivity of the sufferer should be more carefully consulted in discussions about what it is that God imposes on people; this inner perspective should count for more than the objective reports about the suffering of other people.

The Hiddenness of Subjectivity

Before concluding this chapter let us ask about the main obstacle to recognizing the mystery of personal subjectivity. I submit that Newman would say that it is a certain way of seeing human beings "from the outside." This way of seeing yields a relatively complete picture of human life without allowing anything like personal subjectivity to appear. It is a way of seeing human affairs in terms of causal laws. Newman describes it well when he says in a passage of his work that deserves to be much better known: "Nothing happens, nothing goes on in the world, but may be satisfactorily traced to some other event or fact in it, or has a sufficient result in other events or facts in it, without the necessity of our following it into a higher system of things in order to explain its existence, or to give it a meaning.... The sun rises and sets on a law; the tides ebb and flow upon a law; the earth is covered with verdure or buried in the ocean, it grows old and it grows young again, by the operation of fixed laws. Life, whether vegetable or animal, is subjected to a similar external and general rule." Newman discerns this reign of cause and effect in human beings and human affairs; he goes on: "Men grow to maturity, then decay, and die. Moreover, they form into society, and society has its principles. Nations move forward by laws which act as a kind of destiny over them, and which are as vigorous now as a thousand years ago. And these laws of the social and political world run into the physical, making all that is seen one and one only system.... We cannot set limits either to the extent or to the minuteness of this wonderful web of causes and effects, in which all we see is involved. It reaches to the skies; it penetrates into our very thoughts, habits, and will."[34] In this last sentence he seems to admit the rule of cause and effect even into the conscious life of human beings. Thus Newman envisions a way of exploring even the inner man that does not reveal the subjectivity of the person. This law-based exploration takes human beings as objects, not as subjects, and it takes them in terms of universals and does not take them in all their personal singularity. Since this perspective of human affairs seems to be complete, it is easy to overlook the personal subjectivity that it does not reveal.

This passage is taken from a review that Newman wrote in 1841 of a history of Christianity that took Christian institutions in the same external way. The author of this history (Henry Hart Milman, 1791–1868) explained these institutions in terms of social and cultural laws, and lay great stress on the similarity between Christian and non-Christian religious institutions. Newman warns against the danger of thinking that this causal account of Christianity is a complete account. The causal account has its own truth, and Newman affirms this truth forcefully, as we have just seen; but Newman is concerned that the partiality of this account is overlooked, with the result that the mystical, interior, providential dimension of Christianity is also overlooked. He is concerned that this author takes his natural account of Christianity to be so complete that he in effect neglects the supernatural mystery in Christianity. The remarkable thing about Newman's discussion is this: he feels no need to deny the vast reach of causes and natural laws in order to make room for the mystical; he is not tempted to posit a "God of the gaps." Just as water keeps all of its natural properties when it is sacramentally connected with baptismal regeneration, so the causal fabric of the world remains intact, suffering no infringement when God is present working in it a history of salva-

34. ECH II, 191–92.

tion that entirely exceeds the history that can be told in causal terms. Newman is able to insert the relentless reign of causal law into a larger whole that includes grace, divine election, supernatural life.

Thus he says of Israel, considered in the way in which Milman considered it: "The Israelitish polity had a beginning, a middle, and an end, like other things of time and place; its captivities were the natural consequences, its monarchy was the natural expedient, of a state of political weakness. Its territory was a battle-ground, and its power was the alternate ally, of the rival empires of Egypt and Assyria. Heathen travellers may have surveyed the Holy Land, and have thought it but a narrow slip of Syria. So it was; what then?"[35] In saying "what then?" Newman means to say, why should Israel not *also* be a uniquely chosen people, under a special providence of God, destined to play a privileged role in the history of salvation? Throughout his review Newman wants to show how we can conceive, or rather imagine, a divine presence in an earthen vessel. He shows how to resist the reductionist temptation to think that the earthenness of the vessel prevents it from bearing in itself a divine presence. He shows us how to think "sacramentally," and not to be so awed by the natural aspect of Jewish and Christian history as to lose contact with the supernatural life at the heart of it. The central idea of his rejoinder to Milman is this: "We maintain then ... that Christianity, nor Christianity only, but all God's dealings with His creatures, have two aspects, one external, one internal. What one of the earliest Fathers says of its highest ordinance [the Incarnation], is true of it altogether, and of all other divine dispensations: they are twofold, 'having one part heavenly, and one part earthly.' This is the law of Providence here below; it works beneath a veil, and what is visible in its course does but shadow out at most, and sometimes obscures and disguises what is invisible."[36]

35. ECH II, 195.

36. ECH II, 190–91.

The reader will ask just what this has to do with discerning or failing to discern the subjectivity of persons. Consider where Newman finds the most revealing analogy available to him for explaining his sacramental reading of Christian history: he finds it precisely in man, more exactly in man considered as a composition of a law-governed exterior and an interior principle of subjectivity. After asking, "So it was; what then?" Newman proceeds to answer: "Till the comparative anatomist can be said by his science to disprove the rationality and responsibility of man, the politician or geographer of this world does nothing, by dissertations in his own particular line of thought, towards quenching the secret light of Israel.... Its history is twofold, worldly to the world, and heavenly to the heirs of heaven."[37] The analogy with the composite nature of man is even more explicit in this significant passage: "The Creator 'formed man of the dust of the ground, and breathed into his nostrils the breath of life, and man became a living soul.' He first formed a material tabernacle, and then endued it with an unseen life. Now some philosophers ... have speculated on the probability of man's being originally of some brute nature, some vast misshapen lizard of the primeval period, which at length by the force of nature, from whatever secret causes, was exalted into a rational being, and gradually shaped its proportions and refined its properties by the influence of the rational principle which got possession of it. Such a theory ... bears an analogy, and at least supplies an illustration, to many facts and events which take place in this world."[38]

Newman is writing almost twenty years before Darwin began to publish, and is able to envision the idea of an evolutionary account of the emergence of man from the non-human primates. In addition to the laws already mentioned that govern man and human affairs, he glimpses the idea of evolutionary laws at work in the emergence of man. He considers this idea

37. ECH II, 195–96.
38. ECH II, 193–94.

with equanimity, for he is empowered by his strong sacramental imagination to "think together" such laws and the "infinite abyss of existence" in each human being, even though this existential depth, which is nothing other than personal subjectivity, cannot be entirely accounted for by evolutionary laws.[39] Newman is entirely free from that "angelism" (as Maritain called it) according to which a spiritual principle can be acknowledged in man only to the extent that natural laws cease to operate on man; Newman can think the interpenetration of matter and spirit in man in a radically non-angelistic way, that is, in a genuinely "incarnational" way.

Back to our question why personal subjectivity is so easily overlooked in the study of human beings; it is because the causal examination of man that shows us man "from without" gives us a relatively complete vision of man. "The world in which we are placed has its own system of laws and principles, which, as far as our knowledge of it goes, is, when once set in motion, sufficient to account for itself,—as complete and independent as if there was nothing beyond it."[40] One can overlook subjectivity because it does not appear in this relatively complete vision of man.

In order to bring subjectivity to light we have to learn from Newman the sacramental principle, which in this study of his he expresses in terms of "outward" and "inner." What is outward, however complete it seems to be, is not the whole; it is mysteriously interconnected with an inner principle. Newman makes room for both outward and inner; indeed, he is a master of making room for aspects of reality that seem to exclude each other, as we saw in the previous chapter. Once again: "But one aspect of Revelation must not be allowed to exclude or to obscure another; and Christianity is dogmatical, devotional,

39. This "thinking together" can of course sometimes be carried out in objectionable ways. Take, for example, the discussion of free will; the position called "compatibilism" tries to fuse together causal determination with free will, but in such a way as to degrade free will to a shadow of its real self.

40. ECH II, 191.

practical all at once; it is esoteric and exoteric; it is indulgent and strict; it is light and dark; it is love, and it is fear."[41] We can add: revelation is also outward and inward, it is institutional and mystical. Applied to man this means that man is governed by natural laws even while he is at the center of his inner life an infinite abyss of existence. He is commensurable with other beings insofar as he and they are governed by the same laws; but through his existential depth he is also incommensurable with those other beings and with the patterns and regularities of the world.

Subjectivity and Subjectivism

If we keep our point of departure in mind we have to ask whether Newman's deep sense of personal subjectivity creates any problems for his theocentric religion.

One commonly says that the signature of modern thought is a certain "turn to the subject." In this sense St. Augustine has been called "the first modern man" because he explored the inner life of persons as no previous thinker had explored it. Book X of his *De Trinitate* is the first treatise on subjectivity in Western philosophy. The same interest in subjectivity that makes St. Augustine "the first modern man" makes Newman an eminently modern man. Now no one says that the theocentric spirit is compromised in St. Augustine as a result of his turn to the subject; what reason then is there to say this of Newman?

Newman would have come into conflict with his theocentrism only if his modernity and his turn to the subject had played out as a subjectivism, that is, if his turn to the subject were at the expense of acknowledging the objective reality of persons, of the moral order, and of God. But there are no such casualties resulting from Newman's talk of the "infinite abyss of existence" in each person, as we can see in his teaching that this inward infinity resonates with, and awakens in response to

41. DD, 36.

the living God. Our subjectivity and our being *capax Dei* are like two poles of our being. As for Newman's view of the material world, I do admit that there is a subjectivist tendency in this part of his thought. I admit that those philosophers who have explored the embodiment of the human person (Edith Stein, Gabriel Marcel, Erwin Straus, Hans Jonas, to name a few) have acquired something important for Christian personalism that is missing in Newman. But this lack in Newman is not the kind of lack that tends to compromise his theocentric religion; it is not the kind of lack that could compromise his religious fear and zeal and his adherence to the dogmatic principle.

7

"The Creative Principle of Religion"

Our question in this final chapter is: what is, for Newman, the primordial knowledge of God that engenders an awakened religious existence? And in particular we ask: what is distinctly personalist about Newman's conception of our primordial religious knowledge?

From the Theological Intellect to the Religious Imagination

Let us first consider what this primordial knowledge is *not.* Christians have sometimes tried to explain it in terms of proofs and demonstrations. They have said that we can reason from the finite world to God as the cause and ground and governor of the world. Four of the five ways to God offered by St. Thomas Aquinas are of this kind. What has been traditionally called natural theology consists of such proofs of the existence of God, along with demonstrations of the main attributes, or names, of God, such as one, omnipotent, omniscient, just. While Newman does not reject the traditional approach, and even presupposes it, he also does not make much direct use of it; his personalist way to God is different. Even if all the proofs contained in natural theology are as rationally successful as the theologians claim them to be, they are all matters of formal inference, and as a result they all lead only to notional apprehension of God. But Newman is looking for a primordial religious knowledge that involves a real apprehension of God. Sometimes he makes a contrast between "the theological intellect" and "the religious imagination," and says that proofs and demonstrations are carried out by the theological intellect, whereas he is concerned with knowledge that appeals to the religious imagination. He is looking for a primordial knowledge of God which is "existential" knowledge, that is, knowledge that engages the whole person, knowledge that we can live by, and not just knowledge that appeals mainly to the intellect. He says in a famous passage of his *Apologia,* in words that could only have been written by him: "I am far from denying the real force of the arguments in proof of a God ... but these do not warm me or enlighten me; they do not take away the winter of my desolation, or make the buds unfold and the leaves grow within me, and my moral being rejoice."[1] He is looking for primordial religious knowledge that speaks to his heart, not just to his mind.

In one place Newman sketches out the monotheistic concept of God as elaborated in natural theology: "I speak then of the God of the Theist and of the Christian: a God who is numerically One, who is Personal; the Author, Sustainer, and Finisher of all things, the life of Law and Order, the Moral Governor; One who is Supreme and Sole; like Himself, unlike all things besides Himself which all are but His creatures; distinct from, independent of them all; One who is self-existing, absolutely infinite, who has ever been and ever will be, to whom nothing

1. Apol., 241.

is past or future; who has all perfection, and the fulness and archetype of every possible excellence, the Truth Itself, Wisdom, Love, Justice, Holiness; One who is All-powerful, All-knowing, Omnipresent, Incomprehensible." Newman thinks that God so understood can be apprehended only notionally, and he explains why: "It is an assent following upon acts of inference, and other purely intellectual exercises; and it is an assent to a large development of predicates, correlative to each other, or at least intimately connected together, drawn out as if on paper, as we might map a country which we had never seen."[2] In these last words Newman vividly evokes notional apprehension: it is apprehension of something that you aim at with your mental intention but do not really see; it is apprehension based more on concepts and definitions than on the intuitive presence of the reality apprehended in its unity. Newman longs for more than a notional apprehension of God, and so he goes on: "So far is clear; but the question follows, Can I attain to any more vivid assent to the Being of a God, than that which is given merely to notions of the intellect? Can I enter with a personal knowledge into the circle of truths which make up that great thought. Can I rise to what I have called an imaginative apprehension of it? Can I believe as if I saw?" It would seem that, if ever intuitive presence is beyond our reach, surely it is beyond our reach in the case of God, who is a hidden God, and apprehensible only in faith. With Him one would think that in this life nothing more than notional apprehension is possible. But Newman is not deterred, for he writes, "Yet I conceive a real assent [to God] is possible, and I proceed to show how."[3]

Conscience

He claims that our primordial religious knowledge arises in our conscience. It is through our sense of being morally obliged that we can gain a real apprehension of the reality of God. New-

2. GA, 102, DA, 294.

3. GA, 102.

man says, "Were it not for this voice, speaking so clearly in my conscience and my heart, I should be an atheist, or a pantheist, or a polytheist when I looked into the world."[4] So Newman's way to God is not cosmological, in the sense of starting with the external world and reasoning back to God as the cause of it; Newman's way to God passes through his moral interiority.

But in order to understand how Newman finds God in conscience, we have to distinguish with him between two levels of conscience. There is first of all conscience in the sense of the mental power by which we understand right and wrong. For instance, it is by conscience that we understand that it is wrong to shed innocent blood, or to distort the truth for my convenience, or to be ungrateful to my benefactors, or to break my word. We often say that someone who understands these things has a well-formed conscience. But there is a more proper sense of conscience and this is the one that mainly concerns Newman. Suppose I come into a particular situation in which I am tempted to distort the truth for my convenience, or to break my word, and suppose that at this moment I have the strong sense that I must not yield to these temptations. I might say that my conscience *warns* me not to yield, that it *commands* me not to do wrong. The thought of doing wrong fills me with a certain shuddering; I realize that I will compromise myself in an ultimately serious way if I do the wrong that tempts me. Or suppose that I have yielded to the temptation; then I say that my conscience *accuses* me, and I am tormented knowing that it rightly accuses me; I feel that all deeper happiness in myself is now undermined. This is the second level of conscience, and is the one with which Newman works. Conscience in the first sense gives me moral knowledge, knowledge about the wrongfulness in principle of lying or of breaking my word. We need this knowledge in order to have a conscience in the second and more proper sense. For it is only when I see myself and my actions in the light of these moral universals that conscience in

4. Apol., 241.

the more proper sense awakens. Conscience in this sense involves not just moral universals, but also my concrete existence, exposed to the light of the universals. It is in the setting of this encounter of myself with the moral law that the mysterious admonitions and accusations of conscience make themselves felt. Newman says, "And hence it is that we are accustomed to speak of conscience as a voice ... and moreover a voice, or the echo of a voice, imperative and constraining, like no other dictate in the whole of our experience."[5] Our understanding of moral universals, by contrast, has more analogy with seeing than with hearing a voice. So we have conscience as a moral sense, by which we come to know the natural moral law; and we have conscience as a dictate, "imperative and constraining," which challenges me in a definite situation. It is conscience in this latter sense that especially concerns Newman.

Newman proceeds to examine the affections that go with conscience in the second sense. He gives particular attention to the affections that make up a "bad" conscience, emotions such as shame, fear, dread, sense of responsibility, but he also gives attention to the positive affections of awe and of hope and of the peace of mind that make for a "good" conscience. He first argues that these affections taken together represent one basic kind of personal experience; just as there is aesthetic experience, and sense perception, so there is also, at just as fundamental a level, a kind of experience that might be called "conscience experience." He then argues that if we draw out the "lines of meaning" contained in the affections proper to conscience, we can discern in them an interpersonal structure. He says that conscience (in the second sense) always implies "the recognition of a living object, towards which it is directed. Inanimate things cannot stir our affections; these are correlative with persons. If, as is the case, we feel responsibility, are ashamed, are frightened, at transgressing the voice of conscience, this implies that there is One to whom we are respon-

5. GA, 107.

sible, before whom we are ashamed, whose claims upon us we fear.... These feelings in us are such as require for their exciting cause an intelligent being: we are not affectionate towards a stone, nor do we feel shame before a horse or a dog." Many readers of Newman will accept his description as long as this interpersonal dimension of conscience is explained in terms of some human other. But Newman proceeds to suggest that the person to whom the affections of conscience refer cannot be merely human; he goes on to say that

> conscience excites all these painful emotions, confusion, foreboding, self-condemnation; and on the other hand it sheds upon us a deep peace, a sense of security, a resignation, and a hope, which there is no sensible, no earthly object to elicit. "The wicked flees, when no one pursueth"; then why does he flee? whence his terror? Who is it that he sees in solitude, in darkness, in the hidden chambers of his heart? If the cause of these emotions does not belong to this visible world, the Object to which his perception is directed must be Supernatural and Divine; and thus the phenomena of Conscience, as a dictate, avail to impress the imagination with the picture of a Supreme Governor, a Judge, holy, just, powerful, all-seeing, retributive, and [it] is the creative principle of religion.[6]

Note the expression "the creative principle of religion." This is the kind of knowledge of God that Newman seeks, the knowledge that can engender religious existence. Newman wants to encounter God in a way that does not just appeal to the theological intellect, but also to the religious imagination, and he finds this encounter in conscience.

One should beware of converting Newman's train of thought too quickly into a formal argument, as if the affections typical of conscience were taken by him as an effect, and as if Newman were arguing that only a divine being is a sufficient cause of them. Though the letter of his text sometimes suggests this interpretation, I read him instead as articulating the sense of a divine person that is from the beginning implicit in the intentionality of

6. GA, 109–10.

these affections. He is not attempting to prove by inference that a personal God exists; rather he is attempting to render explicit that sense of a personal God that is implicit in the affections of conscience. If we do not read Newman like this, we will tend to absorb his train of thought on conscience back into the theological intellect and miss the appeal he is making to the religious imagination.

Above we heard Newman asking, "Can I believe as if I saw?" He claims that through conscience I can indeed come to believe as if I saw. He argues for this by way of drawing an original analogy between conscience and sense perception. He says that there is a great gap, easily overlooked, between receiving sense impressions and discerning material individuals. A person born blind who suddenly receives his sight, as we saw in chapter 5, at first perceives only a riot of color and shape, but not yet an ordered world containing distinct individuals standing in definite spatial relations to each other. What he perceives at first is like what we perceive when we look at a tapestry on the wrong side. It takes some time and some work of interpretation to learn to see the tapestry of the external world on the right side, that is, it takes some time and work to find in the sense data the distinct individuals that exist around us and also to find the spatial relations in which they stand. What interests Newman is that we do not infer to, or reason our way to, the material individuals; we do not, for example, reason that they are the only thing that could have caused the sense data. We apprehend the individuals, not indeed with the immediacy with which we experience the sense data, but still somehow directly; we apprehend them in the sense data, and in a way that forms a contrast with the act of deducing from the sense data that those individuals must be there.

Now Newman argues that the affections of conscience (in the second sense) subserve our apprehension of God just like our sense experience subserves our apprehension of distinct, spatially situated individuals. We can recognize God in these affections, just as we can recognize distinct individuals in the sense data. The parallel that Newman draws between conscience and sense perception is at first surprising, because material individuals seem to be directly present to us, whereas God seems hidden. Newman overcomes our hesitation about the parallel by showing, first, that the material individuals are not as immediately present to us as one might think, certainly not as immediately present as the sense data themselves, and by showing, secondly, that the God of conscience is more present to us than one might think, since God is not deduced as the cause of the emotions of conscience, but is rather discerned as the veiled object of those emotions. Of course, this kinship with sense perception holds only for the real apprehension of God in conscience and not at all for the notional apprehension of God in the theological intellect. In fact, Newman, after articulating the monotheistic concept of God that emerges in theology, complains, as we saw, that this concept is like "the map of a country that we have never seen"—he complains of a lack of seeing. But there really is a certain seeing of God in conscience, and this is the point of the parallel that Newman draws between conscience and sense perception.[7]

So far I have been presenting Newman's thought on conscience as if he were in dialogue with an agnostic and were trying to show the agnostic where we encounter God in our experience. But in fact his thought on conscience hovers between this dialogue and another one, namely, the dialogue with someone who indeed believes in God but who apprehends Him only notionally. In the famous passage in the *Grammar of Assent* that I have been interpreting, it is this believer more than the agnostic who is the real addressee of Newman's discourse. In this pas-

7. A striking sign of the deep kinship of spirit between Newman and the phenomenological personalism of Max Scheler is the first pages of Scheler's great essay on repentance, found in his *On the Eternal in Man* (Hampden, Conn.: Shoe String Press, 1972), 35–36, where he draws out the religious significance of conscience in exactly the way Newman does, and even brings in the parallel between sense perception and a kind of "perception" of God in conscience.

sage Newman says that he is addressing someone who has a full notional apprehension of God, and that he is trying to awaken that person's religious imagination by appealing to his or her experience of conscience.[8]

It is important to notice this dialogue with the notional believer, because we discern in it something of great importance that may remain hidden in the dialogue with the agnostic: we discern the unity of the real and the notional apprehension of God. It is the same God who is first notionally apprehended by the theological intellect—apprehended as "One who is self-existing, absolutely infinite, who has ever been and ever will be, to whom nothing is past or future; who has all perfection, and the fulness and archetype of every possible excellence, the Truth Itself, Wisdom, Love, Justice, Holiness"—and then really apprehended in conscience by the religious imagination. It is remarkable that Newman effortlessly and without any argumentation recognizes the one who speaks in conscience as being identical with the one who is spoken about in theology. It is for him self-evident that in conscience he experiences from within the very one about whom he thinks in theological discourse. And so what results for him in conscience is a composite—a sense of God composed of experience and understanding, of real and notional apprehension.

A word now on what is distinctly personalist about Newman's way to God through conscience. It is natural to explain this aspect of Newman's personalism in terms of real apprehension: in conscience we apprehend God not just abstractly but imaginatively, not just intellectually but affectively, not just from a distance but with full personal engagement, not just as an object of cognition but in an interpersonal encounter. And yet we cannot completely explain Newman's personalism in terms of real apprehension. Though a *merely* notional apprehension of God is weak in a personalist respect, the composite of real and

8. He observes here (GA, 104–5) that the same appeal to conscience can also be made in dialogue with the agnostic.

notional, of which we just spoke, makes an important personalist contribution of its own to the religious act. But for the notional elements contained in Newman's account of monotheism, the pure religious experience would remain vague, and our religious existence would lack focus. We discussed this important point in chapter 2 and we will return to it at the end of this chapter.

We have been talking about Newman's personalism as expressed in his approach to God through conscience. Let us notice the significant fact that this personalism is not far from Newman's theocentrism. Though these two aspects of Newman's mind seem in some sense to be antithetical, they both spring from a common source. It will be recalled that, in explaining his theocentrism in chapter 1, I made a point of referring to his teaching on conscience, and in fact to his teaching on conscience in the second and more proper sense. I said that conscience as a "magisterial dictate" intimates the high authority of the one who speaks in conscience; conscience does not just concern my happiness and flourishing, but subjects me to the divine judge, thus imparting a theocentric form to all of Newman's religious thought. It now turns out that it is the same conscience that is "the creative principle of religion." The very aspect of conscience that founds Newman's theocentrism also supplies the experiential energy that converts the notional apprehension of God into a real apprehension.

Newman and the Phenomenology of Religious Experience

We will be able to give a fuller account of Newman's approach to God through conscience if we make use of Rudolf Otto's phenomenology of religion as laid out in his classic study *The Idea of the Holy* (1917). Indeed, Otto's work may even enable us to understand Newman better than Newman understood himself.

Otto says that the German word *heilig* (holy) has been reduced to having a merely moral meaning, as in Kant, for whom *"ein heiliger Wille"* is simply an unconditionally conscientious moral will, a will entirely given over to duty and untouched by inclination. Otto goes on to say that *heilig* used to have also a specifically religious meaning, a meaning irreducible to all meanings expressing moral excellence, and that he wants to recover this specifically religious meaning. He forms a new term, *numinous,* to express that which is irreducibly religious and not merely moral in the idea of the holy. When I shudder on hearing some piece of sacred music, such as the *Te Deum* of Bruckner, I apprehend something numinous in the music. When the apostles were overwhelmed by what they experienced on Mount Tabor, it was the numinous mystery erupting from Christ that filled them with a certain religious shuddering. One speaks in this case of *numinous fear,* which Otto carefully distinguishes from *natural fear,* that is, fear of being harmed. The apostles did not expect to be harmed by what they experienced on Tabor, but they feared greatly in the sense of numinous fear. Otto proceeds to distinguish with great sensitivity and subtlety different numinous aspects. Thus he analyzes the primitive numinous phenomena that we call "uncanny." Among the higher numinous phenomena he distinguishes those that draw us and fascinate us *(mysterium fascinans)* from those that make us shrink away and keep a distance *(mysterium tremendum).* And so on. He lays great stress on the fact that the numinous is something simple and indefinable; each person has to experience it for himself. It is not something else like moral excellence, but it is itself and is nothing else. Thus Otto tells his readers early on that, if they cannot find the numinous in their experience, they should not read on in his book, for they will not know what he is talking about. By the end of his book he has rehabilitated the holy by restoring its irreducibly religious core.

It is certain that Newman would have been fascinated by Otto's phenomenology of religious experience. But more to our purpose is that the concept of numinous experience and numinous objects can be very fruitfully used in interpreting Newman. Thus we can say that the power of Newman's sermons lies not just in what he says but in what he evokes, and that he knows how to evoke the numinous dimension of Christianity. A sermon like "The Religion of the Day" (PPS I, sermon 24) is seething with numinous energy; it is charged with numinous fear and numinous awe. But still more to our purpose is this: the "magisterial dictate" of conscience is full of numinous mystery for Newman. Conscience is not just a matter of morality for Newman; moral obligation is also something distinctly religious; a *mysterium tremendum* breaks through in moral obligation, filling Newman with numinous dread.[9] When we do wrong, our conscience registers not just *wrongdoing* but *sinfulness,* which is a numinous category; the wrong we do, once exposed to the light of the numinous and the holy, takes on the uncleanness of sin. *This* is why conscience is the creative principle of religion. Without the concept of the numinous we might take Newman's teaching on conscience as reducing religion to morality, as Kant did. We would also be at a loss to understand how conscience can have such power to turn our religious beliefs from notional assents into real assents.

Once we think of Newman in the light of Otto's phenomenology of religious experience, we can understand better why Newman expected so little from Paley's design argument for the existence of God.[10] Newman thought that even if arguments like that of Paley are as successful as claimed, they do not awaken any strong numinous shuddering; they do not lend

9. But notice that Newman never takes the religious dimension of conscience in a voluntaristic sense, as if moral obligations derive from arbitrary divine commands and prohibitions. The way in which Newman roots the "magisterial dictate" of conscience in the first sense of conscience secures him against any kind of voluntarism.

10. On this issue in Newman's thought see the instructive study by Kevin Mongrain, "The Eyes of Faith: Newman's Critique of Arguments from Design," *Newman Studies Journal* 6.1 (Spring 2009), 68–86.

themselves to serving as a foundation for revealed religion. He said that the adherents of decadent "the religion of civilization" "lay much stress on works on Natural Theology, and think that all religion is contained in these; whereas, in truth, there is no greater fallacy than to suppose such works to be in themselves in any true sense religious at all. Religion, it has been well observed, is something relative to us; a system of commands and promises from God towards us. But how are we concerned with the sun, moon, and stars? or with the laws of the universe? how will they teach us our duty? how will they speak to sinners? ... We see nothing there of God's wrath, of which the conscience of a sinner loudly speaks. So that there cannot be a more dangerous (though a common) device of Satan, than to carry us off from our own secret thoughts, to make us forget our own hearts, which tell us of a God of justice and holiness, and to fix our attention merely on the God who made the heavens."[11] Otto would say that Newman, when he says that the design arguments are not "in any true sense religious at all," is in fact deploring their numinous barrenness. Newman wants to say that his approach to God through conscience, by contrast, is numinously rich. Otto would take Newman's talk of the "wrath of God" not only as an expression of God who avenges human injustice, but also as an expression of God who fills us with numinous fear. Otto would say that Newman is quite right to discern in conscience a sense of sin; as we just said, we experience our wrongdoing as sin whenever we confront it with the holy. The design arguments cannot deliver any sense of sin because they approach God in a highly rational way that does not evoke the numinous mystery. This is why no one goes away from the design arguments with a longing for redemption, whereas Newman thinks that this longing does indeed awaken in conscience. It is also why no one goes away from the design arguments with a sense of *tua res agitur,* whereas Newman thinks that this sense of existential urgency does indeed belong to conscience.

11. PPS I, 317–18.

There is something else in Otto that ought to be brought into relation with Newman. Otto distinguishes within the idea of the holy between "rational" and "non-rational" moments. When we unfold the holy in terms of "morally good," "omnipotent," "omniscient," "eternal," "personal," we employ the rational names of God; but when we speak of the holy as "numinous" we aim at something non-rational in it. The full "idea of the holy" contains both rational and non-rational moments. Otto's work of rehabilitation consisted not only in retrieving the non-rational numinous and but also in trying to comprehend the unity of rational and non-rational in the idea of the holy. He had no intention of playing the non-rational off against the rational, or of using the numinous so as to discredit the rational; hence the subtitle of his book: "an inquiry into the non-rational factor in the idea of the divine and its relation to the rational." Otto says that when the rational is overdeveloped and the numinous is neglected, the holy turns into the god of the philosophers; religious men and women then strive to recover a sense for "the living God," "the God of Abraham, Isaac, and Jacob." Otto discerns in Christianity a "classical balance" of rational and numinous; in Islam, by contrast, the numinous is developed disproportionately and the rational side of the holy is neglected.

One readily sees the parallel with Newman: Otto's "rational" moments of the holy are known by what Newman calls the "theological intellect"; Otto's non-rational numinous is apprehended by the "religious imagination." Or in other words, the rational moments are objects of notional apprehension, whereas the numinous is the object of real apprehension. The unity of rational and non-rational that Otto sought is not unlike the unity in Newman of notional and real. It is also very helpful to think of Newman as an ally of Otto in resisting the "god of the philosophers" and to think of him as asserting his personalism by standing with those who would make religion center once again around the "living God." But despite the far-reaching parallels between the two thinkers, there is one important point of discrepancy between them, as we will see at the end of this chapter when we set Newman in relation to theological "modernism."

Some Objections

Now we will develop Newman's personalist approach to God through conscience, and will develop it by considering some serious objections that have been raised to it.

A first objection says that conscience is an unreliable path to religious knowledge, since there are after all many unbelievers (and many merely notional believers) who have an alert conscience. Religious significance must not belong intrinsically to conscience, otherwise people who lack or reject the religious significance of it would have to have a diminished conscience. This objection is readily overcome as soon as we recall the two senses of conscience. It is certainly true that unbelievers can discriminate between right and wrong; they know as well as believers that they ought to keep their promises, to tell the truth, to thank their benefactors, etc. They can have what Newman calls the moral sense; they can have conscience in the first sense. But let us recall that Newman's path to God through conscience goes through conscience in the second sense. Now conscience taken in the second and imperative sense can be blunted even while conscience in the first sense remains alive. It can be blunted by thinking of moral requirements as if they were mere social conventions and by thinking of morally upright behavior as being nothing more than loyalty to one's tribe. Or it can be blunted by thinking of moral requirements in evolutionary terms, that is, as nothing more than conditions for survival. And then it is not surprising if the moral life, after being conceived in some such reductionistic way, seems to be devoid of intrinsic religious significance. But persons whose lived moral experience is unencumbered by reductionistic theory, who are therefore capable of feeling moral obligation in all its binding force, will find it difficult not to discern some numionus mystery surrounding moral obligation. Once conscience in the second sense of Newman is experienced by them without any theoretical obstructions, their *sensus divinitatis* (as Calvin called our sense for the numinous) is unavoidably awakened.

Another objection says that Newman's position leads to a strange and even shocking consequence. Suppose that someone sincerely thinks that he is bound in conscience to sacrifice his children to the gods. He will feel in his conscience a dictate, "imperative and constraining," directing him to do this, he will feel something that admonishes him before he acts, and accuses him if he fails to act. He will have exactly those experiences of conscience that Newman says yield a real apprehension of the living God. But is it credible that God is really present in an obligation that rests on so serious a moral error of ours? Would God not be absurdly divided against Himself if He were really admonishing us to do something that is in itself wrong and that He could not possibly want us to do? Yet Newman's position seems to imply that we encounter God just as much in an honestly erring conscience as in a well-formed conscience, since both are equally filled with those emotions of shame, responsibility, dread, etc.

Let us consider that the experience of the numinous mystery is not necessarily discredited by mistakes about the circumstances under which this mystery appears. Perhaps for a "primitive" person a clap of thunder is full of numinous mystery that it does not have for a modern person who knows about the discharge of electricity in the clouds. But the breaking in of the numinous surely provides for the "primitive" just as much real apprehension of the divine as it does for the religious person who experiences the numinous without committing any mistake about the natural world. It would, of course, be different if one thought that all numinous experience is essentially tied to some scientific error, and that this experience vanished entirely in the minds of those who are fully informed about the natural world. But if there is such a thing as numinous experience, then it can hold its ground even in the midst of all kinds of errors about the natural world. It is, then, not so surprising that the intimation of the numinous mystery as it presents itself in conscience can hold its ground even in the midst of mistakes made at the level of the moral sense. Even while I wrongly think that God is commanding me to sacrifice my children, I rightly experience a numinous mystery surrounding that which presents itself as morally obligatory.

And there is something else that can reconcile us to what at first seems paradoxical. Consider how we come to know the essence of a thing. We start with concrete instances of an essence and then try to make our way by some process of abstraction or eidetic intuition to the essence taken universally. Thus if I want to understand what friendship essentially is, I turn over in my mind concrete cases of exemplary friendship, or concrete cases of disorders or "pathologies" of friendship. Working through these concrete cases I come to understand, for example, that the "friendship" of parties to a contract is not friendship is the most proper sense, and I come to understand other essential traits of friendship, many of which are articulated by Aristotle in his admirable treatise on friendship. Now let us suppose that the concrete cases I was working with turn out to be illusory. Suppose I had before me the friendship of Bill and Susan and that I discerned in it many essential features of friendship; but suppose that I was deceived about that friendship and that Bill and Susan were just using each other and were never really friends. The remarkable thing is that the essential knowledge I gained by considering that concrete case remains intact even while the concrete case dissolves into illusion. If in thinking about Bill and Susan I came to realize that there is vastly more to a friendship than persons doing business together, this essential knowledge holds its ground and retains all its validity even after I acknowledge that Bill and Susan never had this "more" in their relationship. And so if the concrete cases that support my concrete perceptions can turn out to be illusory even while my essential knowing remains intact, it is hardly surprising if the sense of God that I gained in conscience remains intact even while the ethical basis on which my conscience spoke turns out to have contained errors. Of course we do not mean that the "step" from a sense of being obliged to a sense of the numinous is a step from the concrete to the universal, as in the case of friendship. What we want to get out of the parallel with friendship is simply the idea that the "basis" for an experience can have some defect without undermining the experience itself.

But we should perhaps grant this much to the objection: the image of God arising in conscience is sure to suffer distortion to the extent that it is based on serious moral errors. If God is thought of as commanding cruel deeds (and even if I take these deeds under the aspect of "good" and "right"), this cannot fail to color my sense of the voice speaking in conscience. As we have said, my experience of that voice is not a completely self-sufficient source of knowledge of God; it forms a unity with the notions and concepts of the moral law and of God that I bring to the experience of conscience. If these are true notions then my knowledge of God is deepened through my experience of conscience, but if they are false then this knowledge is to some degree compromised.

Newman vs. Freud

We said above that Newman spontaneously and effortlessly identifies the voice of conscience with the God of Christian monotheism. We come now to an objection that contests this identification; the objector says that the voice of conscience is really something quite finite and is not to be identified with God. This objection comes from Freud and is based on Freud's concept of the superego. It is perhaps the most challenging of all the objections.[12]

12. It is an objection that is also raised by one of Newman's most acute critics among the Anglo-American philosophers, J. L. Mackie, in his *The Miracle of Theism* (Oxford: Clarendon Press, 1982), 103–6.

Freud begins by considering what it means to say that a child internalizes the commands and prohibitions of its parents. If the child is tempted to some wrongdoing, it hears the parental voice within itself warning against the wrongdoing. If the child has done some wrong, it hears the parental voice within itself, condemning the wrongdoing. The child is not merely afraid of parental punishment; the internalization goes deeper, for the child feels bound by the parental commands even if it thinks it can escape punishment. This internalized parental voice is the Freudian superego. It is a voice that in many ways resembles conscience in Newman's second sense. Besides being like a voice, it is full of higher authority; it commands and prohibits; it is highly personal. It could easily be taken for the voice of God. But Freud argues that this is the voice of a merely human parent and not of a divine parent. He thinks that the process by which the parent gets internalized is an entirely natural psychological process, and can be explained without bringing God into it. Of course, there is no objection to Newman as long as conscience and superego are distinguished; the Freudian analysis of the superego gets its edge against Newman from the claim of Freud that conscience is nothing but the superego.

Newman did not live quite long enough to hear of Freud's work in psychology. It would be fascinating to see how he would have encountered Freud. Here is my response to Freud made in the spirit of Newman's personalism: what Freud calls the superego is a pre-personal and in many cases a depersonalized form of moral life, whereas what Newman calls conscience is an eminently personal form of moral life; therefore Newman's conscience falls outside of the Freudian superego and cannot be reduced to it, or explained in the terms in which the superego can be explained. The naturalistic explanation that Freud offers for the superego does not threaten conscience in the sense of Newman, because it is an explanation for something entirely different from conscience.

Let me explain first why the superego represents a sub-personal form of moral life. If we ask what this internalization of parental commands really is, we find that it is based on the child existing as a kind of moral extension of its parents. Consider how the child repeats the opinions of its parents. The child does not exactly agree with its parents, it just distinguishes very little between itself and its parents. The parental opinions are quite naturally the child's opinions, since the child experiences himself as being "of one piece" with its parents. The child does not yet live very much as its own person, with a mind of its own, but it lives largely "in" its parents. When the child hears parental commands, it takes these into itself just as it takes the parents' opinions into itself, or perhaps it is better to say that these commands invade and inhabit the child, thus giving rise to the parent *in* the child, which is the superego of the child.

It is not difficult to see from the formation of the superego what it would take for the superego to get broken down and eventually destroyed in the child. It would take the child's coming into its own as person, gaining its own moral understanding, forming its own moral judgments, thinking for itself in moral matters. Then the child, now grown up morally speaking, becomes related to its parents not as a moral extension of them but as a fellow person, an equal of theirs in the kingdom of persons. If the child should agree with its parents on moral matters, this agreement has an entirely different meaning from the "agreement" based on the superego, for this new agreement exists between two independent persons, whereas the agreement of the superego exists between one dominant person and the extension of himself into a dependent person. By the way, this process of the child developing a moral mind of its own may begin much earlier than Freud thought, and it may be that from a very early age the superego is always to some degree limited by some moral judgment of the child's own. In other words, the superego may be a useful limit concept that hardly ever adequately describes the concrete state of moral development of any real child. In any case the superego, wherever it occurs, is a matter of a child's existing as a kind of extension of its parents, and hence existing in a sub-personal or a pre-personal way.

But conscience in Newman's second sense is the very opposite of the superego with respect to moral maturity and to being alive as person. What we just said about the breakdown of the superego enables us to understand this. Remember that conscience in the second sense is based on conscience in the first sense, that is, it is based on the person understanding right and wrong by means of what Newman calls the moral sense, and understanding them with his own mind. Conscience in the second sense arises, as we saw, when a person confronts his concrete moral existence with the laws of right and wrong. And when it arises, when a person knows himself to be morally bound to do something, he comes alive in the center of his moral existence; he is pierced by a sense of his distinct personhood. This experience receives an admirable expression in *A Man for All Seasons.* Thomas More feels bound in conscience, for weighty moral reasons, not to acquiesce in the second marriage of the king, and in one place he speaks about what he is experiencing in his conscience: "I will not give in because I oppose it—I do—not my pride, not my spleen, nor any other of my appetites but *I* do—I."[13] This is the way people speak when they are morally bound; they say "I" with this emphasis, which expresses a strong sense of personal selfhood. They say in effect, "Not my parents, not any internalized human authority, but I, I myself, will to fulfill my obligation." The person living at the level of the superego and being a kind of moral extension of an internalized person, cannot say "I" like this.

One might object that the exuberant sense of self expressed by Thomas More is not always found in the real consciences of real people. It is well known that conscience can be oppressive in many ways, beginning with a scrupulous conscience, in

13. Bolt, 123–24.

which a person is neurotically tormented by the fear of doing wrong, and this sometimes to the point of being crippled in acting. Such a person may not feel any more alive as person than the one who is subject to a strong superego. This seems to put into question my way of contrasting conscience and superego. I would respond that I am assuming that the reader can readily find in his or her experience a normal or standard case of feeling an obligation in one's conscience. When Aristotle discusses friendship in *Nichomachean Ethics* VIII and IX, he assumes that his reader can discriminate between friendship properly speaking and friendship in its quasi forms as well as in its pathological forms. So here; it is not difficult to see that a neurotic conscience is a deformation of a normal conscience. It is not difficult to see that a person who once was neurotically scrupulous, and then freed himself from scruples, now enjoys a more "normal" conscience than he formerly had. And so when I contrast conscience and superego I take conscience, or the sense of being under an obligation, in its normal, typical, untroubled, non-pathological condition. Suppose I were discussing the contrast between the non-human primates and human persons; I would of course take persons in their normal, typical, non-pathological state; it would not be to the point for me to compare a severely mentally handicapped human person with a very clever primate.

The objection of Freud, then, looks threatening only as long as one thinks that conscience in Newman's sense is nothing other than the Freudian superego. Once we see how fundamentally different conscience and superego are, Freud's naturalistic account of the superego does not touch Newman; even assuming the validity of this account, it does not interfere, or even seem to interfere, with Newman's claim to find deep religious significance in conscience. One cannot say, therefore, that the God appearing in conscience is just an internalized parental voice, for this God respects me as person in the sense of letting me say "I" more emphatically than I can otherwise ever say it, whereas the internalized parental voice inhibits me as person, preventing me from saying "I" with emphasis.

By responding to Freud's objection, we are able to bring out more fully the personalist content of Newman's approach to God through conscience. For there is not only the personalism that lies in the personal encounter in conscience with the living God, which we have already discussed in its contrast to *thinking about* God; there is also the personalism that now emerges for the first time and that lies in the fact that I "quicken" into life as person in this encounter, that I come into my own as person in it. The understanding of the cosmological demonstrations of God's existence, by contrast, does not give me anything like this experience of my personhood.

Perhaps we can even use this new personalist insight to reinforce the sense that it is God whom we encounter in conscience: perhaps the depth of personal existence that I experience in conscience—the infinite abyss of existence—can only be experienced when it is the Absolute Person who stirs the waters of my existence.[14] *Abyssus abyssum invocat.* In articulating this awakening of the person who encounters God in conscience, we go beyond the text of Newman, but in such a way as to offer an entirely natural personalist "development" of his thought on conscience.

Newman and "Modernism"

Let us finally consider an objection that comes from the Catholic theological tradition. Well known is the "modernist crisis" that absorbed the Church in the early years of the twentieth century. In 1907 Pope Pius X condemned "modernism" in his encyclical *Pascendi.* Many admirers of Newman at the time were shocked because some of the papal condemnations

14. I discuss in greater detail the difference between conscience and the Freudian superego in my paper "Conscience and Superego," in *Personalist Papers* (Washington, D.C.: The Catholic University of America Press, 2004). Newman plays a large role in this earlier discussion of mine, as does Max Scheler.

seemed to refer to certain teachings of Newman, especially his teachings on conscience.[15] The pope condemns in the encyclical those modernists who say: "In the religious sentiment one must recognize a kind of intuition of the heart which puts man in immediate contact with the very reality of God, and infuses such a persuasion of God's existence and His action both within and without man as to excel greatly any [rational] scientific conviction" (para. 14). So Newman's appeal to conscience and the heart, and his reservations about the traditional proofs and demonstrations, would seem to place him among the modernists. He seems to be among those who are rebuked for not knowing "that sentiment and experience alone, when not enlightened and guided by reason, do not lead to the knowledge of God" (para. 39). What made matters worse was that some of those modernists who were undeniably the target of the condemnations, such as the British Jesuit George Tyrell, cited Newman as an authority, as a thinker by whom they had been deeply influenced. The objection we have to face is this: Newman's personalism, if it turns out to be a species of modernism marked by anti-intellectualism, is a very problematic part of his legacy, and is not worthy of the warm reception that I have been giving it.[16]

By way of response to the objection I quote a passage from Newman that sounds very different from all that we have heard in this chapter. In his work *The Idea of a University,* he says: "The

15. Wilfred Ward, friend and biographer of Newman, wrote to a friend right after the publication of *Pascendi:* "It is not any subtle interpretation of J. H. N.... but his notorious characteristic lines of argument which are at least apparently included in the [encyclical's] account of 'Modernism'—his way of proving Theism, his arguments for Catholicism and Christianity from the needs of the human heart, his account of the symbolical character of propositions relating to the Infinite God, his analysis of the process whereby dogmatic formulae have been framed and very much else." Quoted in Edward Kelly, "Newman, Wilfred Ward, and the Modernist Crisis," *Thought* 48 (1973), 515.

16. For a competent account of Newman and modernism, and for a balanced argument that Newman did not hold the modernism condemned by Pius X, see Stefan Hofmann, *Religiöse Erfahrung—Glaubenserfahrung—Theologie* (New York: Peter Lang, 2011), 473–91.

religious world, as it is styled, holds, generally speaking, that religion consists, not in knowledge, but in feeling or sentiment. The old Catholic notion, which still lingers in the Established Church, was, that Faith was an intellectual act, its object truth, and its result knowledge.... But in proportion as the Lutheran leaven spread, it became fashionable to say that Faith was, not an acceptance of revealed doctrine, not an act of the intellect, but a feeling, an emotion, an affection."[17] This does not sound like the author who distanced himself from proofs for the existence of God on the grounds, as we heard above, that "these do not warm me or enlighten me; they do not take away the winter of my desolation, or make the buds unfold and the leaves grow within me, and my moral being rejoice." In these words Newman seems to be very dependent on religious feeling, whereas in *The Idea of a University* he sounds almost like Pope Pius X himself in *Pascendi,* deploring the modernist reliance on religious feeling. How can we put these different sides of Newman's thought together?

I submit that the knowledge of God that Newman derives from conscience is a composition of real and notional apprehension, of conceptual understanding and religious experience, of intellect and imagination. Already in chapter 2 we showed the unity formed by notional and real apprehension, and in fact we made a great point of this composition. In the *Grammar* Newman mainly stresses the real, the experiential, and the imaginative; he thinks that these have been underdeveloped in Christian teaching and apologetics and need to be brought to the fore. But as we saw in chapter 2 he takes for granted the indispensable place of the notional and the intellectual. He takes for granted the God whose various names—one, infinite, omnipotent, eternal, personal, etc.—he surveys in a passage quoted earlier. Even though this concept of God is like "the map of a country one has never seen," it is a map that

17. Idea, 27–28.

has its own truth. Take for instance the statement that God is one, not several; as a result of affirming this we are monotheists, not polytheists. But this truth about God is not clearly given in conscience. The "higher authority" experienced in conscience is veiled; whether there is one or multiple centers of authority cannot be easily discerned. Newman takes for granted that this higher authority is centered in the one God of Christian monotheism. Newman interprets the imperativity of conscience in the light of the unicity of God as propounded by Christian theology. Or again: does the higher authority making itself felt in conscience admit of no shadow of change or becoming, does it dwell in eternity? This cannot be answered simply on the basis of the experience of conscience; the eternity of the God who speaks in conscience emerges for us by interpreting the experience of conscience in the light of the theology of the divine eternity. And in many other ways the religious imagination and the theological intellect collaborate in forming our apprehension of the God who speaks in conscience. Newman does not often reflect on this collaboration, but he takes it for granted, and he sometimes adverts to it, as when he says that "religion cannot maintain its ground at all without theology. Sentiment, whether imaginative or emotional, falls back upon the intellect for its stay ... and it is in this way that devotion falls back upon dogma."[18]

This goes far toward clearing Newman of the suspicion of modernism, for it makes clear that he never played the religious imagination off against the theological intellect, and that he in fact recognized that the latter anchors the former. He quite agrees with Pius X writing in *Pascendi* "that sentiment and experience alone, when not enlightened and guided by reason, do not lead to the knowledge of God" (para. 39). Newman took indeed a particular interest in the religious imagination, but he never disparaged the theological intellect, and always relied on

18. GA, 121.

it. Not only that, but he was himself a major theologian, producing works like his *Lectures on Justification* and his *Essay on the Development of Christian Doctrine*. He did not dream of trying to solve by an appeal to the heart all the theological issues that he discussed concerning justification and doctrinal development.

Let us turn back to Otto and let us point out a certain modernism that one can discern even in him. Otto tends to make the rational elements in the idea of the holy subordinate to the non-rational, and this in a manner that is foreign to Newman. Here is an example of what I mean. We saw above how Otto analyzes the concept of *sin*, showing that it does not just express moral wrongdoing, but is a numinous category. But when Otto proceeds to speak of the doctrines of original sin, of atonement for sin, of the regeneration of the believer, he speaks as if these doctrines, rightly understood, simply aim at describing some aspect of our numinous experience. Thus the truth in the doctrine of original sin is simply a description of that deep-rooted profaneness that we experience in the presence of the holy; all theological talk about the representative function of Adam, the loss of original justice, becoming subject to death, the need for a redeemer, has no other meaning than to express that numinous sense of sinfulness. Insofar as these doctrines introduce new ideas not directly contained in the numinous experience, they are for Otto nothing more than non-binding attempts at thinking concretely about the numinous experience; nothing is really lost if we drop them or replace them with different attempts at thinking concretely about the numinous experience.

Otto is letting the dogmatical principle be undermined by religious experience, and Newman would strenuously object. Newman would say that there are other sources of our knowledge of God besides numinous experience. When for instance believers affirm the divinity of Christ, they are relying not only on the numinous impression made by Christ on those who knew Him and know Him; they are relying on other sources, such as His own solemn declaration about His oneness with the

Father, or such as the Nicene Creed. To the extent, then, that Newman does not subordinate the theological intellect to the religious imagination in the way that Otto seems to, he is free from the suspicion of modernism that attaches to Otto.[19]

But after we have distanced Newman from modernism, we have to go back and say that the truth contained in modernism is fully present in Newman. There is a great appeal to works such as William James's *The Varieties of Religious Experience* or Rudolf Otto's *The Idea of the Holy;* they seem to express important experiential truth that had not been previously expressed. And yet they (and James far more than Otto) represent exactly what the pope meant by modernism. Newman was able to be mistaken for a modernist because he understood this experiential truth and expressed it everywhere in his work because he was working toward a new Christian personalism. But he is in the end no modernist because this personalist truth exists in fruitful tension with Newman's dogmatical principle. For among the many polarities that characterize the mind of Newman, and impart to it its inexhaustible plenitude, is just this polarity of his theocentrism and his dogmatical principle, on the one hand, and his concern with the personal and the experiential, on the other. It follows that Newman, far from being a modernist, is in fact the strongest possible critic of modernism, and this for the very reason that he knows how to incorporate the truth of modernism into a larger whole.

A Personalist Approach to Revelation

Throughout this chapter we have been examining Newman's thought on "natural religion," the religion born of conscience and available to everyone both inside and outside the Christian orbit. Before concluding we should say a word about

19. Max Scheler was a personalist philosopher who combined Otto's attention to religious experience with a much greater respect for the work of the "theological intellect" than Otto had, as we can see from Scheler's great work *On the Eternal in Man.* Working within the same personalist tradition, Josef Seifert has made important contributions to philosophical theology, as in his work *Gott als Gottesbeweis.*

"revealed religion" in Newman, and especially about the personalist profile of it. In the previous chapter we already encountered this side of Newman, as when we examined his sermon "A Personal Providence Revealed in the Gospel." Here we want to make a brief mention of another sermon in which Newman gives forceful expression to his Christian personalism.

In a sermon preached when he was just twenty-nine, "The Influence of Natural and Revealed Religion Respectively," Newman contrasts "natural religion" with "revealed religion," saying that the latter discloses to us the divine Personality in a way in which the former cannot. Natural religion "was not without provision for all the deepest and truest religious feelings, yet [presented] ... no tangible history of the Deity, no points of His personal character."[20] In the hands of the philosophers natural religion might include "a conviction of the Infinitude and Eternity of the Divine Nature," but it gives "no circumscribing lineaments nor configuration of the Immeasurable, no external condition or fortune to that Being who is all in all," as Newman expresses himself in explaining the lack of concreteness in the God of the philosophers.[21] "Here, then, Revelation meets us with simple and distinct *facts* and *actions,* not with painful inductions from existing phenomena, not with generalized laws or metaphysical conjectures, but with *Jesus and the Resurrection.*"[22] And he says, "The philosopher aspires towards a divine *principle;* the Christian, towards a Divine *Agent.*"[23] Here we have an early declaration of Newman's personalism, spoken with respect to revealed religion. It is true that in the third edition of his *Oxford University Sermons* of 1871 Newman had to correct one sentence in this sermon, the sentence in which he says that natural religion "gives little or no information respecting what may be called His *Personality.*"[24] He had to correct this, of course, because conscience, "the creative principle of religion,"

20. OUS, 23.
21. OUS, 22, 23.
22. OUS, 27.
23. OUS, 28.
24. OUS, 22.

gives significant intimations of His Personality. But the important truth that Newman here articulates is that *the free actions of the Christian God that constitute salvation history* convey to us, in a way that conscience cannot, a God who is personal, "living and seeing." In this sense Christianity is a far more personalist religion than is religion based on conscience alone. Only the actions of God in history give us a God who is concretely "configured" and "circumscribed," as Newman quaintly says.

We will understand Newman better if we make a certain contrast with Kant. In his *Religion within the Limits of Reason Alone,* Kant contrasts the core of authentic religion, which for him is moral integrity, with the contingent historical events of revelation. Kant thinks that doctrines like the Incarnation, the Atonement, the fall of man cannot be taken seriously and literally because of the historical contingencies on which they rest; he thinks that they have meaning for us only insofar as they reinforce our a priori moral knowledge and our sense of duty. If a person can live a resolute moral life without believing in the historical revelation that constitutes Christianity, so much the better; his religious existence lacks nothing essential. By contrast, Newman sees in the historical events of salvation history not suspicious mythic elements, not something that embarrasses pure reason, not something that needs to be reduced as quickly as possible to our a priori moral consciousness, but *he sees God acting as living person in our midst, drawing us into dimensions of interpersonal life with God that could never be reduced to doing our universal duty.* Where Kant sees mere historical contingency, something a-rational, Newman sees the freedom of persons, human and divine, making salvation history.

We come to the conclusion that Newman's personalism shows itself in his account of natural religion based on conscience, and that it in fact shows itself here both in the interpersonal encounter with the living God, and also in the way in which the human person comes to himself in this encounter. His personalism also shows itself in his account of revealed religion, which he understands as God freely and inscrutably entering into human affairs.

We have already seen, by setting Newman in relation to theological modernism, that his personalist approach to God through conscience does not interfere with his theocentric religion, just the contrary. Let us now add that the personalism that he shows in his account of revealed religion also lends support to his theocentrism, and this in different ways. For one thing, the God who reveals Himself in history is encountered in His inscrutable freedom, and hence in all His otherness. If we think of God only in terms of His essential "names" as these are elaborated in rational theology, we do not have the same kind of encounter with His otherness. And Newman makes another important point in this early sermon: he says that this encounter with God as living Person wards off a certain pantheistic danger and reinforces the sense of our creaturehood. He points out very perceptively the pantheistic danger that lies in thinking of God in terms of Platonic Ideas: "In whatever degree we approximate towards a mere standard of excellence, we do not really advance towards it, but bring it to us; the excellence we venerate becomes part of ourselves—we become a god to ourselves. This was one especial consequence of the pantheistic system of the Stoics, the later Pythagoreans, and other philosophers; in proportion as they drank into the spirit of eternal purity, they became divine in their own estimation."[25] But when God is experienced by us as a living and seeing person who acts in our midst, then the divine goodness toward which we aspire cannot be thought of as our own; for one person can never absorb another person into himself. Each person is himself and is no other. However much I pattern myself on another, and want to grow into the image of another, as person the other always retains for me a certain otherness. If the other is God, then we call this otherness His transcendence over the creature, and this transcendence blocks any pantheistic encroach-

25. OUS, 28.

ment to which I may be tempted, and confirms my creaturely personhood. And with this the truth of Newman's theocentric religion is confirmed. The confirmation comes right out of his personalism.

Conclusion

Having now arrived at the end of this study, let us look for a way of recapitulating its main theme. Perhaps it can be said that all that we have examined in Newman shows his resolute anti-rationalism, or, better, his anti-intellectualism. His personalism emerges in debate not primarily with a naturalistic reduction of man, but with a rationalistic constriction of man. When Newman shows the limits of the "theological intellect" and tries to revive the "religious imagination," he is pushing back against a certain intellectualism, or a certain overrating of the place of deductive operations in the religious existence of human beings. When in speaking of the proofs for the existence of God he says, "But these do not warm me or enlighten me; they do not take away the winter of my desolation, or make the buds unfold and the leaves grow within me, and my moral being rejoice," he is seeking reasons of the heart. In taking as his motto "heart speaks unto heart," he is pledging to give his readers more than arguments. The knowledge by connaturality that I claim to find in Newman is a knowledge by which Newman gains a highly personal voice, a voice that he could not have by speaking only on the basis of knowledge *per cognitionem.* As for communicating religious truth, Newman knows indeed how to craft powerful arguments, but he says that "if I am asked to convert others by it [Paley's argument], I say plainly I do not care to overcome their reason without touching their hearts."[26] Newman also resists a certain intellectualism by taking seriously the informal reasoning carried out by the illative sense, that is, by the "spontaneous living intelligence" of the thinker. And if we

26. GA, 425.

think of the paradigm of scientific objectivity that privileges the third-person perspective, we can see in Newman's turn to the first-person perspective ("egotism is true modesty") yet another aspect of his anti-intellectualism.

One may think that Newman goes so far as to depreciate the intellect and to depreciate reason, as when he says, "To most men argument makes the point in hand only more doubtful and considerably less impressive. After all, man is *not* a reasoning animal; he is a seeing, feeling, contemplating animal."[27] By now we know how to interpret such a passage. The "reasoning" refers to formal, calculated reasoning, and the "feeling" and "contemplating" are understood by Newman as capable of their own nationality and their own world-openness. What he opposes is a one-dimensional reason that constrains the existence of persons, and what he seeks is that plenitude of reason by which a person really "quickens" as person. Reason is abundantly at work in motivated affectivity, in the religious imagination, in knowledge by connaturality, in personal influence, in the Athenian spirit, in oral education, in the illative sense, in the first-person perspective, but it is a kind of reason that engages the whole person. It is an exercise of reason that does not spend itself in abstraction, but that gives us truth in the concrete. It concerns not only the universal but the personal as well. The reason at work in Newman is exercised not only through his propositional teaching but also through the passion of his personal existence.

I conclude my study of Newman with the assessment of him with which I opened: Newman "stands at the threshold of the new age as a Christian Socrates, the pioneer of a new philosophy of the individual Person and Personal Life."

27. DA, 294.

Bibliography

Aquinas, St. Thomas. *Summa Theologica. Biblioteca de Autores Cristianos: Matriti, 1961.*

Barry, William. "Newman, John Henry." *The Catholic Encyclopedia.* Robert Appleton: New York, 1911. Also available at www.newmanreader.org/biography/biography.htm.

Benedict XVI. *Spe salvi (Saved in Hope).* Boston: Pauline Books, 2007.

Bengtsson, Jan. *The Worldview of Personalism.* Oxford: Oxford University Press, 2006.

Boekraad, A. J. and Tristram, Henry, eds. *The Argument from Conscience to the Existence of God according to J. H. Newman.* Louvain: Editions Nauwelaerts, 1961.

Buber, Martin. "Distance and Relation." In *The Knowledge of Man,* 59–71. New York: Harper, 1966.

———. *I and Thou.* Translated by Walter Kaufmann. New York: Charles Scribner's Sons, 1970.

Burrow, Jr., Rufus. *Personalism: A Critical Introduction.* St. Louis, Mo.: Chalice Press, 1999.

Church, Richard. *The Oxford Movement.* London: Macmillan, 1922.

Clarke, Norris, SJ. *Person and Being.* Milwaukee: Marquette University Press, 1993.

———. "Living on the Edge: Man as 'Frontier Being' and Microcosm." In *The Creative Retrieval of St. Thomas Aquinas,* 132–51. New York: Fordham University Press, 2008.

Crosby, John F. "What Is Anthropocentric and What Is Theocentric in Christian Existence? The Challenge of John Henry Newman." *Communio* 16 (Summer 1989): 244–56.

———. "The *Coincidentia Oppositorum* in the Thought and in the Spirituality of John Henry Newman." *Anthropotes* 1990/2: 187–212

———. *The Selfhood of the Human Person.* Washington, D.C.: The Catholic University of America Press, 1996.

———. "Conscience and Superego." In *Personalist Papers, 93–112.* Washington, D.C.: The Catholic University of America Press, 2004.

———. "The Empathetic Understanding of Other Persons." In *Personalist Papers, 33–63.* Washington, D.C.: The Catholic University of America Press, 2004.

———. "A 'Primer of Infidelity' in Newman? A Study of the Rhetorical Strategy of Newman." *Newman Studies Journal* 8.1 (Spring 2011): 6–19.

DeLubac, Henri. *At the Service of the Church.* San Francisco: Ignatius Books, 1993.

Dessain, Charles Stephen. *John Henry Newman.* London: Thomas Nelson and Sons, 1966.

Froude, J. A. *Short Studies on Great Subjects.* Vol. 4. London: Longmans, Green, 1899.

Hofmann, Stefan. *Religiöse Erfahrung—Glaubenserfahrung—Theologie.* New York: Peter Lang, 2011.

Husserl, Edmund. *Lectures on the Phenomenology of Internal Time Consciousness.* Translated by James Churchill. Bloomington: University of Indiana Press, 1964.

Inge, William Ralph. *Outspoken Essays.* London: Longmans, Green, 1923.

James, William. *A Pluralist Universe.* In *William James: Writings 1902–1910,* 625–819. New York: The Library of America, 1987.

———. *The Varieties of Religious Experience.* In *William James: Writings 1902–1910,* 1–477. New York: The Library of America, 1987.

———. "The Will to Believe." In *William James: Writings 1878–1899,* 457–79. New York: The Library of America, 1992.

Kant, Immanuel. *Critique of Practical Reason.* Translated by Lewis Beck. New York: Bobbs-Merrill, 1956.

———. *Religion Within the Limits of Reason Alone.* Translated by Theodore Greene and Hoyt Hudson. New York: Harper & Row, 1960.

Kelly, Edward. "Newman, Wilfred Ward, and the Modernist Crisis." *Thought* 48 (1973): 508–19.

Kierkegaard, Soren. *The Journals of Kierkegaard.* Translated by A. Dru. New York: Harper and Row, 1959.

Lockhart, William. *Cardinal Newman: A Retrospect of Fifty Years.* London: Burns & Oates, 1891.

Mackie, John Leslie. *The Miracle of Theism.* Oxford: Clarendon Press, 1982.

Merrigan, Terrence. *Clear Heads and Holy Hearts: The Religious and Theological Ideal of John Henry Newman.* Louvain: Peeters Press, 1991.

Mongrain, Kevin. "The Eyes of Faith: Newman's Critique of Arguments from Design." *Newman Studies Journal* 6.1 (Spring 2009): 68–86.

Mounier, Emmanuel. *Personalism.* Notre Dame, Ind.: University of Notre Dame Press, n.d.

Neville, William. "Note on Cardinal Newman's Preaching and Influence at Oxford." Appendix to John Henry Newman, *My Campaign in Ireland.* Aberdeen: A. King, 1896.

Newman, John Henry. *Via Media of the Anglican Church.* Vol. 1. London: Longmans, Green, 1901.

———. *Sermons Bearing on Subjects of the Day.* London: Longmans, Green, 1902.

———. *An Essay in Aid of a Grammar of Assent.* London: Longmans, Green, 1903.

———. *Verses on Various Occasions.* London: Longmans, Green, 1903.

———. "The Biglietto Speech." In *Addresses to Cardinal Newman with His Replies,* edited by William Neville, 61–70. New York: Longmans, Green, 1905.

———. *Discourses Addressed to Mixed Congregations.* London: Longmans, Green, 1906.

———. *Apologia Pro Vita Sua.* London: Longmans, Green, 1908.

———. *Discussions and Arguments on Various Subjects.* London: Longmans, Green, 1907.

———. *Essays Critical and Historical.* Vols. 1–2. London: Longmans, Green, 1907.

———. *Parochial and Plain Sermons.* Vols. 1–8. London: Longmans, Green, 1907–9.

———. *The Arians of the Fourth Century.* London: Longmans, Green, 1908.

———. *Lectures on the Doctrine of Justification.* London: Longmans, Green, 1908.

———. *Lectures on the Present Position of Catholics in England.* London: Longmans, Green, 1908.

——. *Sermons Preached on Various Occasions.* London: Longmans, Green, 1908.

———. *An Essay on the Development of Christian Doctrine.* London: Longmans, Green, 1909.

———. *Historical Sketches.* Vol. 2–3. London: Longmans, Green, 1909.

———. *Fifteen Sermons Preached before the University of Oxford.* London: Longmans, Green, 1909.

———. *Autobiographical Writings.* Edited by Henry Tristram. New York: Sheed and Ward, 1957.

———. *Letters and Diaries of John Henry Newman.* Edited by Charles Stephen Dessain et al. Vols. 1–10 (Oxford: Clarendon Press,1978–84), vols. 11–22 (London: Thomas Nelson and Sons, 1961–72), vols. 23–31 (Oxford: Clarendon Press, 1973–77).

Orwell, George. "Politics and the English Language." In *The Collected Essays, Journalism, and Letters of George Orwell,* Vol. 4. New York: Harcourt, Brace & World, 1968.

Pieper, Josef. "The Philosophical Act." In *Leisure,* 69–127. New York: New American Library, 1963.

Plato. *Symposium.* Translated by Michael Joyce in *The Collected Dialogues of Plato,* edited by Edith Hamilton and Huntington Cairns. New York: The Bollingen Foundation, 1961.

———. *Plato's Epistles.* Translated and annotated by Glenn R. Morrow. Indianapolis: Bobbs-Merrill, 1962.

Price, H. H. *Belief.* London: Allen & Unwin, 1969.

Sacks, Oliver. *The Man Who Mistook His Wife for a Hat.* New York: HarperCollins, 1990.

Scheler, Max. *Man's Place in Nature.* New York: Farrar, Straus, and Cudahy, 1962.

———. *On the Eternal in Man.* Translated by B. Noble. Hampden, Conn.: Shoe String Press, 1972.

———. *Formalism in Ethics.* Translated by Manfred Frings and Roger Funk. Evanston, Ill.: Northwestern University Press, 1973.

Seifert, Josef. *Gott als Gottesbeweis.* Heidelberg: Universitaetsverlag C. Winter, 1996.

Shairp, John Campbell. *John Keble.* Edinburgh: Edmonston & Douglas, 1866.

———. *Aspects of Poetry.* Oxford: Clarendon Press, 1881.

Sillem, Edward. *The Philosophical Notebook.* Vol. 1. Louvain: Nauwelaerts, 1961.

Sokolowski, Robert. *Introduction to Phenomenology.* Cambridge: Cambridge University Press, 2000.

———. *Phenomenology of the Human Person.* Washington, D.C.: The Catholic University of America Press, 2008.

Turner, Frank. *John Henry Newman: The Challenge to Evangelical Religion.* New Haven, Conn.: Yale University Press, 2002.

Von Balthasar, Hans Urs. *Dare We Hope That All Men Be Saved?* San Francisco: Ignatius Press, 1988.

Von Hildebrand, Dietrich. *Ethics.* Chicago: Franciscan Herald Press, 1973.

———. *The Heart.* South Bend, Ind.: St. Augustine Press, 2009.

———. *The Nature of Love.* South Bend, Ind.: St. Augustine Press, 2009.

Weatherby, Harold. *Cardinal Newman in His Age.* Nashville, Tenn.: Vanderbilt University Press, 1973.

Wojtyla, Karol. "Subjectivity and the Irreducible in the Human Being." Translated by Theresa Sandok. In *Person and Community,* 209–17. New York: Peter Lang, 1993.

Index

The Personalism of John Henry Newman was designed in New Baskerville and composed by Kachergis Book Design of Pittsboro, North Carolina. It was printed on 60-pound Sebago and bound by Maple Press of York, Pennsylvania.